Valley of the Skunk

The Story of a Haven

by

Roland Paulson

THE NATIONAL WRITERS PRESS

Disclaimer: The pilot, Gordon Grand, is a composit of many
pilots' limitations that I observed, endured and remembered
from flak-filled rides through hell and back. In no way is this
character intended as a portrayal of an individual person,
living or dead.

Published in the United States of America by
The National Writers Press
1450 S. Havana St.
Aurora, CO 80012

International Standard Book Number: 0-88100-091-4

Library of Congress Catalog Card No.: 96-69428

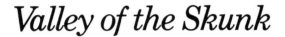

Valley of the Skunk

Dedications

To my wife, Earlene, for all her help and patience,
and to my many high-school classmates and long-time friends
for their encouragement.

To my twin brother, Rodney, my older brother Ralph, and
all the other Ames boys who didn't survive one or the other—
World War II and Korea.

To my editor, Jim Ayers, who used his
invaluable talents to provide objectivity, balance and pace.
I couldn't have done this without him.

About The Author

Roland Paulson was born in Ames, Iowa, and educated at
Iowa State University and the Harvard Business school. He
served eight years of active duty in the Air Force during World
War II and Korea.

His 25 years of varied and highly adventurous experience
in private industry took him to over 40 countries in North and
South America, the Far East, Western Europe and finally,
Africa.

He was run out of Liberia, West Africa, after the bloody
coup in 1980.

Now retired, he lives with his wife, Earlene, in Colorado.
They share his long-time love of history and travel.

He began his career as a writer in 1992. *Valley of the
Skunk* is his first book. The second, a non-fiction book about
his Liberian adventure, will be published in the spring of 1997.

Comments From Some Who "Were There"

"By the time they were ten, the twins had lost everything but each other. Their father had left. Their hard-working mother could not be with them, and their childhood was abruptly shortened by the urgent necessity to 'help out.' No wonder they 'dropped out,' 'lurched from fantasy to fantasy,' and 'acted-out with feats of defiance and daring.'"

Dr. Carrold Iverson,
ex-marine and psychiatrist

"Uncle Neal said their mother was the Iron Lady of Ames. Who but Louise could have had the strength and will to, as a single parent, hold her brood of five together through the depths of the Great Depression?

You and Rod got into more trouble than any four of us. We were in fifth grade when the bragging started about that gun. Ten-year-olds sneaking out to hunt with a shotgun. We all thought you were bigger liars than Pinocchio."

Dr. Earl Feldman,
a neighborhood friend

"Our sloppy, strung-out formation of 28 planes was an engraved invitation to the 160 enemy 109s and 190s waiting for us. They shrieked savagely through us in waves of ten and 20, ripping B-17s out of the sky like sitting ducks. Five minutes later, with half the group already destroyed, the fighters left us to their flak gunners...raw, naked devastation blooming in red, orange and black. It was the 301st's bloodiest day of the war."

Rodney Paulson,
tail gunner

"Arriving at the war with innocence and high hopes, the twins soon discovered they had sleep-walked into an alien place of eternal fear and bloodshed...."

Ray Dominy,
co-pilot on the B-17 FUBAR

What People Are Saying About This Book

"A surprisingly intense and intimate book that leaves you wondering about the lengths to which people can go out of necessity."

Rosemary Long,
librarian

"A powerful story of courage and loss; a struggle which mirrors life itself."

Thomas Kelly,
attorney and former Air Force pilot

"From its opening to its close, a chronicle of the American exerience. Compulsively readable."

Dr. Richard Day,
professor and author, University of Southern California

"A tribute to the author's skill as a writer...he told stories that kept me turning pages."

Joan Moores

"From experience he writes believably about the faces of love, poverty, stupidity, brutality, death and the fate of people."

Arjes Youngblade,
artist and writer

"Credible and insightful . . . fresh and enjoyable without redundancy—each chapter is a special treat."

Erna Hereford,
wife of retired Air Force Academy faculty member

"A compelling story about his lfie and times that does not suffer the usual malady—too much or not enough."

John Brant,
attorney and historian

Prologue

June 1992—Ames, Iowa

Thirty-eight years since he died and it still hurt to be near my brother's grave. It was a hard, cold, isolating kind of hurt that hadn't changed much over the decades. Devastation? Yes, it was like that, but it was more, worse. A husband losing a wife, a mother losing a child—that's devastation. Rod and I were identical twins. Losing him was a kind of amputation—the loss of half of my brain, half of my heart, half of my spirit. The wound never stopped bleeding.

Rod and Mother are buried on a green knoll in the Ames Cemetery. I looked up into the branches of the ninety-year-old oaks above them. The leaves were full. Birds sang in the branches. Idyllic—lonely, horribly lonely.

Why the hell had I come back here? What had drawn me? I had told myself it was Earl Feldman's incessant nagging about coming to the fiftieth reunion of our high school class.

"Everybody is going to be here, at least everybody who's rumored to be still breathing. You should consider yourself blessed to be a member of that group and get your butt back to Ames to remember the good old days."

Remember? They were Earl's good old days, not mine and not Rod's. Ames High School was excellent by any standard. Compared to the rest of the country, Ames students excelled in scholarship and athletics—everyone but Rod and me, it seemed. Depending on who you asked, we were "the twins"; the troublemakers; the sons of a crazy man; Louise's kids ("poor Louise"), the Daniel Boones of the class. We attended high school under protest. We were space cadets before that condition had a name, occupiers of our own, private planet. All we seemed to have was each other. That's all we wanted and all we made room for. Only one reunion mattered to me and where I stood was as close as I would ever come to it. Rod was dead.

I looked out toward the valley of the Skunk River. A hundred yards from where I stood, Rod, Mike, and I entered the woods on our first squirrel hunt almost sixty years before. Mike was our beloved "mixed breed" hunting dog, the best squirrel dog around.

The woods had changed; more people called them home. As kids, Rod and I thought of the valley and the woods as ours, a haven. I think I understood at that moment, though not in words, that I was where I had to be. I wasn't here for a reunion or to visit Rod's grave again and rekindle the cold fire of my pain and guilt. I was here to say goodbye. I'd never been able to do that, not really. Instinct started me down into our beautiful Valley of the Skunk. If I was going to get it done this time, I had to know what I was leaving behind.

Rodney   Roland
Three years old

Roland Paulson

Rodney Paulson

Back row: Gert, between twins.
Front row: Ralph (left), Leonard (right).

Chapter One

April 1934, Friday night—Rod swung and expertly buried the blade of our small ax in a log. Chunks of stove wood split off, and I quickly set up another log for him. It was already dark outside. We had to hurry if we were going to finish in time for Jack Armstrong on the radio. Splitting stove wood had been our favorite chore, but lately the stove had been going all the time just to heat water. We had to split more each day to keep up.

Melvin suddenly appeared in the dim light of the single overhead bulb. Silent as an assassin, he grabbed the big ax.

"Run!" Rod yelled. He scooted one way and I the other. We always did that and it had always worked because we were ten years old and faster than him, and he was usually drunk when he came after us anyway. It kinda of figured that I'd be the one to break our record of clean escapes; I slipped. Melvin swung the axe handle at my rear end. I stuck out my right arm to block the blow. Like a bolt of lightning, pain raced up my arm and down to my toe nails. I thought I heard a bone crack. I ran screaming and crying to the back door of our house. Mother took one look at my arm and sent Gert, our older sister, to fetch Doctor Fellows. It turned out to be a bad sprain. It was only after the doctor was gone and my arm was safely tucked up in a sling that Mother went looking for Melvin, but he was long gone by then. Good thing for him.

Saturday, dawn—All of us older children were having breakfast. Rod and I had turned ten just four days before. We were identical twins. Our brother Ralph was eleven. Our sister Gert was twelve. Leonard was three and wasn't up yet. Gert looked out the back window. Surprise registered on her face.

"Well, Melvin has come back and done what he should have done a month ago—borrow a horse and plow from Shorty and plow the garden."

We all went to look. Melvin wasn't plowing. Mother and he were arguing furiously. Mother was much taller and towered over him. She never hit him, or used her size against him, though. Mostly she tried to reason with him, even though it hardly ever worked when he was drunk. Sometimes she cried, more lately. We went back to breakfast.

"That's what he should be doing for a living," Gert said, speaking in her very grown-up way. "Lately, Mother has been telling Aunt Dorothy and me, 'Melvin should still be farming. He farmed from the time he was old enough to sit on a cultivator until he was twenty. He loves farming and he's good at it. What is there for him in Ames? Nothing but frustration— no job, no income. I don't know where he is most of the time... which may be for the best.'"

Mother earned our entire family income by cleaning Bourn's Motel and taking in laundry. We *existed* because of her. Melvin was an anchor, but she loved him.

Saturday, afternoon—Mother and Gert were still doing laundry. Ralph was working in the garden. Leonard was napping. Melvin was across the road at the Browns'. Mr. Brown and Shorty were part-time farmers and Melvin's drinking buddies. Mother helped Mrs. Shorty in return for chickens, eggs, milk, butter, and meat sometimes.

Rod and I had been in the woodshed for several hours. Rod stopped splitting wood to help me load our red wagon. I was loading with my good arm. Our big, red, wooden wagon with sideboards was a marvel. It had been a Christmas present from Aunt Dorothy when we were seven. We hauled Leonard and groceries around in it. It also doubled our wood production because we didn't have to make so many trips to the house.

"Sure you can do this without hurting your arm? Do you need to take a break?" Rod asked.

"Only hurts when I bump it....I'm about to get rid of this sling. It's an awful nuisance," I said.

"You can't do that! Doctor Fellows said it had to stay on

2

for at least a week."

"Maybe I'll get the hang of it....You know, it would be perfect if your right arm was the one in a sling. That way Old Dumb Dora would have to let you write left-handed." Dumb Dora was our teacher. She was trying to break Rod of being left-handed because its just not normal.

Rod thought for a minute. "Hey, we can still do it. We both go to school with right arms in a sling. We'll both have to write left-handed. Dumb Dora'll have a fit."

I giggled. "She won't even be able to tell which one is actually the left-hander."

"Don't you wish! You can't even write right-handed, let alone left."

"Anyway, Gert writes a note, supposedly from Mother: 'The twins had an accident...'"

Gert would never have done it, but we had a good laugh anyway. When the wagon was full, I grabbed the handle and was about to start for the house. We heard yelling outside — not close, but loud and violent. Rod and I looked at each other a moment, but got back to work. This was nothing new.

I pulled the wagon outside in time to see Mother drop her washboard and run across the road toward the Browns' house. Before she could get there, a woman screamed and Melvin bolted out the Browns' back door, across the road, and into our house through our back door. His face was livid with rage. That was nothing new either, but I stopped. He was inside the house and I didn't want to be anywhere near him. It was quiet a minute, then we heard a siren. Soon after that, a police car squealed to a stop in front of our house. Most of the neighborhood had come out to see. Ralph, Rod, and I rushed over to Gert. Officer Tom and his partner were headed our way. They had their guns out.

"What's Officer Tom doing here?" Ralph asked. "Is he going to arrest Dad and put him in jail?"

Gert seemed untouched by it all. "Heaven only knows," she said. "He may really have done it this time."

Officer Tom looked at us all, then at Gert alone. "Any guns in the house?"

"No...at least, not that we know of."

Officer Tom circled round to the front door and his

3

partner went to the back. They went in. They came out seconds later with Melvin between them. He was calm, meek, stone-faced, and handcuffed. They took him to their car and left.

Ralph was crying. "Will we ever see him again?"

No one answered. I looked at Rod. He knew I was thinking we were better off without Melvin.

Mother came home soon after that and fixed supper. Usually a noisy meal, that night we ate canned beef, boiled potatoes, and turnips in silence.

Finally, after our Saturday-night baths in the kitchen in the laundry tub, Mother had us gather round in the living room. She turned off the radio, something silly we were listening to. In the dim light of a floor lamp, she dabbed her eyes with a cloth from her apron. "I've been living in mortal fear of this or worse." She broke down and had to stop for a minute. "I've been terribly wrong, not doing something sooner to protect you children. I've tried, Lord knows, but there was simply nothing I could do to keep him away."

"Was it our fault?" Rod asked. "Did we make him do it?"

Mother started to cry, then she got angry. "Of course not! All of you have suffered enough without taking that on. Not even Dr. Fellows knows why, except that he thinks your father's problems go way back....But it was all my fault, what happened to Roland last night. It was bound to happen. I hope you can forgive me, all of you. Now, at last, it's finally over with."

"What do you mean. What's happened?" I asked.

"You're too young. You'll know soon enough," Gert said quietly in her grown-up voice.

Between sobs Ralph asked, "Now what happens?"

Mother stopped crying. The iron will we were most used to strengthened her face. "We are now, finally and forever, really on our own....But pulling together, we'll find a way."

We learned later that Melvin had hit Mrs. Brown. A review board composed of doctors, lawyers, and other experts declared him insane and he was committed to the state mental hospital at Mount Pleasant.

Mother took charge after that. On a Friday, we moved and our lives changed completely. Through most of that first night at our new (new to us anyway), modern house, Mother baked pies, cakes, and cookies. Saturday morning she had everything neatly wrapped and ready to go. Without even so much as a chance to explore, let alone comprehend, the wonders of the indoor plumbing and basement furnace this house contained, we older kids were sent to sell Mother's pastries door-to-door. We earned seven dollars that weekend. We could live for a week on that amount, plus the fresh produce from our garden and the government surplus food that Rod and I had to go and get with our wagon.

Ralph said he felt like a beggar. We all did. The ignominy of door-to-door peddling had an unintended consequence. It drove all of us, including Mother out of pity for us, into quickly finding other employment. Meanwhile, only Mother knew how she managed to move us to a neighborhood whose residents included doctors, lawyers, and business owners. It didn't take long for us kids to begin feeling like the only have-nots in a world of haves.

Early summer, 1934 — Rod laughed as he wrestled Mike in the soft grass. I was trying to divert stupid Ike into chasing his tail rather than tear up the garden. With Melvin gone, pets were allowed, although Mother wasn't thrilled when we showed up with two dogs.

We were lounging in the shade of a cherry tree full of birds. One order for the day was to pick those cherries before the birds did. Another was to hoe and weed the garden. We were going to get to it, but on that morning we'd never had it so good. We'd been in our new house for a month. We'd just finished a record week doing lawns and garden chores. Best of all, it was Sunday morning and we weren't in church. That had never happened before and wasn't likely to happen again.

Rod tossed a green apple for the puppies to fetch. "We got off scot-free. I never thought we'd get away with it. She's never made a mistake like that, but she did — no clean, ironed clothes for us to wear to church."

"Even if there had been, she'd never have sent us to church alone," I said. "Not after last Christmas."

Rod roared and rolled in the grass. Cowardly Ike yelped and ran for cover. Ike was mine, the larger of our three-month-old pups. He should have been the braver, but he wasn't. "Rolling those steel balls down the aisle—no one would have been any the wiser if it hadn't been for Melvin."

The Sunday before Christmas, the Johnson boys brought marble-size steel ball bearings to Sunday school and dared us to roll them down the center aisle. Our problem was not *whether* we should do it, but when and how. We pondered that for days. Finally Rod had an idea: Christmas Eve would be the best time, when the choir came down the aisle and the church was dark except for the candles the singers carried. We would roll the balls behind them. I was the trouble-shooter when we planned things and I pointed out that Gert and Ralph were in the choir, which meant we would be alone in a pew with Mother, Melvin, and Leonard. That would make it next to impossible to sneak to the back of the church, especially with "Eagle Eye," the assistant pastor, in the back on look-out.

Rod came up with the answer, as he usually did. We had been saddled with the privilege of passing out collection plates. Christmas Eve would be our first time. We would say we had to go back and see old Eagle Eye to make sure we knew what to do and when to do it. While we were in his office, one of us would have to go to the bathroom and be outside free and clear while the other kept Eagle Eye busy.

It worked pretty well. The fact is, there probably wouldn't have been any fuss at all if one of the girls in the choir hadn't stepped on a steel ball and fallen down. When she did, Melvin jumped up and run out of church. At home that night he screamed at Mother. "I can't stand it anymore! I won't be humiliated by your children, especially those two!" He had no evidence we'd done it, but he assumed we had.

Mother was sure we had done it, but what could she have done anyway? Expel us from church? Not likely

Rod and I thought we were too smart for words, but we paid a price. From then on the pew smack in front of the pulpit was reserved for Louise (Mother) and her troop. It was never written down, it just happened that way and nobody ever challenged it. That's also when Mother started carrying a switch to prod us when we nodded-off in front of the preacher. Melvin was too mortified to even show up in church after that.

"But we're not in church this morning," Rod said, "and

6

we didn't have to go with them to visit Melvin at Mount Pleasant."

"He's been there over a month," I said. "It's better without him."

"He never was much of a dad.... Has Gert told you what they do at an asylum?"

"No. All she talks about is how hard Mother works. 'Five in the morning till ten at night, six days a week. I don't know how long she can keep doing it.'"

4 July 1934, just before dark—Out in the backyard we limbered up our green apple cannon. It was made from a cast iron floor waxer minus the handle. The ammunition was jawbreaker-size green apples. The propellent was one-inch firecrackers. The need to get even with Mattie was the mother of our invention. Her back porch was our target, across the alley and about as far as we could throw. With the cannon we could manage ten rounds a minute, which was how long it would take Mattie to storm to the alley, we figured.

We loved the neighborhood almost as much as we loved tormenting the girls who lived in it. Mattie was a special case. Soon after we moved in, she was there to spy on us. She had long, flaming red pigtails, and she wore glasses. She always spoke without a hint of a doubt. In our first encounter she clarified our place in the social structure of the neighborhood:

"I heard you came from the South Side. So, where's your father? With five of you, how can your mother keep you off Relief?"

"We're Rodney and Roland. What's your name?"

She stuck out her hand. "Mattie Taylor! My father's a professor."

It went downhill from there. We mostly tried to avoid her, but this was different. This was inspired. I loaded and Rod fired. We blasted the back of her house with twenty rounds before we heard the back door slam. We got off another five in the time it took her to race around their garden and arrive at the alley, out of breath.

"What took you so long?" Rod smiled.

"Are you trying to kill us?" she whined between gasps for air.

7

"You poor little things. Did any of you get hurt?"

She put her hands on her hips and smirked. "No, but we might have. This isn't very nice. I told father he should call the police."

We looked at each other and shuddered. "Go ahead!" Rod snarled. "Make a federal case out of it!"

"I *would,* but father thinks it's funny. He said if he knew how he'd make his own cannon. He said, 'those twins and I, we'd have a good old-fashioned artillery duel.'"

Fall, 1934 — It was our first week in our new school and we had managed to make a lasting first impression. Five of us fifth-graders were in the principal's office.

"I've heard some ugly rumors. Why was Bill Buck absent today?" Mrs. Mitchell demanded, glaring at Rod and me. People always looked at us when there was trouble. Even in a small crowd like the one in the office that day, people like Mrs. Mitchell always looked at us. It was only later that we learned that our reputation for trouble "to the power of two," as Mother put it, followed us. All we knew for sure then was that everybody just assumed we had done whatever had been done. They were right a lot of the time. Anyway, we knew Mrs. Mitchell already knew the answer to her question. So much for new friends. One of them has already squealed. We knew there was no point in beating around the bush.

"It's our guess that Bill would rather stay home than come to school with a shiner," Rod said.

I thought Mrs. Mitchell was going to smack him, but she didn't. "What caused that black eye?"

Whitey Smith spoke up. He was nicknamed "the Old Coot" because he looked old, probably from the day he was born. His voice was low and full of gravel. "Six of us were on the corner of Tenth and Grand. Somebody thought we should have a fight so we chose up sides, the twins and I against the three upper-crusts."

Mrs Mitchell frowned, "Upper-crusts! What is that supposed to mean?"

I wondered how she could be so dumb.

"Their dads are dentists and a state highway engineer. The twins and I don't even have so much as a dad between

8

us," Whitey said calmly.

"So that's it? Now we have class warfare and ten-year-olds trying to right social wrongs by fighting?"

"It just came out that way, three against three," Rod said. "We didn't mean anything by it."

"That's exactly right," Whitey said. "Nothin' happened till one of them called the twins 'little brats.' Then's when Rod poked Bill in the eye." He patted Rod on the head. "Criminy, look how small they are. Wasn't even a fair fight."

"Besides, what we do three blocks from school is none of your business," I said. Rod and I suddenly were alone in the room. No one had left, but they were all looking at us like we were crazy.

Mrs. Mitchell gasped. She was livid and stunned. "Well! So now ten-year-olds are laying down the law, and explaining my job to me!" she stammered. She hunted up her yardstick and we were paddled.

Early December, 1934—Home alone with an earache, I found the gun and shells. It was a rusty old single-shot, sixteen-gauge, basically a discarded relic, but it quickly became our most prized possession. Frustrated nearly to death until we could sneak out and use it, we eased the pressure by fooling with it in the basement every night for a week. We cleaned and polished inside and out until the metal gleamed and the wooden stock practically oozed the linseed oil we had rubbed into it. It was a thing of beauty. While we cleaned and polished, we planned.

Julius and Earl Johnson, the source of the steel balls we turned loose in church, lived northeast of town on a farm, about six or seven miles up the Skunk River. They claimed to have hunted with their dad. Saturday morning, after finishing our newspaper route, we'd sneak out and go up there. If we came home with rabbits, we'd tell Mother that we'd gone to visit our Sunday school friends—she'd like the Sunday school part—and their dad had taken us hunting. The only hitch was money for ammunition. That need was answered when it started snowing Friday. Before it was through, there was a foot on the ground. We shoveled snow until midnight and earned $2.25, according to Rod enough for

9

twenty shells, three gallons of skim milk, and three loaves of day-old bread.

We were up well before the alarm clock that Saturday morning. By a quarter to five, Mother, Mike, Rod, and I were out the door to walk the ten blocks to downtown. It was a perfect morning for it—crispy cold with no wind and a foot of new, trackless snow crunching under our four-buckle overshoes. Mother's destination was the Sheldon-Munn Hotel where she worked as pastry cook. Rod and I always stopped there long enough for leftovers from the day before. Just across Main Street was the office where we picked up the *Des Moines Register* newspapers we delivered.

We made that trek seven mornings a week, although Mother slept in on Sundays. This day was going to be really something, the biggest day of our lives.

We got home from doing the papers before seven. As the designated cooks, we fixed the usual cornmeal muffins for everybody, and left at dawn. No one else was up. In fifteen minutes we were out of town, traveling along a country road. The only blemishes in the fluffy snow were animal tracks, a good sign, we figured. I sported the gun crooked in my left arm. Rod had our gunny sack game bag thrown over his shoulder. We looked like we knew what we were doing, but we didn't.

"What are all of these fresh tracks from?" I asked. "There's so many Mike won't know where to start?"

"Why would he? He's still only a pup, and this is his first hunt, too....Let's see if we can get him to stay in the weeds along the ditch. Isn't that where the rabbits should be?"

"I guess."

As it turned out, Mike knew more than we did. He was soon on the trail of a cottontail bobbing along ahead of him. Rod was right beside me up on the road, but he yelled anyway. "There he goes, shoot!"

I raised the gun and fired. It clicked. I'd forgotten to put in a shell. Meanwhile, the rabbit ducked into a culvert. That was the end of that. Mike went on down the ditch, hot on another trail that led him to a huge white cat. It darted into a corn field with Mike yapping at its heels. The next opportunity was a shock; a huge pheasant, cackling a blue streak, flapped out of the weeds right under Mike's nose. I didn't come close to getting off a shot. Several more rabbits ducked into culverts. It went that way for the first hour. Sensing we were in over our heads, we paused to regroup, except for Mike who sniffed on.

"This is getting us nowhere. What do you think?" I asked.

Rod looked around. "Let's go back and check out that last culvert." On the way he frowned at me and took the gun. "You keep forgetting: Carry the gun open and empty until you get a shot. If you don't get the shot, empty it again before you do anything else."

At the culvert, I leaned the empty and open gun against a fence, and we dropped down on our knees to look inside. We could see through to daylight on the far end. About midway we could see the rabbit's ears. Our sagging spirits soared.

"What would it take to get him out of there? Or do we have to sit and wait?" I asked.

"If all they have to do is duck into a culvert, it'll be a long day with lots of waiting," Rod said.

"What about Mike? He could easily get into it?"

"No way! What if he tried to turn around and got stuck? That would be the end of the little guy. A hundred rabbits wouldn't be worth taking that chance."

I got an idea and reached in my coat pocket for some of the twine we used instead of belts for our pants. Rod's face lit up. "Who'd have thought our twine would be good for something besides holding up britches," he said.

'Okay, we give it a try," I said. "But first we figure out who does what. I'll go on the other side and wait for the rabbit to come out. Once I'm in the ditch, I'll load the gun and be ready."

"Okay, then I'll send Mike in....But don't forget: If that rabbit decides to come toward me, you can't shoot—right? That's rule number one. And, we'll take turns, okay?"

We tied the twine to Mike's harness so we could extract him if he got into trouble, but it never came to that. He went in and out came the rabbit. Twelve shots and many culverts later, we had seven nice fat rabbits, but it was no thanks to me. The Super-X loads we were using gave the shotgun a kick like a mule. Just one shot left me with a sore shoulder and a bruised cheek. It hurt enough that I flinched in anticipation of the second shot. None of that afflicted Rod. Rod missed his first rabbit, then hit seven out of nine. When we ran out of the Super-X shells, we replaced them with lighter, cheaper loads, but it was too late for me. Flinching was a hard thing to cure.

We never made it to the Skunk River or the Johnson farm. Home before dark, we cleaned the rabbits. We hung three of them in the rafters in the garage. The other four were rolled in flour and fried in time for supper when Gert and Ralph got home. They were surprised, but not impressed. Cooking was one of our chores. We never got all that good at it.

Mother never let on that she knew about the gun. On the other hand, she was neither stupid or indifferent, and she stood six intimidating feet tall—a head and straight, sturdy shoulders above us. She could easily have stopped us, but she never did. Was it because she worked herself to exhaustion nearly every day and simply didn't have the energy to ride herd on us as closely as she wanted to? I don't think so. I think that allowing us to believe we were getting away with it was one of many examples of her wisdom. She could not have missed our wild enthusiasm for hunting. Finally, we had found something we cared about. I suspect she allowed us to nurture our interest without interference. I also suspect she spent a lot of time worrying about us shooting ourselves.

Christmas week, 1934—Avis Cole, sixth-grade teacher and a very nice lady, lived five blocks from us in a big white house high on a hill sloping toward the street. Her's was the largest lawn we mowed, and the one of which we were the most proud. The lush expanse of green was so large that it took us five nights after school just to rake the leaves. All that was done for the year, but we'd made a deal with her. She had lots of trees, including some dead elms. Six of them were small enough for Rod and me to cut down, cut up, and haul home. We'd do that in return for being able to keep the wood.

Coming down the alley with our ninth wagonload of wood of the day, we spotted a coal truck in our driveway. There was no reason for it to be there. We couldn't afford coal, and besides, that's what the wood was for.

The truck driver had been waiting long enough to be

cross. He stormed over to us and demanded instructions on what to do with the coal. We were equally cross with him.

"Whose bright idea was this in the first place? You've got the wrong house."

He waved a slip. "It says here, one ton of coal to 615 11th Street."

"Says who!"

"Right here on the slip, if you punks can read. 'Dr. Joe Fellows.'"

It was a gift and would be the first of many that week. Every day, something appeared on the front porch—food, clothing, even toys. Often, there was no card, leaving us to wonder who it was who cared that much about us.

We kidded Gert over some used clothing that came for her. She was stoic and philosophical about it. "Ruined finery from a previous century. Oh well, beggars can't be choosers." Gert had a way with words. She only drove us crazy when she used too many of them and expected us to pay attention.

Fall, 1935—"Cripes! It's cold! My teeth are chattering!"

"Yeah," Rod said, slapping himself against the pre-dawn chill. "I wish we'd stopped to eat. I'm starved."

"Well, Uncle Neal said this is educational," I said, shivering. "We've already learned we should have eaten first."

We had gone as far as we could in the dark, following Uncle Neal's directions to the entrance to the woods. We listened to the night sounds as we waited—the hoot of an owl, the call of a pheasant rooster. We knew that sound from a time when Dad had taken us along on one of his infrequent hunting treks into the woods.

"It sounds like it's coming from the moon," Rod said. "I really like the night sounds now. Remember last winter, coming back from Johnson's farm? I was scared then."

"Me, too....I'm freezing! This is killing me!"

"It was your idea."

It had been. We had risen in the predawn stillness, after a night of tossing anticipation. Even Mike, our fifteen-pound, curly-tailed companion, spent a restless night. We rushed out of the house with nothing to sustain us but the old rifles Uncle Neal had given us and twenty rounds of ammunition apiece.

Ike wasn't with us because he'd run away and never come back. We'd tried taking him with us on our hunting trips, but one shot sent him hightailing for home and we could never break him of his fear. As a hunting dog, he been a dismal failure. On the other hand, as far as Ike was concerned we were dismal failures as owners.

Frowning, I looked to the eastern horizon. "Does it seem like it's getting light yet? Can you tell?"

Rod followed my gaze. In the moonlight, mirror images stared far off for a glimpse of encouragement. As we watched, a faint glow in the east began to grow. Within minutes, silhouettes of trees and a windmill appeared.

Not long after that, we were able to get our bearings. Look for the cemetery sign, Uncle Neal had said, and there it was in the half-light: Ames Cemetery. No Trespassing. Soon enough, we were able to look down from the hill into the Valley of the Skunk.

We had seen it many times before, but never had it looked so grand and regal as it did from where we were—above it all, with the rising sun glistening off the hillsides' fall coat of reds, yellows, and greens. The Skunk River meandered between them, through golden fields of harvest-ready corn and lakes of green alfalfa. We could tell the river's course by the line of wispy fog that snaked its way through the valley. We continued to look in awe as a nearby solitary oak shimmered in the glow of the sunrise.

Suddenly, Rod pointed into the valley. "I know exactly where we are! See the bridge? That's where Dad took us on our Sunday rides!"

I found the bridge and remembered the infrequent Sunday afternoon drives. We'd stop and throw rocks into the river. The rides stopped even before Melvin left. I hadn't thought about those times until that moment. I dismissed the memories. He wouldn't be part of any new memories, and the old ones were colored with disgust.

Just then, a rattle turned our attention back to the road. Two older boys were nearing on brand new bicycles. They were dressed to the teeth, pictures right out of *Outdoor Life* in their new hunting gear. Unblemished walnut stocks disappeared into oiled leather scabbards on their bikes.

Outdoor Life was the only magazine we read. In it, shooting editor Jack O'Conner explained everything about guns and the right and wrong way to hunt any game animal. Mom had gotten the subscription for us. I don't know how she afforded it, but she did.

There we stood, our bare heads packed with O'Conner's wisdom, our bodies dressed in traditional blue-striped bib overalls, gray sweat shirts and clodhoppers—more like something out of *Farmer's Almanac* than *Outdoor Life*. Our guns were old. I was wearing a khaki hunting vest borrowed from Uncle Neal. It was stained with the blood of his past glories. Beside us, little Mike paced and yapped.

"You kids waiting to go in there?" one of the boys asked, gesturing toward the woods.

"Yeah," Rod answered warily. "Been here half the night. Where you guys headed?"

"Right here."

No, not here, I thought. I knew Rod was thinking the same, not because I looked or I could see it in him, just because I knew. We always knew.

"Hey!" one of them said. "What do ya think of the four of us working together? We'll split whatever we get."

"Naw," Rod said before I could. "We wanna see what we can do on our own."

The boy nodded, looked at his partner, and shrugged. "Okay, suit yourself," he said. "We'll go on to the other side....You going in with *him*?" He looked down at Mike, who was careening like a pin ball. "Peppy little mongrel, but he sure don't look like any hunting dog I ever saw."

I bristled. "He ain't a mongrel. He's a hybrid, half black and tan and half wire-haired. We hunted rabbits all last winter and did real good. He practices on squirrels at home every day."

The boy sniffed and chuckled. "Squirrels in there may be a lot smarter."

"We gotta go," Rod snapped.

They mounted their bikes. "Well, good luck," the boy said. They rode off.

We turned and headed into the woods with no more discussion of the meeting. It wasn't necessary. Once well inside, we stopped. I slipped a five-round clip into the bolt-action, Rod stuffed fifteen rounds into the pump. Mike watched. The second we were ready, he went to work. We followed him deeper into the woods.

"Jack O'Conner says squirrel hunting is mostly patience," I said quietly. We separated by about twenty yards and moved as quietly as we could, but the ground was covered with fallen leaves that crackled beneath our feet, especially under all four of Mike's.

"He sounds like a horse!" Rod whispered. "Every squirrel for miles can hear us! We're gonna get skunked!"

Just then, Mike's special bark told us he had something treed. We moved ahead and found him staring and barking up into the branches of an oak. We circled the tree and saw nothing. Whatever had been there seemed long gone, driven away by our noise. We were about to move on when Rod stopped, looked into the branches, then silently motioned for me to join him.

"Remember at home?" he whispered. "When Mike has a squirrel?"

I nodded, remembering. We moved back twenty yards, separated by the same distance, and sat down—careful to take the opposite side of the tree from Mike. Mike continued to bark, we remained perfectly still. Within a few minutes, we saw movement and heard rustling thirty feet up on our side of the tree. We waited silently for the head shot that O'Conner said was a must for squirrels. A few tense moments later, the opportunity came. Rod took careful aim and fired.

The squirrel seemed to flutter to the ground more slowly than a September leaf. Mike rushed to it, shook it a few times, then dropped it and set out in search of another. We headed him off long enough to hug him. "Not like any hunting dog I've ever seen," the jerk on the bike said? Nope. Better! We let Mike do the work from then on. Seven more squirrels, and we called it a day and set off to explore.

We came out of the woods onto a high, flat knoll. Smoke curled up from the stone chimney on the side of the huge log cabin, the most prominent feature of Camp Canweta, at least from our side of the fence. The map Uncle Neal had given us had led us there. As we watched, two giggling girls left the cabin and headed for the outhouse. They went in giggling, they came out giggling, and they were still giggling when they washed their hands at the pump outside the cabin.

Girls were strange enough, but this was a true mystery. In all the years that we had suffered under the yoke of being one of the few families in Ames still to use an outhouse, we had never found it a reason for laughter. On the contrary, when the wind shifted, it seemed half the town blamed the smell on the Paulsons' outhouse. Never mind Shorty's pig sty, located just across the alley. No, if it stunk, it was the Paulsons. We didn't have that problem any more. But still, the reputation clung to us like muck to Shorty's pigs.

As the girls finished at the pump they saw us and screamed. They hot-footed it back into the cabin. In seconds, the screened porch was full of jabbering girls. Two finally ventured out—Mattie and Liz Ann. Mattie was nagging before she even got to the fence.

"You boys aren't supposed to be here!"

"Who says?" I challenged. "Besides, we're not in there, we're out here."

"Mike's in here," she said smugly.

"So what! He's a smart dog, but like most two-year-old's, he can't read No Trespassing signs," Rod said, smirking.

"Smart aleck."

"Look, we've been going since four this morning. We could sure use a drink...and maybe an apple from that tree?" I asked.

They didn't invite us in—thank goodness with that many girls around—but they did bring us apples and water. It was not, however, to be a free lunch.

"Why are you boys out here?" Mattie demanded. Liz Ann just watched.

"It's none of your business, but we've been hunting squirrels," I said.

"Killing squirrels? That's terrible! You kill rabbits, too! You should be ashamed."

"What do you mean? Squirrels are a game animal. There's a hunting season on them. We only kill for food," Rod said, clearly as amazed as I was at her stupidity. "Besides, don't you know hunting is educational?"

"Oh, really!"

"Yeah!" I said. "Do you know how to read a map?" Blank faces told us they didn't. I fished the map out of my vest pocket and opened it to show them. I explained its many features and how we had used it to come to that very spot.

"Hunting also teaches you how to clean and dress game," I said proudly. We proceeded to show them. We realized it was a mistake when they screamed at the first cut. Mattie recovered quickly, however.

"What's that stuff?" she asked.

"Guts," Rod explained with authority.

Liz Ann turned away, her hands over her face. Mattie flinched, but continued. "I'll bet you learned about that when you hunted last winter," she said slyly.

We went pale. How could she know about that. No one was supposed to know about that. "How'd you know that?" I asked.

"I heard my folks talking about you. My mother said it was awful to let ten-year-old boys go out alone with a gun. She said, 'What kind of person is their mother?'"

Both of us scowled at her. "It wasn't mother's fault. She didn't even know. She has to work all the time," Rod growled. "We just did it. Besides, rabbits are good to eat. Would your mother rather we go hungry?"

Mattie shook her head. "You won't go hungry. You're on Relief."

"So what?" I said.

"Oh, don't feel bad. Father says people on Relief shouldn't feel bad. They're not bad, they're just people down on their luck. Mother says people on Relief shouldn't spend money on foolish things like bullets."

"We shoveled snow to pay for shells!" I said angrily. "One sidewalk paid enough for ten rabbits—that's enough for two meals for us kids!"

"Doesn't your mother like rabbit," she asked, too sweetly.

"She works at the Sheldon-Munn. She eats there. She never gets home in time—these eight squirrels took twelve shells. That's twelve cents for two meals!"

She looked at Liz Ann and smiled knowingly. She turned back to us. "We heard your father was in an insane asylum."

"It's called a mental hospital," Rod said, disgusted. "He

was there, but he's not now. He's not crazy, he just had a nervous breakdown."

"What's that?" Liz Ann asked.

"We don't know," I conceded. "But he got out."

"He doesn't live with you," Mattie pointed out proudly.

"No," Rod said. "He's on a farm in South Dakota. Sometimes he lives here with our grandmother. We—look, do you want to learn about hunting and maps or not?"

Mattie smiled. "Why? All we have to do is look around to know where we are."

"Not if you were out here instead of in there. Out here, you can get lost if you don't know what you're doing. I'll bet you'd get lost in a minute!"

"Oh, really!"

"Yeah, really."

"You boys kill cats!"

"Cripes! We don't kill cats! Mike kills cats."

"You sic Mike on the cats. It's the same thing! What if he gets hurt? You two are trouble makers. And you're mean, to Mike and the cats."

A whistle blew from the porch of the cabin. Lunch time for the girls saved us from Mattie's wrath. More to the point was how we would go about keeping Mattie from knowing more about us than we did.

We circled the cabin to the east, to the edge of a steep bluff. The whole valley spread out far below us. Miles and miles of fields and farms, and hills covered in fall golds and reds. From there we followed the map down to a place at the river where a tree had fallen on the bank—a perfect perch for dangling feet in the cool water. We listened to the birds chattering, doing our best to identify them. We heard a pheasant rooster again. We had come too far for it to be the one we heard that morning.

"Maybe we should join the Boy Scouts," Rod said.

"Maybe. Mother thinks we need to spend more time with other people."

"Like Mattie?" Rod laughed. "How can anybody want to be around girls?"

"I don't know. Earl does, though. He carries Liz Ann's violin for her."

"It's a good thing Gert doesn't play anything bigger than a flute or we'd probably have to carry it for her," Rod said.

"Gert works awfully hard for us. We should do more. Maybe we could iron," I suggested without conviction.

"Naw. Mother would never allow that. It wouldn't be good enough. Our clothes have gotta be *perfect,* just like the house."

"Geez! I'm tired of hearing how messy the house is," I complained.

"Me, too. I bet Mother's room is perfect."

"Are you kidding? Of course it is," I said.

"Have you been in there?" Rod asked, surprised.

"No, of course not. But it's her room. How else would it be?"

"Yeah."

The pheasant rooster called again. A fearless muskrat swam by with house-building material in its mouth. I pulled my feet from the river and watched the water drip from them. "Do you think Melvin will come back?"

Rod thought for a moment, then shook his head.

"Good," I said. "Who needs him. Should we ask Mother about nervous breakdowns?"

"I don't know," Rod said, swirling the water below us with a stick. "You remember when we used to work in the garden together? All of us? I miss that."

It was already dark when we got to our alley off Thirteenth Street. We had a choice between going home or to Judd's for a lime soda in honor of our victories that day. Home could wait. Judd's was a two-pump, one bay service station where full service usually meant shooting the breeze with Judd or listening to his radio. As we approached we saw a pair of shiny bicycles parked outside.

The dandies were inside, gulping down Baby Ruths and sucking on sodas. The pile of wrappers and platoon of empty bottles on the table said they had been there long enough to spend a fortune. Judd and a couple of his cronies were huddled around the radio listening to football. Judd acknowledged us with a smile.

We stopped beside the dandies. "How'd you do," I asked.

"Hey, it was too hot," one of them said. "The squirrels

weren't out. You little kids got skunked, too, I imagine."

Little kids? We pulled ourselves up straight and proud. "Nope. We woulda been without Mike here," Rod said pointing at our dog snoring in the corner. "We got a few."

"So, how many's 'a few?' "

"Eight."

"Eight? You punks think we were born yesterday? Eight! Tell you what, we'll give you a nickel for every squirrel you pull from that cruddy vest."

"Who needs your money," I said proudly. "We don't care whether you believe us."

"A pop each and a dime for each squirrel, then," he challenged.

There's pride and then there's opportunity. As the fifth squirrel left the vest, they slapped the money down on the table and beat a hasty retreat. We scooped up eighty cents and began sipping free lime soda.

Judd joined us. "You got them good," he said, chuckling. "How long you been squirrel hunting?"

"Just today," I said.

"And you got *eight*? Good Lord. How'd you do it?"

"Mike did it," Rod said. "He's a heck of a dog."

Judd nodded. "You know, my mother know's your mother. She admires her for all she's done. They go to the same church."

"Really? She goes to our church? You go? We haven't seen you there."

"Nope. Quit when I was seventeen."

"Seventeen? We've got a long way to go," I said mournfully.

"In years, maybe," Judd said. "But I watch you two coming and going, always working, trying to help out. Those other two are seniors in high school and don't know half as much about what it means to be grown up as you do at what, ten or eleven?"

"Eleven last April," Rod said. "We gotta go. Thanks for the pop."

Outside, we walked slowly toward home, an exhausted Mike limping along behind. Poor little guy. I picked him up and carried him the rest of the way.

"Do you think he's right? Do you think we're more grown up than those high school guys?" Rod asked.

I shrugged. "We hunt better....We do make a lot of trouble for people, though. I don't think grown-ups would do that. They'd do everything better than we do."

"Except hunt."

"Yeah," I said.

Broad, proud, identical smiles covered our faces for the rest of the way home.

It was dawn. Our papers bouncing in the wagon we dragged behind us, we raced to the Sixth Street viaduct. We were a half a block away when the horn wailed. We sprinted the last yards and were there in time to see the silver gleam of the Streamliner, hurtling westward so fast that we had guessed it must be going one hundred miles an hour, or perhaps the speed of sound, whichever was faster. Our older and wiser brother, Ralph, assured us it was the latter.

From our panoramic perch, we watched it pass, feeling the pull of it. It rocketed through Ames every morning at 5:30 sharp, carrying royalty, the rich, and the famous, according to Gert. That's why it never stops here, she said. Why would they want to stop in Ames? At two years older than us, she was even wiser than Ralph, who was but one year our senior.

They say that few things are more inspiring than the sight and sounds of a train arriving, and few things more lonesome than its leaving. I think that's because trains bring possibilities, but they leave you with certainties. We had many certainties that morning, but the most immediate one was that we had papers to deliver and we would again be late with The Old Crab's.

His name was Sanderson. He was very old, very crotchety, and he refused to pay for the paper because we never made his deadline.

"I want it here by 5 A.M. If it is, I'll pay. If it isn't, don't bother coming to my door," he said, every time we went to collect.

His house was the grandest in several blocks of stately homes, so it couldn't have been the money. That's why we called him The Old Crab, which we quickly shortened to TOC.

He'd been treating us that way for months. At our wits

end, we had decided to leave him a note, a written ultimatum telling him he either paid or he didn't get the paper from us. But we had held off on that because of the small chance that we might win the *Des Moines Register* circulation drive contest. The carrier with the most new customers got a ride in the paper's brand new Stinson, a plane who's power and mystery was for us rivaled only by the Streamliner.

Try as we might, however, we could not increase our route. We knew Little Ben, the circulation manager would cluck his tongue and say, "Like I told you, you are way too small for a paper route."

When we were sure there was no hope of winning the contest, we wrote the note:

Dear Mr. Sanderson,
We have checked with all of the other carriers. None of their customers expects a paper before 6 A.M. What is so special about you? Please sign on the dotted line, indicating that no later than 6 A.M. is OK, or you will get no more papers from us.
Yours truly,
The Paulson Twins

That morning, twenty minutes after the Streamliner disappeared, I laid TOC's paper and our ultimatum on his porch. Not long after that, Little Ben called us in. TOC had called him. We showed up, expecting to be fired. Instead, Little Ben told us that TOC had decided to mend his ways, and all because of our note.

"He said you were great kids and that your note was what he needed to 'get me down off my high horse and discover I had become a miserable old crab.'"

He used the word crab! We were amazed, but there was more. Little Ben told us that he had talked the paper into giving us an award for Best Customer Relations. It came along with a ride in the Stinson. We were flabbergasted.

On a bright day not long after, we discovered the sky—a limitless place from which you could look down on Ames, and see all of the Valley of the Skunk.

Chapter Two

Spring, 1936—Ned Jenkins, a huge, pot-bellied blond, slammed down a shot glass. He snatched up his mug and guzzled beer before the whiskey said goodbye to his teeth.

"I'm tellin' you it is!" He wiped his mouth with the back of his hand. "This here scar come from a mustard gas burn!"

His companion at the bar peered at him over the top of his beer and shook his head. "Bull shit, Jenkins. Closest you ever come to a trench was diggin' a latrine."

"Well, I dug me some, that's true," he said, grinning. He guzzled again from the mug. "But I ain't shittin' you, Joe."

"Ha! You'd shit your grandmother if she'd fit! Anybody who come that close to that devilish stuff is dead. You ain't dead."

"No, I ain't, thank the Lord. But that poor soul I drug back behind the line when it was over, now *he* was dead....You don't get no deader 'en that." He drained the mug, drowning the memory.

"You sayin' you got that touchin' somebody else?" Joe Smith, a balding, black-haired, former mechanic, considered that seriously for a moment. He looked hard at Jenkins. His face cracked into a smile. "You almost had me that time. I ain't buyin'."

"It's the truth, so help me." Jenkins turned on the barstool and for the first time noticed the small man drinking alone at a table in a far corner of the American Legion Hall. The man was staring at nothing in particular, occasionally sipping from a glass of amber liquid. "Son of a bitch," Jenkins murmured.

"What?" Smith turned, saw the man, and sneered. "I'll be damned....Come on. Let's us pay our respects to the loon."

Melvin Paulson saw them coming and knew it would be trouble. The response he chose was to continue staring at a dust ball in the corner.

"This here's a veteran of W-W-One, Jenkins. He'll know. Show loony-bird Paulson here the scar. Careful now. Don't let him bite ya. Rabies drives folks crazy. That what got you, Paulson? Rabies? Get too close to them pigs?...Shit, a course not! It was the syph, wasn't it? You got *way* too close to them pigs!" Smith punched Jenkins in the shoulder. Jenkins was giggling, a strange ability for a man of his size.

Paulson didn't show the anger building within him. He could do nothing against these two. He continued to stare. Smith grabbed Jenkins' hand and thrust it in front of Paulson's face.

"We got us *a* argument," Jenkins said. "Ned here claims he got this scar from a mustard gas burn. You was there. Is it?"

Paulson glanced at the ugly scar. He hadn't made it out of basic training, but there was no use in admitting to that. He nodded. Still, he never looked at them.

Jenkins nearly danced with glee. "See? See? I told ya! I told ya!"

"You expect me to believe a loon, you big ox?" Smith scowled down at Paulson for a moment. A sneer slowly curled his lips. "Your wife and kids moved, did ya know that? They got 'em a good house with inside plumbing. *She* did that, Paulson. Your wife did that. You didn't, did ya? All you could give 'er was a stinkin' outhouse and a bunch a raggedy brats. You could never cut it, could ya?" He settled his weight evenly on both feet and waited.

Paulson blinked, that was all.

Seconds later, a frustrated Jenkins spat on the table. "God, you're a worthless sack of shit. Everybody in town knows whose got the balls in your family.... Ya know, Ned? I figure he ain't really crazy."

"Yeah?"

"No, not crazy...just yella."

"Yeah. A chicken-shit bastard."

Rage burned in his belly. He sipped from his glass to put it out. He waited, never looking at his tormentors. Finally, they gave up and returned to the bar. Paulson finished his drink and waited for them to lose interest. It didn't take long and he left unnoticed.

It was late afternoon, a sunny Friday. It was a pleasant day to walk, but what he noticed most was the feeling of eyes on him, judging him, some of them laughing. How had she been able to manage the new house? Slowly, drop by drop, the alcohol began feeding the flames in his gut. Each drop flared as it ignited.

What had she done? She'd taken the kids from him, that's what she'd done. Turned them against him! Turned the whole town against him!...No! She's a good woman. She didn't. It was the break-down. It was all the break-down and that was done, over. He'd worked it out. All he had to do was be careful and not drink too much. He hadn't drunk too much.

Minutes later, he saw the house. It was a great house, small but better than he'd provided. His courage left him and he turned and left. Powered by a pint bottle, he and his courage returned on Sunday afternoon.

Rod and I were in the backyard fooling with a glider, trying various configurations of wing position and elevators to see which kept it airborne longest. Since the trip aloft in the Register plane, flight had become a summertime passion for us. Hunting remained our fall and winter reward for surviving the week. Looking back, I believe flight and hunting had much in common for us. They offered the opportunity for control and mastery without interference: If we failed, *we* failed.

We heard angry, insistent banging from the front of the house and ran around to investigate. We froze when we saw him. He was on the porch, pounding on the door with both fists. Our thoughts? I don't think we had thoughts. It was shock, mostly, and maybe ambivalence—fear and hope, happiness and disgust, and maybe a hundred other emotions we couldn't have understood and dared not allow. And I think we knew what was coming. We knew, but there was nothing we could do. He was small, but we were smaller. If he saw us, he didn't acknowledge us, nor we him. We returned to the backyard and escaped into the air with our glider for a few moments until it lodged itself into a high branch, far out of our reach.

Later the police again took Melvin away in handcuffs. We never found out what he had done, and at the time we didn't know what he was doing out of the insane asylum. We never wanted to know.

Fall, 1936—Like bugs on a fetid lake, greasy scum and bits of garbage floated atop the water. Rod dumped in more soap. The grease rushed away from the spot for a moment. A dish followed with a splash that left an oily film flowing down the sides of the sink.

"Cripes, it's hot! How can it be this damn hot on Halloween!" he complained, wiping his face.

"How can we be stuck *here* on Halloween night," I moaned.

"Don't start!" Rod warned.

"Hell! It's your fault. You volunteered us for maid duty!"

"You would've if I hadn't." He was controlling his temper, and he was right. I would have.

A week before, late on a Saturday night, Mother shook us awake and demanded to know how we dared leave the house in so sorry a state. The answer was pretty simple: Ralph, George, Leonard, Rod, and I had been playing cards and eating popcorn.

Rod and I may have made a habit of annoying people, but never Mother, at least not deliberately. In this case, however, the choice between cleaning up the house or cards and popcorn had been an easy one to make.

She'd complained before, and we'd promised to do better before. But dragging us out of bed in the middle of the night was a new tactic. She looked more tired than usual. She was always tired on Saturday night, the end of a seventy-hour week at the Sheldon Munn Hotel where she baked.

Often, we waited up for her, watching for her from the porch as she trudged into the light of the corner street lamp, turn the corner and then to the house. She'd smile when she saw us. With all the energy she had left, she would hang up her thread-bare, but spotlessly clean coat, and then pull herself slowly up the stairs to bed. On this night, we hadn't waited up. On this night, she'd had it.

28

"I've been slaving for over two years to keep us together and to give you a good home! Look what you've done to it! Is this the thanks I get?...Obviously, it is. Obviously, you just don't care!...I can't take any more! Every day I fight to keep us together, and every day I have to fight again!"

She rose wearily and set about warming a cup of that morning's coffee. Rod and I fidgeted. This time was different, we knew. This time... "We'll clean up on Friday nights," Rod volunteered. "Everything but your room, Gert's, and the back room."

"We haven't been fair to you," I agreed, believing what I said enough at that moment to be truly sorry. "We know it's us — not Gert or Ralph. They have regular jobs and they do well in school. And Leonard's too little. It won't be hard for us." It was clear from her reaction that she would believe what she saw.

"At least we should've waited till after Halloween," I complained.

"Sure, sure. I have a fat picture of that: 'We'll be happy to help, Mother, but we can't start till after Halloween because we got a bushel of tomatoes to throw.' She would've loved that!" He dumped a dish into the rinse water. I plucked it out and began drying it with a rag that had become nearly as dirty as the wash water.

"Cripes! Change that! What's the point of washing if you're gonna dry 'em with that filthy thing?"

I stared at the rag. "'What's the point' is right! Why don't we just put 'em away dirty? If anybody gets sick, we'll just blame it on our cooking....You know, we *do* a lot around here. We cook. We bring home fresh game. We cut down dead trees and drag them home for furnace wood. We bring home money. We do a lot!"

"Yeah!" Rod agreed hopefully.

I got a clean cloth and watched as it brought up a shine on the plate. I could see the distorted reflection of a liar.

"Who are we kidding?" I sighed. "We don't do enough. Gert and Ralph bring home *real* money for the fifty-fifty kitty. Do we make them quit their jobs just so we don't have to clean the house? And Mother — nobody works harder than Mother.

Nobody in the whole town works harder than she does....Let's get this done. We got dusting to do."

We saved the worst for last, and the worst by far was the living room and dusting. The worst of the worst were the dozens of framed photographs on the wall. Each one had to be taken down and individually wiped clean. As we were about to start this daunting task, Gert came home from her job at the drug store. Ralph was with her. He worked at the dairy. She smiled when she saw the doom etched in our faces.

"I see you're getting ready to polish our unnatural history," she said. We cringed. Gert had a brilliant mind. At the age of fourteen, however, she tended to demonstrate it more than we could stand. Once she got on a roll, it took losing her audience to stop her—that or hitting a tree. At that moment, she had that look and tone that said a roll was beginning. There were no trees in the living room, and we couldn't run.

"What do you mean?" I asked, feeling Rod wince and instantly realizing I had made the fatal mistake of encouraging her.

"Our unnatural history. It's in the pictures....Look at them."

We did, but all we saw were the reasons we were going to miss Halloween altogether.

She sighed and reached up to help us pluck them from the wall. If she was going to help, it might be worth the price. We listened. She used time as her guide, pointing out first the baby pictures of all of us, beginning with Gert in 1922—five children in less than four years, and then Leonard six years later.

"Notice how young Mother looked then," she said. "She's aged so much. It's no wonder, with all of us. It's our fault."

"What do you mean?" Ralph demanded.

Gert continued to study the photographs. A melancholy mood swept over her. "I shouldn't have said 'our fault.' I meant that supporting us is what's going to put her in an early grave. We had nothing to do with that, but it's true just the same."

One by one, we looked at the photos. One in particular caught my attention. It was of Ralph, Rod, and me in 1933. We were decked out in our baseball gear. I was holding up a finger. "Look, I'm showing off my mashed finger," I said proudly.

Gert nodded. "I remember that. Doctor Fellows had to come and splint it. Mother and Dad argued about how they were going to pay the bill. Mother really let him have it that time. She was so much bigger than he was. I think he was afraid of her then. I remember her telling him we'd have the money if he didn't drink it all away."

"She should've hit him," Rod said. "He deserved it."

"What good would that have done?" Gert asked.

"He deserved it," I said.

Gert thought about that for a moment, then shrugged. "Maybe he did, but alcohol can destroy people."

"I don't want to talk about this," Ralph said, turning away. "What's done is done."

Gert nodded. "At least she's safe now." Her head snapped up and fearfully stared at all of us.

Ralph scowled at her. "Go ahead. You gotta tell 'em now."

Gert looked at us with special kindness and deep regret. "He used to get violent when he'd drink. After the breakdown, it got worse. The second time the police took him away was because he...hurt her.

In a vague way, Rod and I had known. But to hear it—at that moment, anything we might have felt for him was galvanized and shut away.

"Tell us what you meant by 'unnatural,'" I said softly.

"The pictures show it," she said. "Until 1933, we're a family living in the nineteenth century. A year later, we moved into the twentieth century." She studied our faces and continued when she found no understanding in them. "When we lived on High Street, we lived in the nineteenth century— no indoor plumbing, only a wood stove, no car, but we were a complete family; we had both a mother and father. A year later, we don't have a father, we never see Mother except on Sunday, and we've moved into a house in the twentieth century with heat and plumbing. We moved ahead, but we had to be ripped apart as a family to do it."

"We're together," Rod grumbled. "All but Melvin."

Gert stared at him a moment, then she looked at each of us. Ralph turned away. "After Dad was arrested that spring of '34, "she said slowly, "I heard Mother and Aunt Dorothy talking. They were terribly upset, Dorothy especially. She could barely talk, but she was trying to help Mother figure out what to do with us, what would be best for everybody. They were crying and they talked about the orphanage or foster homes. Was I scared!"

For several seconds, the only sounds in the room were Mike snoring in the corner and the ticking of the clock atop the Atwater-Kent radio. Finally, Rod spoke, nearly choking on the words. My throat hurt, too. "They were gonna put us in an orphanage? Why?" We were close to tears. We could see them in Gert's eyes.

"They talked about it, but not because they wanted to get rid of us. Neither of them knew how Mother was going to support us all. If they had decided to put us up for adoption, it would have been to keep us alive. But Mother didn't do it. She wouldn't break us apart like that. That's why she works so hard. That's why she expects us to."

"Do you understand this?" We asked Ralph.

"I don't know. I try not to think about it. But Gert does. She wrote a report about it."

"Ralph!" She glared at him, then noticed our stares and lowered her eyes.

"You mean a school report? In junior high?" I asked in disbelief. Ralph nodded.

"Cripes, Gert! Isn't it bad enough everybody knows we're on relief? Mattie knows that and everything. Now, you gotta tell the whole world about us?" Rod said.

She bristled. "The whole world does not know! Just my teacher. She said it was senior-high, even college-level work."

"Oh, *that* makes it alright then! You got to show off your brains! Cripes, Gert!"

"What's it say?" I asked. I could feel Rod's eyes burning into the side of my head. I met them. "We gotta know what we're up against," I said. "Maybe it won't be so bad." He snorted in response. With a mixture of regret and pride, Gert explained her sociological inquiry into our "unnatural history."

Thanks to mother's latest addition to our misery index (school, Sunday school, church, junior choir, and now Friday night maid duty), it was eleven by the time we hit the street that night. We left the tomatoes where they were. It was too late for them. By now, Gunner Davis and Whitey Smith — the best arms in the seventh grade outside of Rod — had figured out we weren't coming and no doubt had found some other wonderful way to raise hell. Without a word or a question, we found ourselves headed for Judd's.

What Gert had said was piled all around us like snow — cold, heavy, and covering everything with new reality. But unlike snow, it held no promise.

"Do you remember *With the Indians in the Rockies*?" Rod asked.

It was a strange question, but I was thankful for it. "Yeah, That was years ago."

"I know, but you remember how John was always on the run, always hiding, always having to escape from something?"

"Sure," I said. "Bears, wolves, Indians — somebody was always after him."

"That's the way we are," he said.

"Hey, fellas," Judd greeted us. "How was squirrel hunting this year?" I'll never know whether he did it on purpose or not, but Judd had a wonderful way of giving us sanctuary, both with his place and his interest.

"We only went four times. Too much work to do. Got six each time."

"Six? You birds are pulling my leg."

"Nope. It's like our own private squirrel farm. Six was our personal daily limit."

Judd grinned. "I suppose you had one heck of a Halloween." He lit a Lucky.

We frowned. "Naw," I said. "We got stuck with maid duty. We just got out."

"Maid duty? When did you two get reduced to housework?"

"Reduced is right," Rod said. "We've sunk lower then snakes."

"I know how you feel. My mom — boy, she could tighten the screws. When I was seventeen I decided I'd had enough, so I left."

"You just left?"

33

"Yep. One night, right after our umptieth fight, I packed my bags, headed for Alaska."

Alaska! Judd may have said more, but I didn't hear anything for a few seconds except the echo of the word in my mind. Alaska! Wilderness! Maybe even gold! When I came back to the conversation, Judd was describing heaven.

"It's a fantastic place!...A dream land!...You have to see it to believe it!...No people, great hunting and fishing, good jobs....Wages are two or three times what they are here...."

"So, why did you come back?" Rod asked, obviously as excited as I was.

"Oh, it was a struggle at first up there, but I was doing fine. Then my dad died and I had to come back to take care of this place. As soon as I can sell it, I'm on my way back! You know there's so few roads up there that people fly more places than they drive?"

As we walked home that night, we both knew. We'd talked about it before: In two, but no more than four years, we were leaving. Now we knew where we were going. From then on our money was on Alaska. God's heaven might have been millions of miles away in space. We could hitchhike to ours.

The good news was that late Saturday night the unseasonal heat broke. The bad news was that a merciless rain broke it. It was still raining hard when we dragged ourselves out of bed early Sunday to do our paper route. It was raining when we came home, drenched and dripping, to find Gert doing the Sunday ironing.

"So," one of us asked her, hoping to lift her spirits a little, "what would you like for breakfast? Oatmeal or cornbread?"

"Neither!" she growled. Her Sunday mood was in full force, like a low-grade fever building to a fatal disease. "Both choices are like church — an acquired taste. No one should be required to acquire them. How about pancakes or French toast for a change!"

"We're out of syrup," I said.

"That's no excuse, you lame brains! We have brown sugar, make some!" She glared at me and slammed the iron down on a shirt. She was moving the iron so hard and fast that whoever was destined to wear that shirt would be lucky if it wasn't scorched by friction alone. Gert had been ironing all the family's clothes every Sunday for five years. It was also her job to see that all of us kids were pressed and shined to Mother's exacting standards by 9:30 A.M. sharp every Sunday—in time for the entire troop to be marched by Captain Mother to church. Rain or shine, snow or gale, we walked and we were there dead on time. It was a thankless task for Gert, especially where we were concerned. She rose every Sunday morning as early as we did to be finished in time.

"I assume your Sunday clothes are just where you left them last week? What's your excuse for not doing your laundry yesterday?"

"Since when did you become our keeper?" I demanded. "It's none of your business, but we were up at four, raked two lawns, and didn't get home until dark!"

"Big deal! You should've had that done by noon. Even so, you had plenty of time to do your laundry last night, but no. Instead, you found some way to goof off."

"By the time we finished collecting, it was after ten! Who do you think you are?"

"I'm the one who has to iron your stupid clothes! I'm the one who has to iron everybody's stupid clothes!" She slammed the iron down again. "As usual, Mother will demand we all look perfect. Do you think I like being caught in the middle when you two goof off?... But will you tell me what difference ironing is going to make today? We're all going to look like drowned rats the minute we leave the house!"

She glared at us as if she really wanted an answer or was expecting an argument. She wouldn't get one from us. As far as we were concerned, ironing was *never* necessary.

"Well? Don't just stand there! Go get your clothes! I'll iron them dirty. Lucky for you that nobody will be able to tell after thirty seconds in that rain!"

Maybe we were lucky, but we didn't feel that way. In its own way, Sunday was the toughest day of the week. Sunday school and church in the morning, then waiting there while Mother, a member of the church council, fulfilled her obligation to meet and talk with members of the congregation. Literally a head taller than most people, Mother wasn't just active in church, she was the franchise.

On Sunday evenings, we marched back again for Junior Choir. What there was to sing about when you've already been up for fifteen hours was never clear to Rod and me. Between church in the morning and church at night was family time together. On this particular Sunday, Mother was still pleased with the job we had done on the house. The chicken was perfect, the rolls hot, flaky, and oozing fresh butter. The talk was light and hopeful—all except Gert, who's Sunday malaise seemed to have darkened into fear. When dinner was finished and the dishes were washed and put away, Mother asked us—asked us—back to the table.

We sat waiting for her to speak. Leonard desperately needed something to play with. Gert restrained him, her apprehension as plain as a blood stain.

"Gert told me about the report," Mother began solemnly. We held our breaths. Gert's eyes teared up. Mother studied each of us before continuing. "I think she's done us a favor," she finally said with a small smile. There was a collective exhale. Color rushed into Gert's cheeks. "It's long past the time I should have explained everything to all of you. We've had too many secrets for too long. You all have gotten some idea of what happened from Gert—and just so you'll know, Uncle Neil told her most of what she knew about it. Do you have any questions for me?"

No one spoke for a moment as the relief settled in, passed, and was replaced with the unsettling realization that somehow, for that moment at least, none of us was a child anymore.

"Is Dad crazy?" I asked. "Is he insane? Is that the same as crazy?"

Mother struggled to find the words. Tears formed and glistened in her eyes. "Your father had...a nervous break-down....At times, he was dangerous to be around...like when he hit you with the ax handle, Roland. You know he hit Mrs. Brown. You probably don't know he broke his mother's arm."

"Did he hit you?" I asked, staring straight into her eyes with an authority that until that moment had been reserved for adults.

She looked hard at me, at all of us. "Whatever he did to

36

me, I've managed. We've all managed. I'm very proud of all of you, of everything you've done. I know how hard you work and I wish there was another choice. If there is, I can't see it. I want you to know that I believe that if we keep it up, in a year we won't need help—not from the government, not from the town, not from Neil, not from anyone," she said. Her face still showed signs of stifled crying, but there was pride there as well.

"When you think about your father, I want you to remember what Gert said in her report. This isn't about good people or bad people. He was sick and needed help. They tried to give it to him at the VA hospital, but I guess he had trouble taking it. He left. I suppose, in a way, he's a fugitive...."

"A fugitive?" Rod said. "Is a sheriff's posse after him?"

"No, stupid," Gert snapped. "Dad's back in Dakota on the farm doing a lot better than any of us—or at least he should be. All he's got to worry about is him. The Iowa authorities don't want him back. He's not their problem any more, or ours either."

"Geez! Doesn't anybody care what happens to him?" Ralph said, his voice cracking.

"You don't get it!" Gert shot back. "I'm glad he's back on the farm. He's doing well there, better than he was here or in the hospital. I'm happy for him, but I don't have to be happy that he's a lot better off than us!"

Her eyes still glistening, Mother broke in. "Gert knows many things and understands many things. Your father is better off where he is and we should be happy for him, but I disagree with your sister that he's better off than we are. Maybe he doesn't have to work as hard, but he doesn't have what we have."

Puzzled, all of us looked at each other. Mother smiled. "We have each other," she said quietly. "What does he have that's as good as that?"

We considered that as best we could. Leonard continued to squirm. His arm jerked free from Gert's hold and knocked over the salt shaker.

Chapter Three

August, 1939—We smelled the pie before we hit the back door. Something was up. It was nearly midnight on a brutally hot and muggy Friday. Mother baked twelve hours a day at the Sheldon Munn. Even on those rare nights when she came home with enough energy to do more than just find her bed, it usually was spent on little more than pleasant talk. Usually it was just Mother, Rod, and me, owing mostly to the fact that we were the only ones up. Our Friday maid duties kept us up. Our reward trips to Judd's after the house was clean kept us up even later. She was pulling the pie, an apple pie, out of the oven when we stepped into the kitchen.

Mom and apple pie—symbols of America said with sneers now as though they aren't real and never were. Whether the values represented were ever real depends on how you define them. As portrayed by television during the first twenty years of that medium, the mom-and-apple-pie symbol was about milk, cookies, and bed-time stories told by women who didn't sweat. That was the lie. As a symbol, Mom and apple pie always was and still is about ethics, courage, and stamina. From that perspective, few women personified the symbol as well as our mother. Of course, just a month away from high school on that blistering Friday night, we didn't think of her that way. What we knew was that she made a fabulous apple pie. The question was whether is was for the family or just for us in reward for something Rod and I had managed to do right.

Our faces must have telegraphed the question because she answered it with a smile. "I'm so happy with how clean the house has been, I thought we should celebrate," she said. She set the pie out to cool and we all sat at the table, her sipping coffee, smiling, and saying little. She looked past us to the refrigerator. As she rose, she fetched the ever-present cleaning cloth from her apron, stepped to the gleaming white prize against the wall, and rubbed a speck we couldn't see from it's top. Our mother was a miracle of Creation. It's one thing to *assume* the tiniest fleck of dust might be present and to clean based on that assumption. It's another thing to be able to *spot* *it* from twenty feet and direct a disbeliever to it from that same distance. Our mother could do that.

The refrigerator had been in our home only a week. For us, it was a wonderful source of cold, fresh milk that occupied the space that only a week before had belonged to the old ice box that kept sour milk luke warm; that infuriating, useless thing that kept us trudging to fetch ice and busy cleaning up the disgusting mess in the drip pan. For Mother, the refrigerator was much more, more even than the birthday present we intended it to be.

One of the puzzles we never did figure out is how Ames, a city of ten thousand, could survive with a central business district consisting of six blocks of one street, Main Street no less. Late the afternoon of the Saturday previous to the apple-pie Friday, Rod and I were "downtown." Because we were identical, we drew the usual quick looks and double-takes from the crowd of shopping, strolling, or striding farmers and town folk. The Depression remained in full force, but you couldn't tell from the near-celebration that rippled through the gathering in the full heat of an August weekend. Perhaps we all had carried the burden long enough not to notice it any more.

Sweat-stained and dripping, a cigarette drooping in every other mouth or so, they mingled and talked, and bought and carried, and ate the treats hawked at various stands. Our favorite belonged to blind Billy Roads, who sold fluffy popcorn to shoppers and a hefty bag of the kernels that didn't pop to us. He said we were his best customer for the Old Maids.

We had spent most of the day on yard work. Taken together, our business enterprises were bringing us what we thought was a respectable income, enough for us to consider buying a new shotgun. We had rushed home to change, decided against donning clean clothes because of the heat, and dashed out with our sights set on the second-hand store. We were nearly there now. As usual, we swung wide to avoid the front of the beer and pool hall. The place scared us. We never knew why. We did know it reminded us of Shorty, our one-time neighbor across the alley whose bouts with drinking were legendary — and dangerous for him when his tiny little wife got hold of him.

We paused at the front door of the shop. I looked at Rod — tanned, robust, never tiring, nearly always smiling (possibly because he ate twice as much as I did).

"Putting on clean clothes would have been a mistake," he said. "The worse we look, the better the price we can get from Maxie Duitch and his junior money sharks."

I nodded. Both of us put on our all-business scowls and stepped inside. Max had made his money selling cars. "There ain't no comparancy," he'd said of them to everyone in Story County. Success brought expansion and he opened the second-hand store. Once inside, we separated; Rod to guns and me to the appliance section. It was Mother's birthday. Although our main focus was a new gun, we hadn't forgotten her — or figured out what to get her. The party was set for late that night when she got home. Gert was making the cake and Ralph and Leonard swore they had found her something she really needed. We had thought about a new coat; hot as hell during the day, it could be cool by the time she walked home. What drew me to the appliance section, I don't know. There was nothing there we could afford. Still, the refrigerator caught my eye immediately. It was, literally, a gleaming white pillar in the electrical community. Before I had a chance to investigate, Rod summoned me.

He showed the shotgun to me along with his excitement. Both were as big as a cannon. "Can you believe this?" he said, shouldering the weapon and pretending to track a bird across the store and up to the ceiling. "It's exactly what we *have* to have, and it's as good as new!" Another bird bit the tile. "The stock's a little long, but I can grow into that. The balance is good. It handles great!"

Forcing enough of a frown to cover our grins, I took the gun from him. "Cripes, I can see I should never have left you alone. Start looking at other guns before somebody sees how much you want this one or we'll be paying through the nose!"

Suddenly sober, Rod turned and began testing the heft of other weapons. Within seconds, a smiling junior model of Max Duitch scurried up flashing his own brand of the "ain't no comparancy" smile. He was older than us, but no taller and that put us on equal footing. It's tough enough growing up with people looking from one to the other, never quite sure who they're talking to. It's worse when they're looking down. We were eye-to-eye with the son of Ames' super salesman. His bow tie knotted tightly at his neck, he was dressed to the nines in the midst of a store full of cast-offs and hand-me-downs.

Rod feigned interest in a pump-action twenty-gauge. The Duitch smile beamed. Ships lost in the fog could have been guided by that smile. "You boys have made a dandy choice," he said with somewhat less enthusiasm than his smile warranted. "You'll grow into it in a couple of years and then it'll be the perfect gun for you. It's just five dollars down and three dollars a week for ten weeks."

The smile never wavered, but something about the rest of him told us he held little hope that we could afford more than the fare for the trip out the door. Worse, he'd called us *boys*, almost as bad as *kids*. He deserved our best.

Rod lovingly stroked the stock of the twenty-gauge. "Is that the price for two of them?" he asked innocently. "We need two, of course."

It was less a flinch than a flicker, a barely noticeable brown-out in the glow of his smile. It was quickly gone. "We have some *dandy* single-shot four-tens and twenties. I think we could fix you both up for the price of the pump."

I shoved my hands into my pockets and looked disappointed. Rod laid down the pump-action and surveyed the other choices with disdain. "What's the story on that monstrosity," he said, pointing to the gun. "Who would have been dumb enough to buy it in the first place?"

Just for a moment, Max Junior looked as though maybe he had been dumb enough. He quickly righted himself, however. "That's a man's gun—no offense. It's too big for me. The guy who brought it in was *huge,* said it kicked like a mule. Besides, it's a magnum…"

"We know. It takes three-inch shells," Rod interrupted.

Unimpressed, young Duitch continued. "Not many people can afford them."

"It's for our father," Rod said quietly. "It's his birthday."

"Is he big?"

"Big enough," I said, allowing just a hint of menace.

The smile had become downright tentative. "Well! In that case, its yours for the price of the little pump."

"Only if you believe in magic!" Rod sniffed.

"Oh....Well...that includes four boxes of shells and a sheepskin case."

I took Rod's arm. "We'd better go before Dad finds us and spoils the surprise. We'll come back Monday...if we can."

We left and he didn't stop us. We had reached his limit. We stopped just outside.

"That's an awful lot of money for an awfully big gun. How do we know you can even hit anything with it?"

"Sure, the gun's big. But the three-inch shell holds twice as much shot as the sixteen. I'll do even better, not worse, especially at long range." He wanted the gun badly, but Rod eventually agreed that we should think about it. We were about to leave when I remembered what I had seen in the appliance section. I dragged him back inside.

It was a refrigerator, the clerk said. He wasn't Max Junior, but was clearly another Duitch. He decided at first glance that we were a couple of rubes who didn't know anything. We knew that it was a refrigerator because Grandma Paulson had one. But this one was special, the clerk said, because it ran on gas. Cheaper, better, fewer moving parts, he went on. He had the same stupid smile as his brother, but we were listening.

"How much trouble is it to clean?" Rod asked, getting right to the point.

"You gotta clean an ice box once a week, right?" the clerk asked slyly.

We nodded. The memory of having slogged through that painful task the day before was much fresher than the food in our ice box.

"Well," he gushed and beamed, "all you do with this baby is defrost it *once a month!*"

That was it. We settled some important arguments about

credit worthiness, signed, and were in debt for the first time in our lives. There would be no new gun, and the prospect of *having* to make enough money to cover the debt was frightening. But no more ice box? It was easily worth it.

At nine that night, Ralph and Gert came home together. There, in place of the ice box, stood the refrigerator. They didn't quite get it.

"Put the ice cream in here," we told them. They opened the door and realized for the first time that this wasn't just a bigger ice box. It was cold inside, really cold.

"Does this thing use dry ice?" Ralph was suspicious. "That's going to be expensive."

No, it's a refrigerator, we said.

Gert wasn't buying. "Whatever it is, you can bet it's no good. How could you two pull something on Mother's birthday?"

We explained everything, twice.

Finally, Ralph accepted it. "How long do we get to keep it when you stop making payments? Can you imagine how Mother's going to feel when they repossess it? You two have done some rotten things, but this…" He threw up his arms and turned away.

"Is this on the level?" Gert asked, peering at us.

It took another ten minutes, but we finally persuaded them both. Once they accepted the purity of our motives — we didn't mention the cleaning schedule, but it was a minor point — they were amazed and began demonstrating something we had seldom seen from them: They were proud of us. We even offered to let them share in the credit, but they refused.

At midnight, Mother shuffled through the door and carefully hung up her thread-bare coat. Maybe a new coat would have been a better idea, we thought. The kitchen was dark except for the candles on her cake and she didn't notice the refrigerator at first. When she did, she just stood and stared, frozen in the candle glow.

We waited. She didn't move, she didn't speak. Finally, Ralph could stand it no longer. "Well?"

She stepped to the gleaming white box and opened the door. Inside was the sign we all had made: HAPPY

BIRTHDAY, DEAR MOTHER! IT'S YOURS! She closed the door gently and dropped into a chair at the table. She laid her head in her arms and wept quietly while Gert, in tears herself, served the cake and ice cream. In silence, we watched Mother eat a little of hers. A few moments later, she rose, hugged each of us, and went to her bedroom. She never said a word.

Rod and I were in shock. What had we done? "It seemed like a good idea," Rod said finally.

Gert burst into tears. "It was," she bawled. "It was the very best idea, the best thing anyone has *ever* done for her and of all people to have done it....I'm so proud of you!" She kissed us and hurried off to her room.

Sunday night, Mother was able to talk about it. She wrote Aunt Dorothy and invited her to come up from Des Moines and see it. As great a change as that refrigerator made in our household and in our mother, it was no greater than the change it sparked in Rod and me. We had become part of our family in our own eyes. It was too much to understand all at once and we argued that if they knew the *real* reason we bought the refrigerator, their worst suspicions would be validated. We never told them.

Fall, 1939—Mow enough lawns and you can't help appraising each new one you see in terms of time and sweat. Ames High School was built around an outdoor central courtyard that was covered in green grass. The perplexing part was that there was no access to it—no door, no gate, no apparent secret tunnel known only to the King. How did they mow it? Who mowed it? Rod and I had gotten jobs as janitors in the school and you would think they would have told us, but they never did.

I stepped away from the window and put the push broom I'd been leaning on back to work, guiding it between the rows of double-occupancy tables in the science lab. Rod was across the hall. We assaulted our block with a pincer movement that flanked the remnants of the previous day of classes and drove them into the hall—not as fast as Hitler had plowed through Poland a few weeks before, but just as effectively. At the end of the hall, we joined forces and swept back through.

As I neared the door, I saw Rod already stepping out of the room across the hall. "Come on!" he said. "We're late!" He was right. The student body would be crashing through the main doors soon.

We were beginning our final drive back up the hall when we heard the doors open to the sound of laughter. We looked at each other. Rod frowned, lowered his head and began racing back up the corridor, herding the filth of others before him. I was behind him by less than a second. We strained to move faster, shifting the brooms from side to side with choppy, frantic slaps on the floor. Almost there, almost there...

I would have plowed right into them if I hadn't seen their feet at the last moment. Three pairs rounded my corner just as I approached and stopped dead, my pile of dirt only a few inches from six shined shoes — girls' shoes. Rod had stopped, too. I was aware he was watching, but I was alone. There was nothing he could do.

I looked up into the faces of three town girls. The faces were blank, or maybe indecisive at first. Then two of them scowled and one began to giggle. They stepped around me without a word.

One of those flushes that starts at your toes and gets hotter as it climbs was shooting up my spine on the way to the top of my head. That these were the super students who got to school early because they *wanted* to be there didn't help much. That we were only in the tenth grade and girls remained remarkably strange creatures didn't help much. I felt like a shaken bottle of strawberry soda.

As I looked over at Rod, who was nearly as mortified as I, a boy rounded the corner. We'd seen him before. He was a junior destined to spend his life buried in a laboratory somewhere. He stopped, nodded at us both, unwrapped a stick of gum, wadded up the paper, and dropped it in the pile of dirt in front of my broom. He nodded again and moved on, flat feet pounding the floor, his mind engaged somewhere no one in his right mind would want to go.

Heads drooping, we finished and waited for classes to begin. By the last bell, we had almost convinced ourselves that it didn't matter.

The week before pheasant season began, Mother came home with an early Christmas present: *the* gun. How she managed it, we never knew. We had it all and she gave it to us. That night, safe in the house a single mother had managed to buy for five kids in the middle of the Great Depression, we all had a good cry.

Mother had to work Thanksgiving Day, which was just fine with us — not fine that she had to work, but that we wouldn't have to hang around home. Armed with Bertha (short for Big Bertha, the name we gave *the* gun) and with Mike in tow, we were in our valley — the best equipped hunters in Ames, if not all of Story County, bundled against a bitter, snow-spitting wind. It was noon and with seven shells we had brought down four rabbits and three pheasants. Pheasants, no less, that regal hunter's prize of the corn fields. Any kid could hunt rabbits and squirrels. With Bertha we had been vaulted into the big leagues. Regularly we brought home pheasants, ducks, and geese. For that added variety, Gert and Ralph were grateful. After the bird seasons closed, thanks to Bertha, we were well equiped to hunt foxes and coyotes. Those pelts and bounties brought real money to us, real in those days anyway.

As we emerged from one draw and were about to enter another, we noticed without pleasure that our reserved part of the Skunk wasn't entirely ours. A hundred yards from us, a man and two boys waved like friends. We approached with all the openness of armed guards. Mike grew more wary the closer we came to the trio of interlopers and their spaniel.

"Wonderful day for it, isn't it boys?" the man said.

Boys don't hunt, mister, we responded silently.

"Oh — forgive my lack of manners. I am Doctor Knight, a professor at Iowa State. This is my oldest, Harold, and my youngest, Rollie." I flinched. "And the Springer's name is Joey." The doctor was a big man with a wide, sincere smile.

"Rodney and Roland Paulson," Rod said. "That's Mike." The doctor offered his hand. We took it. That out of the way, we stood waiting, all of us. Even the dogs sat under the weight of the moment. Finally, the doctor said, "Surely its a great day for Thanksgiving, and all that we have to be thankful for. Does this day bring anything special to mind for you fellas?"

After what seemed an interminable pause, Rod said quietly, "The day."

"I beg your pardon?"

"The day itself," I said. "Otherwise we wouldn't be out here."

The doctor's face slowly lit up. "Of course! You're absolutely right. Thanksgiving itself is something to be thankful for.... Forgive me for staring, but it's not often you see twins anywhere, let alone out hunting on Thanksgiving Day. Is your father about?"

"No," I said. "We hunt alone."

"I see. A wonderful place, this. I bring my boys out here as often as I can. Man is intruding on nature on all fronts and I want them to see it. I want them to understand it before it's all gone. Do you come here often?"

"Every weekend," Rod said. It's ours, we added silently. What the doctor didn't know was that we had made a deal with the owner of this section of the valley. Luther was a strange old cuss and had laughed out loud when we'd offered to keep the fox population down in return for rights to hunt on his land. Still, he raised chickens and he couldn't just ignore the logic of it. He'd agreed.

The youngest boy and the dogs had begun to fidget. The doctor was eyeing Bertha. Finally, he could stand it no longer: "I don't wish to be inelegant, but I must say that in the thirty years I've been hunting I've never seen a worse match between gun and shooter. The weapon is huge and, forgive me, but you're not. Can you get it to your shoulder? Does it knock you down? I'm not trying to find fault, but this is fascinating."

At that moment, a pheasant rooster roared up out of a clump of weeds and shot skyward. His direction and angle of ascent gave Rod the only clear shot. He snapped the gun to his shoulder and fired. The bird shuddered, hovered momentarily, and plummeted to the ground. The doctor's spaniel sprinted out after it.

"Great reflexes and a great shot," the doctor said. "One more question, please. Was it luck?"

We showed him our birds. "Actually, these were just luck, too," Rod said. "What happened is that they dropped dead of fright when they saw Bertha here." He slapped the stock.

"I'm impressed. A little man with a big gun and a sense of humor. You should go far. How about you?" he said, looking at me. "Are you that good? Do you take turns?"

I glanced at Rod and grinned. "No," I said, shaking my head. "It takes both Mike and me just to bird-dog what Rod brings down."

Joey returned with the bird and dropped it at the doctor's feet. He nudged his oldest son, a year or so older than us, and pointed at the bird. His son picked up the pheasant and handed it to us, his face betraying nothing.

"Well...good hunting, gentlemen," the doctor said, extending his hand again. We took it once more. "Come on, kids," he said as he stepped away.

We set off again. As I replayed the conversation in my mind, a grin slowly spread over my face. It was there a long time before Rod noticed.

"What?"

"Do you suppose they all talk like that?"

Rod chuckled. "'I don't wish to seem *inelegant...*'"

I chuckled along. "Maybe we're being mean. He was a nice enough guy."

"He was a phony. They're all phonies."

"Who is?"

"All of them. Every damn one of them." He stopped and stared off into the distance.

I followed his gaze to where the crest of the hills met the slate of the sky. I scanned across the hills to the valley opening beyond. Behind us was the entrance, before us the exit from the private world which had never really been private.

"Do you really think they're all phonies?" I finally asked.

Rod studied me a moment. "Probably not. It's hard to tell....Did you notice? He called me a young man, and us *gentlemen.*"

"Well, of course," I giggled, pulling myself up straighter.

"I'll bet you can walk for miles and not see anybody in Alaska," Rod said. "Mike's on the trail of something. Let's go."

Chapter Four

Few things on Earth sap optimism like the sustained heat and humidity of an Iowa summer. The sweat thaws in May and flows until late September, October sometimes. Night and day, the body surrenders all it has in its pitiable hope for relief. Finally, the mind gives up planning and satisfies itself with marking time. Millions of Iowans spend a third of their lives just waiting and sweating.

Or so it seemed to us on just such an Iowa summer day in July 1941. Rod and I had jobs unloading endless piles of heavy, filthy, skin-crusting bags of cement from endless strings of boxcars for twenty-five cents per endless hour. Heat shimmered from the parched, rust-weeping metal casements of the cars. Inside, the air was thickened by constant baking. Gray dust swirled, choked, and resettled with each movement of man within the rolling hells we were sure were invented by people who never planned to work within them.

On that day, however, the apprehension we shared was about choices: We didn't have any. Gert had choices, myriad gleaming choices presented by the college education she was earning. Ralph had choices with Johns-Manville that stretched as far as we could see. All our friends had choices, or had made them already. Up and coming with everything to live for, most of them had bought into the hot trend of going to college. The exception was Whitey Smith. The "Old Coot" was going into the painting business, to take charge of it to hear him talk. We had no reason to doubt him.

But who were we kidding? We couldn't hope to match any of them. College? Not a chance, except for people like Mattie. Over the years she had raced to the top of the class, and we to the bottom in everything except hunting. D students don't go to college except to visit and they do that quietly. Good jobs? So far as we could see, our futures in cement involved choking on it, not building with it.

Alaska had been our one hope, the siren of the wild that sounded long and sweet for two years to the point that no failure mattered. We had believed that all we had to do was go. Once there, it would provide everything we needed for a terrific future. No matter what else happened, she was waiting for us, holding our mountain suites for us. But all that had been blown away like sled tracks in a blizzard.

Late on a Friday in April, Judd was happy to see us. He always was. We were seventeen, eight weeks from the end of our junior year in high school. Judd wasn't that much older than us, not like a father, but he was old enough and wise enough and willing enough and caring enough. That's hindsight, of course. To us then, he was just Judd—a man, a friend, and an ally, the only one of his kind in our lives except Uncle Neal, who we didn't see often enough to really count.

Nervous small talk proceeded from our initial greeting until, fidgeting and unsure, Rod got down to business: "We need to talk to you, but it needs to stay just between us," he said a little too forcefully.

"Understood, no problem," Judd said. He captured and lit a Lucky Strike.

"We've decided. This is the year we go," Rod said.

"To Alaska?" Judd said for him. His crystal blue eyes betrayed nothing. "When? How are you getting there?"

"We're pretty firm on June 15," I said. "By the time we get up there, winter will be over and summer work will be up to speed."

"Makes sense."

"We're going to hitchhike. It shouldn't be any problem. Thirty goes from here all the way to Portland," I continued. "From there, it's two hundred miles on Ninety-nine to Seattle. Then we work our way on a freighter or fishing boat to Juneau or Anchorage. We checked into it. They go back and forth all the time with temporary crew members."

We watched and waited. Judd pondered a moment. "And after you get there?"

"There's defense work all over," Rod said. "We want to stay on the coast, though — Sitka or Kodiak, even out in the Aleutians."

Judd frowned slightly, as though he had a touch of heartburn. "You've got a plan," he said. "You've done your homework." He took a deep drag on his Lucky and exhaled slowly, staring over our heads as he did. "Mind if we see if we can poke a few holes in it?"

"Fire away. We need all the help we can get." I meant it.

Judd nodded and stared over our heads again. His words were measured when he finally spoke. "How many times have you seen a road-kill attract one crow, then another, then another? In fifteen minutes, half the crows in the county are there fighting for their share — so many that maybe one in ten actually gets dinner. That one has to be the toughest and strongest." He locked eyes first with me, then with Rod, and waited. He didn't have long to wait.

We both sighed in resignation to his logic. "We get it," Rod said, dejected. "How could we have been so stupid to think that we were good enough to..."

"Knock it off! You may have reason to feel sorry for yourselves, but not around here! You aren't stupid, far from it. But you are young. I've been around enough to have made some mistakes, some real doozies. Maybe I learned something from them. And maybe you knew that, right? You're in here asking me about your plans, aren't you? Maybe I'm too good to myself, but that doesn't strike me as stupid!

"You listen to me. It's easy to see only what you want to see. People do it all the time, and not just the young. Everybody, even the best educated people, can make horrible mistakes because they only saw what they wanted to see, because they were sure before they actually found out.

"You might be able to make it in Alaska, but not now. It just so happens that your 'book' on Alaska missed a few things. There are desperate men up there who'd eat you for supper and use your skulls for soup pots if it would save their hides. You gotta be as tough as them and you aren't — yet. But you listen to this: You will be...tough enough and smart enough to grab 'em by the nose and kick 'em in the ass."

Through our pain, we smiled at that.

Judd paused, took another deep drag, and shook his head. "You fellas should know I've been dreading this because maybe I've been making a big mistake encouraging you about Alaska for a couple of years now. At first it seemed like a great dream for you...hell, for all of us to have. You don't think I dream of shutting this place and taking out after my own gold mine with White Fang guarding my back? All the time....So, I let it go, enjoyed it with you. And then I started seeing you were serious, that you were gonna do it. I should have known that from the start. You two don't back down. It's like with your hunting — when you raise your guns whatever is in your sights is supper. Bang! It's done. It was never in doubt. So, I've been dreading this, wondering how I was going to let you down easy." He sighed. "I'm sorry, fellas."

For a moment, we allowed that to wash over us — the apology more than the confession. Why we were there had never been less in need of explanation.

"Don't be sorry," Rod said finally. "We already knew. At least we've had some bad feelings. So we talked to George's dad, Professor Hartman — we were riding with him to a track meet and we asked him if he knew anything about Alaska. He didn't, but he said a couple of his students got stranded up there and barely got home. These were big, burly guys, too. It all made sense. It would be stupid to go ahead, but we'd talked so much about it, promised so many things...thanks for letting us off the hook." We both grinned

Stunned, Judd stared at us for a moment. Slowly, he returned the grin. "How 'bout a couple of lime sodas?" he said. "On me." Then he said something we never forgot. "I read this somewhere: Don't expect to win every battle, but at the end of the day, if you are still standing, that sometimes is victory enough."

I dropped a heavy sack of cement atop the pile we were building on the back of a truck, our 211th sack of the day. A cloud of the ever-present choking dust swirled up around it and joined more dust that had mixed with sweat and caked on my face. I tried to wipe it away from around my eyes where it could burn like hell. It didn't work. My shirt was so full of dust I succeeded only in painting another layer across my forehead.

I started back to the boxcar, meeting Rod halfway. He was lugging another bag toward the truck. I stopped him and took hold of one end of the heavy bag. He stared for a moment, then gave me the end and took up position on the other. We toted it to the truck and slung it home.

"Why'd you do that?" he asked.

I shrugged. "Felt like it, I guess."

He nodded. He looked back at the boxcar, and the one behind it, and the one behind that one. I followed his gaze. "Don't they ever run out?" he grumbled.

"Never," I groaned. "But its this heat that's killing us....I have an idea. From now on, why don't we do this at night? And while we're at it, let's see if we can talk Uncle Herb into paying us by the car instead of by the hour. In the cool of the night I'll bet we can earn at least half again as much."

We had absorbed enough cement the night before to be too heavy to move. Sprawled on the front porch the next morning, we saw Gunner Davis heading our way. We were still too tired to care. He was beside himself with something. As he got close enough for us to hear, what we heard kicked the last molecules of adrenaline we had into our blood streams and we were up and running. His brother was home from pilot training — *fighter* pilot training.

It was August. The sneak attack on Pearl Harbor was months away, but news of the war elsewhere had filtered into Ames. We found it hard to believe that so few of our friends paid much attention — like it all had to do with some other planet. Our latest heroes were at war in the skies over China and Britain. Flying Tigers like Scarsdale Jack and Robert L. Scott were in our fantasies along with the mighty fliers of the Battle of Britain. For us, the ground war in Europe and the Pacific existed only for the people on the ground in Europe and the Pacific. We flew right along in the cockpits of the deadly fighters. We only flew Spitfires, however. Second Lieutenant Jim Davis flew America's P-40, no match for a Spitfire, but a fighter nonetheless. He also had the invaluable quality of being real and within running distance of our front porch.

When we got to Gunner's house, his crisply-uniformed

brother was on their front porch. He *looked* like a fighter pilot—dark haired, steely-eyed, easy smile, a little larger than most human beings, cool, logical, sure of himself, but not at all full of himself. That's what we saw, anyway. That and his silver wings. How could anything so simple symbolize the hopes and dreams of every red-blooded boy everywhere?

I don't know how he really felt about all the questions we asked him after he shook our hands (his grip was stronger than most, by the way). I do know that he changed our lives forever by choosing to answer them.

"We'll be at war with the Japs within a year," Davis said with authority and anticipation. "We'll be in it with the Germans soon after. You can count on it. We'll blow the Jap Zeros out of the sky. No problem." He took a long pull from a glass of iced tea. "The German 109s will be something else again. The P-40 is no match for them, not even the Spitfire. But we'll fix that. We'll fix it good." He smiled knowingly.

Like pilgrims at the feet of a messiah, we hung on every word, absorbed every thought and movement. Perhaps too boldly I asked him how we would 'fix it.'

He smiled again and leaned back under the weight of his own wisdom. "Wait till the P-38 and P-47 are combat-ready. It won't even be a contest."

God Almighty—secret weapons! He knew about secret weapons! He told *us* about secret weapons! We gushed with questions: How many guns? How fast? When? *When?*

He shook his head. "The rest is classified," he said, suddenly looking intense and causing us to wonder, briefly but seriously, whether we should check the bushes. "You know, with your interest in flying you boys couldn't have been born at a better time. President Roosevelt has just announced that we're going to build sixty thousand planes next year—twenty times what we have now—and double *that* the year after. We'll be desperate for pilots."

"Where can we sign up? *When* can we sign up?" We said it virtually simultaneously and with enough energy behind it to keep our house lighted for a couple of months. This was it! Alaska be damned, this was it! Finally our dreams *and* fantasies were in easy reach.

Davis threw up his hands. "Whoa! Hold on! There's more

to it than that. We'll need lots of pilots, but first you finish high school. Even that may not be good enough. You may need some college."

From atop the clouds our dreams spun down and crashed in a heap, smouldering with cement dust. Finish high school? That would take nearly a year. Even if college wasn't necessary (and it just couldn't be) it would be another year after high school before we finished pilot training. Two years! No war was going to wait that long. We told him so.

He smiled that easy, confident fighter pilot's smile. "Don't kid yourselves. This is going to be a long war. You still have plenty of time. Actually, you may be lucky. You've got time to improve your chances of getting your wings. If you want them bad enough, you'll get busy and make the most of the time you have."

Had we not needed to know what we should do, we would have left him on the spot and gotten started. As it was, he patiently told us to concentrate on mathematics. If we could, find an E6B, the basic navigational tool, and learn how to use it. Learn something about engines. Take a few flying lessons, but not so many that we would learn bad habits — or even good ones if they didn't match up with the military's way. And finally, he said, good eyesight was critical.

"And don't worry about being small," he said. "It could work to your advantage. I'm big enough that they almost put me in bombers."

We had never seen our size as anything but a handicap, let alone an advantage. Now, it was the one thing we wouldn't have to work on. Our eyesight was normal. Just the same, that night we decided it was not too late to plant carrots in our garden.

Purpose changes everything and now we had one. No longer restrained by fears and doubt, we tended to business in earnest. From the back of the high school pack, we stormed into the leader group in our senior year, at least in physical education. The wars elsewhere had caused a change in the PE curriculum — more toughening, more aggressive activities. We understood; many of our classmates didn't. We pitied them in a way. They just didn't get it. The war was coming to America. Jim Davis said so. We knew it for sure. Our futures were riding on it.

We excelled in boxing. With no one else in our weight class, I moved up one weight class and Rod two. We took the crowns. The PE teacher said Rod had a "killer instinct." Good. Fighter pilots need that.

We stumbled in math. Purpose or not, we couldn't make up for all the day-dreaming years in so short a time. We spent spare hours in the library devouring all we could. We couldn't find an E6B, so we learned how to use a slide rule, which is similar.

On Sunday, December 7, 1941, war swept through Ames like an influenza epidemic. The whole town suddenly understood our purpose. During the weeks that followed, our classmates and their parents were never far from the discussion of conscription, enlistment, and college deferment. George Hartman, Earl Feldman, and Gunner Davis, in fact probably at least half of our class, stuck to their plans to attend Iowa State. Our discussion was never about what, it was always about when: When would we enlist? The answer was April 25, 1942, our eighteenth birthday. We would actually be taken in June, following graduation. We *were* going to graduate.

Our birthday fell on a Saturday. We spent the week worrying. Haircuts were important, we'd been told. We marched into Deek's shop and asked for "Air Corps cuts." Wise man that he was, Deek said, "Why bother? Whatever you join, they're gonna cut it their way."

We had to look good. How would we get our clothes ironed with Gert away so much? Mother solved that problem. She bought us new clothes for our birthday. How could she afford it? Even with all we had to think about, we noticed the change in Mother. She was sad, more deeply concerned. We saw her looking at us more often during that week, as if she wanted to say something to us that she couldn't put into words. But nothing she said seemed extraordinary.

The final question was whether to hitchhike to Des Moines or take the Greyhound. Unwilling to spend the money on the sure ride, we hitched a ride the first thirty miles, hiked the last five, and got there two hours early on

Saturday morning.

Glenn Cunningham was scheduled to compete Saturday at the Drake Relays. To our way of thinking, that meant that every red-blooded American boy in the state would forget about the war long enough to go see the world's best miler. We, on the other hand, would be signing up, taking advantage of the opportunity we were sure would be ignored by most of our competition. What we didn't figure on was the effect of two events half a world away on nearly every red-blooded American boy.

Colonel Jimmy Doolittle staged a daring B-25 raid on Tokyo, a phenomenal boost to morale, for which he was promoted to brigadier general. Meanwhile, the Philippines were about to fall—sobering evidence that the Land of The Rising Sun was not a paper tiger.

The recruiting office was packed. There couldn't have been anybody at the relays. Every one of the guys was bigger than us, and from the number of college letter sweaters, smarter than us. Slide rules swung from the belts of some of them as they swaggered about. You could use them in the tests, we learned. We hadn't thought to bring ours. As much planning as we had done, it suddenly seemed we hadn't thought at all. It was all so obvious. We were out of our league. Once again we had suffered from serious delusions, but we were there, we might as well give it a shot.

When you're young and nervous as hell, it can be hard to tell the difference between confidence and frightened blustering. A fairly big, pock-marked lug latched on to us and started talking. "They make it easy here. Get you signed up then wash you out in Santa Ana. That way they got you either way. Maybe you'll be a pilot or maybe a private, but they got you....Did you know only one guy in fifty makes it through pilot training? One in fifty!" He turned away, surveyed the room, and turned back, pity in his eyes. "I'll bet you didn't know that only ten percent of the pilots who make it through training end up in fighters. The rest go to bombers, transports, gliders, instructing, shit like that. 'Course, no offense or nothin', but you two got no chance anyway. They don't let nobody under five-seven even take the test. They don't want no shrimps for pilots."

He turned out to be as full of it as we hoped he was. Rod sailed through the tests and was signed up. I was stopped by a stethoscope. I had a heart murmur. The doctor explained it was a minor thing that might be caused by bad tonsils, but he made it clear I was 4F, a reject, until it was gone.

But Rod had made it and I would, too. My tonsils would be history soon enough. It was a miracle. It was really going to happen. If we'd known how, we would have danced all the way home.

We had two months to get Rod ready to go. All that remained undone in Jim Davis' curriculum was flying lessons. To pay for them, we sold the Model A we'd been rebuilding to learn about engines, sold our bicycles, and most painful of all, we sold Big Bertha. We consoled ourselves by remembering she could easily be replaced on pilots' pay. We lined up some flying lessons with an instructor named Lucky, whom we ultimately learned got the name because he had survived a dozen serious accidents since 1916. Rod soloed before the money ran out.

A month before Rod was to leave for Santa Ana, Mother got word from Ralph who was working in Waukegan, Illinois. He had joined the Marines and was leaving immediately for San Diego. A new pall settled down around her shoulders, stooping them a little more. The Marines—it caught us by surprise. Ralph had always been there, always living between Gert and us in age, and maybe in every other way. He had stepped out front. Suddenly, we knew more about him than we ever had. We were proud of him.

Two days before graduation, I marched quickly to Doctor Fellows' office, had my tonsils snipped out, and trudged home the same day. This, I had reasoned, should be excuse enough not to have to attend a graduation ceremony where I was to receive a diploma that, as far as I was concerned, I didn't deserve. Mother had other plans. We would both *be there*, along with her, proud and deeply worried all at the same time.

Two weeks later, on a Saturday, Rod and I set out for Des Moines and the train station. He was stiff and crisp in his best clothes. He carried a plain brown suitcase, the only suitcase we'd ever had, and a bag full of food. I was proud and excited.

This was a victory for us both. Mother didn't come. She had to work, but that wasn't the problem. She could have gotten the time off. She said goodbye in her way the night before, the sadness and concern was palpable, but we left for Des Moines by ourselves.

The train station rumbled with the sound of parting. Young men leaned out train car windows and shouted about patriotism, adventure, uncertainty, and home. In the crowd, hugs and tears were epidemic.

We pushed through the throng, the two of us a half a head shorter than most of the others. Even the emotion of these last embraces, handshakes, and long kisses on the platform didn't prevent a few double-takes as we squeezed past. We found the end of a long line headed into the cars. At the head of it, a fresh-faced private first class looked for names on a clipboard and sent civilians-no-longer on their way into an unknown future with a quick mark of his pen.

As we moved forward, we took in the diversity about us as best we could: suits from the cheapest to the most expensive, from the most somber to the wildest. The faces in them grinned and laughed and frowned and worried and showed nothing, in their way, all expressing the same thing. For our part, we stood as tall as we could. Our stances and our faces said we deserved to be there, even if our hearts weren't yet sure that was true.

The PFC marked off Rod's name. We turned to each other and Rod stuck out his hand. I shook it firmly. It was the first time we had shaken hands with each other. He headed up the steps and disappeared into the car. I waited and watched. Eventually, the porters cleared away the steps and the conductor signalled the engineer. The train lurched forward and rolled slowly and noisily out of the station.

That was it. That was the sum of our first real goodbye. To this day, it doesn't seem at all strange to me that there wasn't more to it. For us, there was no thought of separation, not real separation. Rod was going first, that was all. I would be following in a few months when the heart murmur cleared up. He had a head start and there was nothing new about that.

As I was walking home after being dropped in Ames, I

realized he wasn't walking beside me. But that was okay. I was in the train along side him. Still, for the first time ever, I felt empty and numb.

That night, Mother asked few questions about the train station and Rod. She seemed to be waiting for something more from me, as though there was something I needed to ask or tell her. It is only now that I understand why she didn't go to the train station. She had left us alone for that moment, our first real separation. That she didn't understand that it wasn't really a separation, that we could never truly be separated by anything but death, doesn't diminish the gift that she gave us.

Days later, we got our first letter from Rod. It was to Mother, as most of them would be. Rod and I had an unstated understanding that she would come first. This first letter was as hopeful as I expected:

Sunday, June 21, 1942

Dear Mother;

After four days on a train we finally made it. We got here at night so I didn't get to see anything of California. This base is huge. I've heard there are over 20,000 of us milling around. The place seems fairly well organized. Today we were kept busy getting uniforms, hair cuts, shots, and orientation lectures. So far no K.P. or drilling on the parade ground. Tomorrow we start taking classification tests, including another physical.

Coming out here, of the towns we saw in the daytime, the two I liked the best were Albuquerque and Flagstaff. They were real cow towns, with plenty of cowboys and Indians and their horses. Flagstaff is at nearly 7,000 feet, a new altitude record for me. From the train and station, the town looked small and clean. In New Mexico, I saw my first deer, and going west from Flagstaff we saw a herd of elk. Really beautiful animals.

Sleeping sitting up wasn't too great, but the trip went fast. In the daytime there was always a change of scenery. Nobody seemed bored. Most of them played cards and got drunk on beer and whisky. I was surprised they got away with it, but no problem. The guys in charge of us were right in there with them. My friend Glen said it was like a prison where the jailers were more criminal than the criminals.

The food's been pretty good, but there's never enough of it. I have a hard time making it between meals. Glen can't figure out why I don't weigh three hundred.

Glen's a nice guy from Knoxville. He isn't a hunter, but he knows they have great quail hunting. We agreed we'd have to get together after the war and he'd give it a try. His dad is a psychiatrist who works part time for the mental hospital. I didn't tell him we had visited the place a couple of times. Glen said he was really impressed with Ames High.

"The place is either great, or you have an awfully good press." I thought he was talking about our athletics. He said, "That too, but I was thinking in particular about academics. Every time I pick up the *Register*, there's another Ames story about honors of some kind—National Honor Society, debate club, percent of graduates going to college, and so on. My dad said most of the people in Ames must be overachievers, probably the influence of Iowa State."

I told Glen I knew of a couple that weren't, but they were the exception. Glen is quite a talker. I enjoy just listening to him. I asked him where he got his words and gift of gab. He said, "I didn't realize it was that obvious. I guess I can blame my dad and high school drama and debate clubs."

Glen and I passed the time together for the whole trip. I asked him what his plans were after the war. He said he was going to take forestry at Iowa State. I told him I could recommend it because I knew one of the professors. Glen was impressed. He figures I must be well-connected.

He is about my size, so I assumed he couldn't have been much of an athlete. I was surprised. He lettered in baseball and track. I asked him if he was hoping to be a pilot or what. Pilot of course. He was impressed when I went over all the stuff Roland and I worked on getting ready for cadets. He was sorry he hadn't thought to do it. I even reviewed some of it with him. What I knew about navigation fascinated him. Now he's worried that he could have been better prepared.

I felt very proud to discover that Roland and I figured out some things that didn't even occur to really smart guys like Glen. Maybe we weren't so dumb after all. Just different.

I hope Ralph is still doing fine. Is Gert taking all of those summer courses she talked about? She should be awfully proud to be half way through Iowa State already. Mother, have you listened to Dorothy and Gert and slowed down some? I sure hope so.

—Rodney

Three days later, he wrote another letter. His future—our future—was again in ashes, destroyed by a single, innocent comment:

Thursday, June 25, 1942

Dear Mother;

I don't know how to tell you, or Roland, but my cadet career lasted three days. In three days I went from civilian to aviation cadet to just another buck private. As cadets, at least we thought we were somebody. As buck privates, they make sure you understand that you are a nobody.

I never even made it to the classification tests. I flunked some kind of a psychological test. The only thing I know that went wrong was a question they asked about sleep walking. I said I didn't really know, except that you had kidded me about walking in my sleep when I was so young I could still just barely walk. That's all it took. It was like I'd been hit in the back of the neck with a bag of cement. I guess it just wasn't meant to be. Maybe some good can still come out of it. At least now we know so that Roland won't make the same mistake.

This is the most hard-hearted place I have ever seen. It's like a jungle and we are all animals. For a whole day I tried to find somebody to talk to, thinking an obvious mistake had been made and I was at least entitled to a hearing. It just doesn't work that way. All I got was sneers, sarcasm, and insults. If they tell you something, that's it. No ifs, ands, or buts about it. They command and we obey.

"They" is any punk who is in a position to boss you around, like the pimple-faced little monkey of a PFC who doles out bedding. Even he tried to lord it over us. I don't know if this is the way it has to be to fight a war. If this is the way our country normally works, what is there that's worth fighting for?

They also washed-out my friend Glen for some equally stupid reason. He called home and talked to his folks. His dad, who must not be any dummy, was furious. He said, "It seems like the people running the cadet program have the same sick mentality that made the decision to round-up and intern all of the Japanese-Americans. The cadet program creates wonderful fodder for a bunch of sadists."

Glen mentioned to his dad what had happened to me. His dad said, "Our government knows less about the human mind than your average alley cat."

We've heard that so far, at least a third of our group has been washed-out. Some guy said it reminds him of a slaughter house. "Butcher everything that gets in the door." At first I was so depressed I couldn't even think. I was stunned and helpless. Thank heavens for Glen. He's very level-headed. We went out and walked and talked for a long time. Finally we decided this isn't about us. It's about the crazies that run the place.

Then we talked about where we go from here. Neither of us could stomach the idea of being an orderly room flunky or supply clerk. A private in the infantry would be better than that. Gunnery school seems like the best of a bad lot. Why not try that and go from there? Glen summed it all up. "Now that we are stuck in this mess, we better start figuring out how to make the best of it."

That sounded good to me, so I said, "Lets start right now. Why not get a three-day pass and go to San Diego and see my brother Ralph? Maybe the Marines will offer us a better deal."

—Rodney

Chapter Five

Sunday, July 12, 1942

Dear Mother,

Glen and I and a hundred other losers are now in Harlingen, Texas, for gunnery school. There weren't even any guarantees that we would get to do this. For one thing it takes good eyesight. It's hot and humid down here. We are twenty miles from Mexico and thirty miles from the Gulf.

It took a week of shuffling around on trains just to get down here. Glen says if we work at it, we can live out the whole war on a train shuffling from place to place. We'll be experts on railroading and we'll have seen the whole country so we can decide where we want to live. Glen's dad said, "It appears that this war will be mostly motion and commotion."

This place will be a combination of basic training—drill, marching, and that kind of stuff—and gunnery school. The whole thing is supposed to take only about ten weeks. We obviously picked the worst time of the year to be down here. I thought July at home was hot and humid. This is a lot worse.

Leonard is pretty young to work at the dairy. Maybe they hired him because he looks to them like another Ralph. Tell him I'm proud of him. Roland tells me you are not slowing down. That makes me sad. After the last nine years, you deserve a better life.

—Rodney

Dear Mother;

I didn't care much for basic training, but gunnery school is very interesting. I guess I have an aptitude for it — guns and how they work, gun turrets, and shooting. And I accidentally found out how to go from a nobody to a somebody. It happened on the skeet range. You'll be shocked to know that all of our years of hunting were good for something.

Skeet is part of our training. The theory is that if you can learn to hit a clay pigeon with a shotgun, it will help you learn to hit moving targets with a machine gun. They use the same theory in training fighter pilots to shoot down other planes. As it turns out, skeet is a very big thing in the Air Corps. Every big shot wants to prove that he is also a good shot, and every outfit wants the bragging rights of having the best skeet team. I'm amazed at the competition between units just on this base.

So far, in skeet I'm the best in my class and they haven't found anybody on the base that can beat me. It's crazy. Overnight I've gone from an absolute nobody to a celebrity. They also marvel that I do it left-handed. Even the base commander calls me Rod. I'm now on the base skeet team. On weekends, we fly to other bases for skeet tournaments, sometimes both Saturday and Sunday.

Every place we go we are treated like VIPs. We've already been to Laredo, Corpus Cristi, and Randolph Field. What a beautiful place that is. I saw my first P-38 up close. It's the most beautiful airplane in the world. I saw my first three-star general there. He didn't seem to like being beat by a PFC. Did I tell you I have my first stripe? Glen said, "Your career is taking off like a rocket." A lot of other places are on the schedule, even California. So far I've been on a B-25, a C-47, and a couple of trainers. And I'm building up flying time.

Enos Slaughter, one of the most famous Cardinals, is a sergeant down here as a PE instructor. Glen says, "You are better known around here than Old Country Slaughter. You've become a Golden Boy. You should be able to parley this skeet thing into the best gold-brick deal that was ever invented. Another possibility. As this thing develops, you'll be making some good contacts, some really high rank. You might meet one that is in the right place in Training Command. If shooting is such a big deal, why wouldn't some big shot figure they could sure use that kind of shooting ability in the cockpit of a P-38? What if some general thinks he has discovered another Richard Ira Bong. You never know. Play your cards right, you're a cinch to get another chance."

I really like Glen. I'm lucky to have him for a friend. He reminds me a lot of George, except George is bigger. Like George, Glen is smart. He can really figure things out. Speaking of size, you remember when I left home just a little over two months ago I was five seven and one-forty? I've already grown over an inch and gained ten pounds, but I'm not fat. By the way, for years we couldn't wait to start shaving. In the Army they make you shave every day whether you need it or not.

Mother, you might like to know that I'm actually something more than just another skeet shooter. I can't believe it, but I'm number one in class standing. Some of this stuff comes pretty easy, and on some I have to study hard, but at least I'm getting it.

So Ralph is already on his way overseas. The Marines sure don't waste any time. From what we hear, I suppose he is headed for some jungle. I wish there was something I could do or say that would help you not to worry, but I don't know how to do that. In times like these mothers get by far the worst of it.

— Rodney

Sunday, Sept. 20, 1942

Dear Roland,

I graduated yesterday; believe it or not, number one in the class. They asked me to stay as an instructor, which I guess I deserve, but the skeet team may have had more to do with it than anything. Normally, we finish up gunnery school as corporals. They have made me a sergeant. Three promotions in four months is not bad. Actually, the last one is because of skeet.

I'm sure glad Glen is also staying, but now I outrank him. Glen's a good guy. He has even talked me into going to some USO dances. I still can't dance, but I'm trying. Since Glen at least knows how to talk to girls, with his conniving, we have met and dated some girls who are supposed to be off-limits. One is the base commander's daughter and the other is the daughter of some other colonel.

Neither of them is supposed to date enlisted men. As Glen put it, "An order which they were not inclined to flawlessly obey." Glen managed to make it easy for them and their parents with a couple of harmless white lies. He let it be known that his father is a doctor and mine a college professor. Then, just for insurance, he tactfully dropped the hint that both of us have been accepted for OCS and will be on our way early next year.

Glen admitted they could easily check that lie out, but once they are sold on us, nobody will even bother. Glen is a little bit cocky and said the girls will do whatever selling is necessary. On top of that, when Judy's dad, the base commander, met me he discovered his daughter was in the good hands of his star skeet shooter. I think the old boy actually likes me.

I'm looking forward to cooler weather. They say the winters are perfect with good bird hunting.

—Rodney

Friday, October 16, 1942

Dear Rod,

Last Friday I went to Dr. Fellows for the sixth time. The heart murmur is gone. Yesterday I retook the physical and passed, not without a scare. In the six months since that first physical, my left eye is no longer 20/20. I was lucky to pass. The guy giving the eye test was careless. I memorized the line as I read it with the right eye and then pretended I was reading it with the left.

I'm no longer 4F. I'm signed up, but it will be February, another four months, before I can get out of here. What if my left eye gets even worse in the meantime? At any rate, it will be February of '44 before I can finish pilot training. Cripes, I'll be darn near twenty and the war could easily be over.

Do I hate to be around here another four months. There are so few of us left that everybody thinks I'm a draft dodger. I can't believe I was stupid enough to stay here in the first place. Why didn't I leave when you did? I didn't have to stay. I'm surprised we didn't figured that out before you left.

As a 4F I was a cinch to get hired in a defense plant in California, or any place else. I could have at least gotten out of Iowa for the first time. That's what the Old Coot did. With his bad arm he's 4F. That didn't stop him. Off he went to Southern California to work for Douglas. By the way, he went to San Diego and saw Ralph just before he shipped out for the Pacific. Why didn't I do what Whitey did, go to California? I could just as easily monitor the heart murmur from there. For the last six months and the next four I could have been making nearly ten times what I've made here. I feel like I was too big a baby to even leave home.

My God, I'm going on nineteen and still cleaning the house on Friday night. Do you suppose I was worried about Mother; that she wouldn't be able to find anyone else to do it? Was I afraid if I left before I had to it would look like I had deliberately abandoned her, that I didn't care enough for her to stay around and help? Did I feel that with you and Ralph gone it wouldn't be right for me to leave?

Like a good little boy, I'm still going to church every Sunday. Everybody else is gone and I show up at church looking like a 4F. Besides being a pain, going to church is now humiliating.

Now that I'm signed up, its too late to go anywhere. They wouldn't hire me for only four months. I tried at the plant down at Ankeny. Why am I just now getting all of this figured out? I can't believe I'm so stupid. I guess I needed you to do my thinking for me. Does it take both of us to figure out anything? Maybe without you I have only half a brain. But that doesn't seem to be the case with you. You are doing just fine without me.

Which reminds me, thanks for the new shoes. I'm lucky you are still looking after me. I'm now getting blisters breaking them in. That sure makes a lot more sense than getting the blisters out there. I'm glad you thought of that. But will they still fit me when I get there? Since you left I've kept pace with you in size—grown two inches and gained twenty pounds. I don't think my feet have grown any.

I haven't done any hunting this year. It just isn't the same, doing it alone. By the way, Earl and George got snagged by the draft, and Gunner has gone to Santa Ana. I'm the only one left in the neighborhood.

You mentioned OCS in a letter a while back. What are your chances of doing that? That's how Uncle Neal got his commission.

—Rolly

Every time I wrote a letter to Rod it made me lonely and restless. The next morning, for something to do, Mike and I got up, slipped out of the house in the dark, and set out to redo that same route we took seven years before on our first squirrel hunt. This time I was dressed warmer and not in bib overalls. We didn't leave until five, took a lunch, but no gun. We were at the cemetery just before dawn. While waiting for the sunrise, I didn't hear any rooster pheasants but I did hear a fox bark, coming from the vicinity of that den at the bottom of the ridge.

We paused at the cemetery. The sunrise and everything else were, if anything, even more beautiful. The fall colors the best I had ever seen. Either that or I was taking more time to enjoy them. That view across the valley is still my favorite.

We turned and went on up the ridge. Mike stopped at the oak where we got the first squirrel. He always does. The little rascal either has fond memories of the tree or there's always a squirrel in it. As usual the woods along the ridge were full of squirrels, crows, and blue jays.

Camp Canweta was deserted. We went down to the river, and on north. Not long after, we were hit by a snow storm, a freak for early October, forcing us to hole up under the big cottonwood. I built a fire, ate my sandwich instead of eight-year-old pork and beans, sardines, and sliced peaches. Soothed by the whistling wind, the warm, crackling fire, and Mike's snoring, I laid back and drifted.

My ETA (estimated time of arrival) was up. I rolled my P-38 into a vertical bank, and looked down. Ten thousand feet below was a medium-size town flanked by tree-lined streams, Squaw Creek on the west and Skunk River on the east. A major highway ran through the town, north and south, a highway and railroad, east and west. The airport was where it was suppose to be....I was home.

I throttled back, turned, started my decent, and contacted the Ames airport. A girl was in the tower. No doubt her predecessor had gone off to war. Her voice sounded familiar. "Is that you Mattie?"

"That I am."

"What are you doing on the radio?"

"During the week I'm at Iowa State, weekends I'm here as a warrior, of sorts. And you're one of the twins....Seems you have taken a giant step up from your cats-killing days. Welcome home neighbor. Your's is the first P-38 I get to bring in. That's exciting. Use runway 34, wind north at five. Knowing you as I do, I shouldn't have to ask, but would you mind giving us a little dust-up, kind of personalize the war for us. Good for hometown morale you know."

I had written Leonard that I would buzz Eleventh Street so he and Mike would know I had arrived. But at that moment, landing was my second priority. First, I had to cruise the valley. Circling to the southeast, I leveled off at fifteen hundred feet and approached the road bridge from the south.

Beyond it was ten miles of river meandering through our solitary, fragrant woods. The winding, often rushing waters of the Skunk nourished lush pastures and rich corn fields. Here and there, picturesque farms were tucked under a hill, out of the bitter winter winds.

I came around again, dropped down to eight hundred feet. Full flaps slowed me to fifteen miles per hour above stall. With my engines throttled back to just a whisper, my war bird and I sailed and soared over the valley, our valley.

For our peers, weekends had been about pep rallies, marching bands, ball games, dances, and parties. For Rod and me, they had brought the challenge of an all-day blizzard or the healing of deep silence in the lonely woods on snowy, windless days. Our drum major was a redheaded woodpecker hammering on a dead cottonwood, our cheerleaders crows, jays, and kingfishers.

The student body soon forgot ninety-yard runs and thirty-foot jump shots. I still marveled at how Mike could persuade a chattering red squirrel to make its last mistake. We might trudge ten, fifteen miles in a drenching rain in search of a Christmas goose. Even if we never got a shot we still thought ourselves better off than those who spent Saturday afternoons in the dark of the matinee.

Above our favorite cornfield, I saw the image of a pheasant, roaring up before Rod and streaking for the sky. A blast from Big Bertha ended the flight.

I turned, dead ahead was our refuge, bringing to mind snow above our knees and twenty below zero, more likely fifty below with wind chill. Luckily, we didn't know about wind chill. Numb ears, fingers, and toes forced us to take shelter, where feeling returned before a blazing fire.

I flew directly over the swimming hole where we learned to swim, but not before Rod nearly drowned. I stood by petrified as an older boy pulled him out. It was just one of the near-fatal mistakes our mother never knew about.

The river led me north to Luther's farm. Our No Hunting signs were still on his fence. The Old Geezer was out in the barnyard shaking his fist, no doubt swearing a blue streak.

I crossed over and flew down the east side. Near the south end I checked out that beautiful little woods, the one above the bridge on the east bank where Mike tangled with a skunk. From there I flew east, up the hill and across Stagecoach Road to the watermelon patch. Poor Earl got caught by the farmer, and we got off scotfree....I felt something cold against my cheek. Mike was nudging me. The fire had died down. Outside, it was quiet. The storm had blown over.

Sunday, Nov. 15, 1942

Dear Mother;

Glen and I have decided we aren't cut out for the good life. It just doesn't seem right. There's a war on and we are living like we had joined a country club. Glen leaves for OCS after the first of the year. He tried to talk me into going with him. I didn't think I would have a prayer of passing the test. Glen insisted, "Anyone who breezes through gunnery school at the top of the class can get into OCS. They will feel lucky to get you. In ninety days we'll get our commissions and we can go from there."

I don't think high school D students have any business even trying to get into Officer Candidate School. Besides, I have a different plan. I start aircraft mechanic school in early January. I'll be finished in October. About six months later, Roland will finish pilot training and soon after be ready for combat. By then I'll have enough experience so I can be the crew chief on his P-38, P-47, or P-51, whichever one he draws.

We should be able to pull that off. I've checked up on it. The Sullivan Rule prohibits brothers from being in combat together, not from being in the same unit if only one is actually in combat. I think it would be great if Roland is in combat and I am there to make sure that every time he flies, his plane is in the best shape possible. Also, being a good aircraft mechanic might be very useful after the war.

— Rodney

Dear Mother;

How do you like my timing? My first letter home is on Valentine's Day. We've been here a week, but I've been too busy to write. Eight months ago, when Rod came out here, it was a four-day trip. For some reason it now takes five. As you know, when I arrived I was a little better equiped than Rod. I had shoes that were broken in and I knew better than tell them anything.

My left eye gave me a scare again. I had to finagle around to pass the eye test. From now on, every time I take a physical I'll have that to worry about. So far I haven't had a chance to field-test the shoes, but the rest of it went okay, sort of.

I qualified for everything, so they are sending me to bombardier school. One of my fellow victims said, "That is like being tried and found innocent. So instead of being shot, I only lose an arm and a leg." For some reason I thought I could do something about it. I ran around all day until I found a major who agreed I could talk to him. That's not exactly how it went. In his office, while I stood at attention he said, "How long have you been in the service, Private?"

I said, "Five days, Sir."

He said, "That's long enough to get it through your thick skull that it no longer matters what you want. Actually it's simple: Do as you are told. Get out of here!"

The "do as you are told" part must not have fully registered with me. The very next day I made an explicitly forbidden trip to the PX and got caught. They have organized special goon squads just to deal with such malicious behavior. The punishment was twenty demerits. Each demerit is an hour of marching on the parade ground with rifle and field pack.

Still convinced that not being allowed in the PX on my own time was unreasonable (besides, I needed toothpaste) I tried again, with the same result. Now I have forty demerits. I guess I'll have to borrow toothpaste for awhile. How many times should I have to be kicked in the teeth before I figure out that reasonable doesn't seem to have much to do with anything around here?

Thanks to Rodney, the broken-in shoes will be a lifesaver. Forty demerits turns out to be a total of about 120 miles. The worst part of spending forty hours on the parade ground will not be the marching with rifle and pack. The stream of P-38s from a nearby field will be rubbing salt in my wounds—a constant reminder: "Tough luck, Buster, that's not where you will be going."

I read in the Santa Ana paper that a guy from Ralph's class was killed a few miles from here in a P-38 crash. Have you heard anything about that?

One of the side-effects of the forty demerits is that in the six weeks that we will be here for pre-flight, I will not get off the base. Since I've not yet seen anything of Southern California, I don't know how painful that will be.

—Roland

Sunday, April 4, 1943

Dear Mother;

Here we are in the first week in April. It took us three days to get here. Most all of the trip was desert. Pre-flight went okay. I worked hard and ended up doing better than average. We studied a lot of different stuff and none of it was really that hard.

I started out here with a pleasant surprise. Lt. Simms, our class adjutant, called me to his office. He began by saying, "Your class standing at Santa Ana doesn't indicate you are a troublemaker, but the demerits. You started with forty and still have eighteen to go. What is that all about?"

After hearing my story he said, "Everybody in Santa Ana is crazy. Here you will start with a clean slate."

So far, Lt. Simms has been my only pleasant surprise. He's a ninety-day wonder. That's what they call graduates of OCS (Officer Candidate School). It must be a pretty good deal. From what I hear, all enlisted men have to do, even recent draftees, is pass the test and in ninety days they are second lieutenants. I would think Earl and George could easily do that. Maybe that's why they waited to be drafted. They knew they were smart enough to get into something like OCS.

We knew that cadets could expect a certain amount of hazing and harassment. In some war movies we've seen how mean a drill sergeant can be. We expected that kind of thing. What we are getting is far worse than anything we could have imagined. It's so bad that some of these clever guys decided, for our own good, we had to turn it into something we can laugh about. I think they did a great job. Here is what they came up with:

"The Goon Squad is such a stupendous collection of sadists that we felt we must give each of them special recognition: The leader of the pack—tall, gangly, and grotesque—we shall call Heydrich, the infamous Butcher of 43-13 (that's our class number). His special gift is bestiality. His second in command and number-one henchman is none other than the ghoulish Himmler himself. He looks and acts remarkably like the real thing. Number three is Goebbles, known as 'The Viper,' because he looks like one. He will also be known as Leo, the worst of foul-mouthed lion tamers. What more can we say? They are all unspeakable."

Our class has speculated on where the Air Corps found this gruesome threesome. The consensus is: "Such bizarre behavior and capability to provide high voltage shocks to anyone who strays within a mile has prompted the deduction that they are of a different order of being not of planet Earth."

—Roland

Dear Mother;

Hitler's SS Squad has left us to go and attack and warp the next class. Since their departure, life has been pleasant and time has flown. We've had a class track meet. I shocked myself by winning the mile run. They didn't time us but I doubt I'll be a threat any time soon to George or Glen Cunningham.

We finished skeet, another shocker. In the beginning I was just average, but in no time, the best in the class. We were supposed to each shoot ten rounds. Some of the guys didn't want to shoot at all, and the instructor didn't care, so I shot about fifty rounds. Can you believe it? For eight years I couldn't hit the broad side of a barn. Now, after a few rounds of skeet, I don't have to take a back seat to anybody. I hope after the war my new-found talent works as well on live targets.

We've finished most of our ground school courses. The most important one covered the entire bomb-sight. I got a hundred on the final. Obviously it was a fluke. Nobody around here can remember that ever happening. Who can explain it? How in one year did I manage to go from last to first? I do know one thing for sure: It helps to work hard.

Two of my buddies, Josh from Brooklyn and Sam from Utah, and I studied all weekend for that final. I hardly ever go into Roswell. Instead, I stay home and study. Weekends are the best time to study. Nearly everybody else goes to town and its quiet around here. I can't quite figure out what the attraction is for all of these guys in a town that's smaller than Ames. You would think, if nothing else, they would get sick of seeing each other.

I've flown my first practice bombing mission. Another shocker: I don't know what in the world got into me. I did so well nobody could believe it. My instructor said, "I now believe in reincarnation. You were a bombardier in a past life."

I felt sorry for the other guy. Two students go up

on each practice mission. We each drop five blue whistlers. I went first and couldn't miss. Poor James had to witness all of that. It was a hard act to follow. By the time it was his turn he was so demoralized he couldn't hit anything. I can't wait to go back up and try it again.

Its nice to do something well because it makes your instructor look good. Now mine can't do enough for me. All of a sudden, everybody is trying to claim me as "their boy." They are even trying to talk me into becoming Cadet Captain. I'm afraid the headaches of that job would outweigh the benefits.

I'm sorry about all the bragging about me I've done in this letter, but it sure feels good to at least have something to brag about.

—Roland

Sunday, Aug. 27, 1943

Dear Mother;

We graduate on Sept. 6, and then I get a three-week leave. I have it all figured out. In deciding where I wanted to go, I had a choice of six bases. The one that works the best for me is Moses Lake, about one hundred miles southwest of Spokane. It's B-17s and it's the farthest from here so it pays the most travel pay and per diem. Also, I wanted to see that part of the country. More important, from here I can come home and spend two weeks. Then on my way to Moses Lake, I can go through Utah and see Rod. Do you realize we haven't seen each other in fifteen months? I'm afraid me being an officer will be hard for him.

I'm sure looking forward to graduation. What a great experience all of this has been, except for two things: Number one, it sure wasn't pilot training. Another thing. You remember the Goon Squad? I thought they were the only evil thing going on around here until yesterday. When we started here there were fourteen Jewish boys in the class. That in itself was news to me. I still don't know how to tell a Jewish boy from anybody else. Anyway, only one out of the fourteen will graduate next week.

In the five months we have been here they have systematically eliminated thirteen out of fourteen, including my little pal Josh. It took them two months to get him. The only one they didn't get is Big Jake, also a pal of mine. He's a happy-go-lucky redhead from New York City. I'm not sure how he managed to be the sole survivor of the local Gestapo—quite an achievement. Jake is the one that told me this story. Pretty sick isn't it?

—Roland

I was concerned my being an officer would be hard on Rod. It turned out to be harder on me. I was proud in that uniform. My newly-won golden bars were a testament, not to accomplishment so much as to belonging, equality, even reliability. The closer my bus came to Ames, the more my golden bars turned to brass—which was, after all was said and done, exactly what they were.

It didn't help that all my Ames friends were elsewhere, on their own missions. Mother still worked constantly, Gert was in school, Ralph was on a jungle island somewhere trying to stay alive, Leonard was working to help support the family. And me? I was there in my uniform with nothing to do but wear it. In my heart, I knew I was living proof to the people of Ames that anyone could become an officer. This was a battle lost the day I was born. I retreated into the Valley of the Skunk almost every day.

As Mike (who was *very* happy to see me, by the way) and I wandered through our woods, I reminded myself that while I wasn't a pilot and couldn't claim a first-class citizenship, I was one of the best bombardiers in my class of sixty-five to actually finish the course. That was worth something.

Now, the warning that "you can't go home again" flashes through my mind. There are many people who hear that warning and nod with understanding. I am one of them. For us, home was never much more than a mirage, a temptation, and a wish.

I planned my leave to allow me time with Rod at Hill Army Air Force Base in Ogden, Utah. From there, I would go to Moses Lake, Washington, for the next leg of my training. As the bus rumbled out of Iowa, I mused about the irony that I was traveling Highway 30, the same highway Rod and I would have taken had we held on to our Alaskan dream instead of our fighter-pilot dream. We wouldn't be realizing either dream, but this reality wasn't so bad. Besides, Moses Lake was 1,700 miles closer to Alaska than Ames.

By the time I got to Hill, my concern returned about how Rod was feeling about me outranking him. I settled into Bachelor Officer Quarters and made my way to his squadron's orderly room.

The young captain stuck out his hand. "Joe Thompson," he said as if the difference in our rank meant nothing to him. I took the hand and sat down, instantly comfortable. Thompson sent someone to pull Rod in off the flight line. For the next half hour, Thompson talked of nothing but my brother's accomplishments and talents:

"We're going to lose him in two weeks," Thompson said, glancing at a calendar on his wall. "We've tried to talk him into staying as an instructor or going to OCS, but he won't have it. He could be an officer here, or he could be an engineering officer. As it stands, no matter how he does on his final exam he can't rank any lower than fifth in his class.

"We have a few ulterior motives for wanting to keep him, I have to admit that. He didn't have time to be on our baseball team, but he worked out with them. And he has a hell of a left-handed hook shot. The base commander, Colonel Blair, says it's not fair: 'One kid with so many talents, and some of us have none.'

"But Rod has this—I'm not sure what to call it—such a zest for life, but also a mission, a sense of duty or honor. He feels an absolute obligation to go into combat. Whatever it is, it's a private thing for him. He can't accept that fighting a war takes all kinds and that not all of them can be in combat. I sometimes wonder if he's just naive about war. Surely he knows about the horrible losses in the Eighth Air Force."

I said nothing. I suppose I could have tried to explain it. *I* was going into combat. That meant *we* were going into combat. In that sense there could be no separation. To even try would be no different than Thompson sending his right arm into battle while his left arm stayed in the rear to answer the phone.

"Anyway, Rolly, you brother is really something, maybe one of a kind," Thompson continued. "Does he have any talents we don't know about? Hell, maybe I don't even want to know!" he chuckled.

I had spotted the shotgun in the corner behind his desk. "Well," I said slowly and innocently, pretending to think hard, "Have you seen him on the skeet range? I hear he's pretty good, although I haven't actually seen him shoot—skeet, I mean."

Thompson got excited. Skeet was his passion, his and Colonel Blair's. Again with all the innocence I could muster, I suggested that perhaps he and the Colonel might want to go head-to-head with Rod and me, a friendly competition.

"Let's do it tomorrow morning if the Colonel's available," Thompson offered. A flicker of a frown crossed his face as he studied me. "Are we being set up?"

I shrugged. At that moment, Rod walked into the office— tall, muscular, tan, and happy. Our embrace was one no one could see, the physical distance between us at that moment was meaningless. Had anyone chosen to look, however, they would have seen the beginnings of tears in our eyes.

We were walking. "I feel good about what I'm doing," Rod said. "I love being around airplanes. On the flight line, I get to see a lot of different ones come and go."

"Are you still going to get on a crew? Which plane?"

He shook his head. "Everybody here thinks I'm stupid for not staying, or going to OCS. They keep telling me it would be perfectly honorable and they'd give their eye teeth for the opportunity I have....I understand what they're saying. Cripes, I even agree with 'em sometimes, but they don't understand about us. We both go into combat or neither of us does. I quit trying to explain it. Anyway, since I've got a choice, I'm going to Moses Lake, too, and get on a B-17. We'll see what happens from there."

"Rod, in a way, what you just said makes me feel bad. You have chosen combat because of me. I haven't told anyone this, especially Mother. When I graduated, I had three choices: Stay in Roswell as an instructor, go to training command as a member of the skeet team, or combat."

"Skeet team? How did that come about?"

"A brigadier general was in Roswell for a week, heard about me, and challenged me to a couple of rounds of skeet. It wasn't even a contest. I figured he'd be a sorehead about it. Instead, he offered me a job....What if I had accepted, instructor or skeet?"

"In the first place, you wouldn't have. So, what's there to discuss?"

I filled him in on Mother, Mike, and Ames. The next day, we trounced Captain Thomson and Colonel Blair in skeet. That evening, Colonel Blair invited us to dinner at his home. If Rod had the slightest concern about being the only NCO there, he never let it show. He was as comfortable and at home as I had ever seen him. The conversation turned to the outdoors and hunting. Colonel Blair suggested various locations in the Wasatch Mountains. He made his staff car available to us the following day, and a driver, since neither of us had ever driven a car.

On Sunday, Rod and I toured Salt Lake City and heard the Mormon Tabernacle Choir. It was a long time ago, but when I think of it now, the phrase "the everlasting hills" comes to mind. I don't know why.

Chapter Six

Fall, 1943—Few things can focus the mind to the exclusion of all else. Love and terror are the most obvious entries on a short list. For me in the fall of 1943 it was which plane would I get and who would be flying it. That's why it meant nothing to me that Moses Lake Air Base was surrounded by a hundred miles of sage brush and winter wheat fields. Spokane was a hundred miles northeast, the Cascade range a hundred miles to the west.

To understand an obsession with both pilot and plane, it's helpful to remember that for a crewman, being assigned to a pilot was like being issued a team leader, perhaps even a wife, who called all the shots. Among the shots was your survival, and sometimes more important, your prestige. The plane had similar importance, but each model could be bragged about in one way or another. That wasn't always true of pilots.

Early on a blue-sky Tuesday morning, decked out in my new summer flying suit, and excited and anxious to take up my duties as a bombardier, I trotted from the BOQ to the flight line. I was a week early. For no good reason I can think of, I bounced into the Ready Room. It was a half hour before daily briefing.

The place was deserted, except for a few guys sitting around a table. Pacing before them with casual, athletic grace was a tall, flaxen-haired, broad-shouldered, all-American type. He was in charge, and no doubt the pilot. His appearance was perfect, every crewman's wish and dream, but there was something wrong. Usually the atmosphere of a Ready Room was easy and light, serious attitudes saved for actually doing the work of learning to survive. The men at this table were frozen in their seats, at attention with pads and pencils in perfect order before them. They were angry, seething. Something was wrong.

The pilot spoke. His voice was a nasal whine. His message was his superiority. I had blundered into a disciplinary affair, not a good way to make a first impression on my first day on a new base. I backed away and turned.

"Get your ass back here, *Lieutenant* Paulson! You're already late!" The words slithered out in a whine so nasal it made me want to shower. His emphasis on "Lieutenant" was intended to put the entire crew on notice that his brand of second lieutenant's bars were superior to ours. I froze. I had entered the room in the first place on the chance these guys might know where to find *my* crew. This could not be *my* crew. I stood there, probably gaping, waiting for someone to say, "Oh, sorry. Wrong Paulson. Your crew is out running laps with your pilot, who looks very much like this one, except he isn't a pompous ass." Nobody said that. As the reality of my situation closed in, I felt like a fly who'd come too close to a frog and was trapped and squirming on the end of a long, disgusting, sticky tongue. Old anger bubbled up. I should have been a pilot, not a goddamned bombardier. But I was a goddamned bombardier. The Air Corps owed me one. This sure as hell wasn't it.

"At every briefing that seat is yours," he whined, gesturing weakly toward an empty chair at his right hand. "Every briefing will begin one hour ahead of the posted time." I sat down. There may have been an audible thud. If there was, it was my life.

His name was Charles Grand. When I was as still as the rest of the crew, he resumed his simple-minded, insulting collection of bromides and slogans. As he droned on, I peered across the table at a disheveled, sandy-haired man who reminded me of a lumpy teddy bear. I soon learned he was my roommate.

Charles continued his lecture for an hour, a deluxe tour of his world of irrelevance. He showed emotion only when he was pleased at some sick joke he ventured. We knew he had made a joke because his head bobbed back and forth, his lips twisted, and he snorted. Finally, mercifully, he stopped. He ordered us to get our gear and form up outside.

It was a half-mile to the planes. The other crews piled into buses. We ran there in formation — "double-time" in military vocabulary. It was clear Charles had decided we were going to be special, unique. It was never clear who he hoped would notice.

He had us form up at attention in front of the plane. He looked us over and focused on me. "Paulson, don't expect to get by on your laurels from Roswell. Around here, I hand out the laurels. They have to be earned every day."

He folded his arms, a smirk of superiority on his face. He hadn't just been expecting me, he'd been lying in wait for me. His eyes were clear — not clear like deep fonts of wisdom, but clear like the rancid oil that comes to the top of old peanut butter. I was staring into them when I heard myself respond. "I didn't work hard at Roswell for the privilege of becoming one of your lap dogs. 'Getting by' has never been my style. Taking crap from you will never *become* my style. Today had better be the last time or so help me, whatever it takes, including court-martial, I'll find another crew!"

His lip quivered, his mouth dropped open, his complexion paled a shade or two. His arms fell to his sides and he stared. I stared back and waited for it, whatever it would be — formal charges, a punch in the face, or more whining, which would have been the worst of the lot. He walked away. He stayed away from me for the rest of the day.

Pending doom hung over me the rest of the day, but it felt good to get acquainted with the rest of the crew and the mighty B-17. The practice bombing mission went well. I felt good for awhile. By that night, the good feeling was gone. Only the deep trouble I was in remained.

John "Steve" Stever, my wide-bodied roommate, and I were in our BOQ room. A chunky five-foot-ten bundle of nervous energy, he was not a pretty sight, but he was instantly likeable, despite his chain-smoking of Kools. I wondered how he got through navigation school carrying at least fifty conspicuously-extra pounds? In Steve's case, I soon learned, it was the best of all possible answers: If you are good enough, a few pounds are easily overlooked. He broached the subject weighing on both of us.

"I've had a week to study him. Do you know what he

reminds me of—that pretty boy, nasal-whining, holier-than-thou-or-anybody, prince charming?"

As tragic as it was, I had to laugh. Thinking *horses ass*, I shook my head.

"A poor excuse for a preacher who failed at his profession and was forced to look around for gainful employment. Unable to find any, he joined the Air Corps, became a pilot."

I exploded. A minute later, my sides still hurting from laughing, I was able to speak. "What do you think he'll do? He scares the bejesus out of me."

"Do?...Not a thing." He sat up on his cot and grinned. He put his finger to his lips and spoke softly. "Rolly, my soon-to-be good friend and bunkmate in Hell's Restroom, you nailed him for all of us. I've been trying to figure him out for days now. You did it in a few hours."

"I don't understand."

"Our leader is *not* simply the pompous, preposterous lover of chicken shit I thought he was. I thought he specialized in the absurd or was simply crazy, but you showed me the light and now that I understand, we have him. He's ours to manipulate." He lit a Kool and leaned against the thin wall of our two-man room. Our cots, footlockers, shared closet, and drafty floor were the highlights. The smoke prompted me to open our only window.

"Steve, what the hell are you talking about?"

"He backed down. He's a coward, totally insecure in what he's doing. He makes up for it by trying to impress us with his beauty, and expertise in everything—everything but his job, which we will need to worry about later. But for now, he collapsed like a wet bag when you confronted him. We can use that; we can intimidate him into leaving us alone."

I shook my head. "You're losing me. How do we know all that?"

"We know that and much more. We know he backed down from you, the newest man, in front of the whole crew. What you may not know is that he has read all of our 201 files. He knows how sharp you are, and the rest of us. What he doesn't know is that I've read all those files, too—including his. I can assure you, he needs us a hell of a lot more than we need him. If his IQ has three digits, he knows that, too. We also know he's vain. The preening, the attention he pays to his appearance speaks to that. We can use that, too."

For Steve to assume that attention to appearance indicated vanity struck me as a greater insight into his character than Chuck's. Chunky and frayed around every edge, Steve paid only the required attention to his appearance, a trait I could never share. I wasn't long in discovering Steve was brilliant, yet he had the engaging charisma of the unvarnished. Free of all pretense, he had a gift for words, and a warm, open character — all of which I quickly grew to trust and admire.

"Rolly, my boy, we can control him. We don't have to take any of his shit.... Hot damn, we might even be able to make something of him!"

My spirit was soaring. "Assuming you're not as loony as he is, what's the plan?"

He hopped off his bunk and grabbed his cap. "Let's go get a beer." He slapped my shoulder on the way by. "We'll talk about it."

They didn't have lime soda at the Officer's Club, so I settled for a Coke. Steve got right back to the plot at hand. "The bad news goes like this: He's like a clogged drainage system — slow, haphazard, confused, and leading to no concrete destination. As a product of false premises, he's about what one should expect."

"False premises? I don't get it."

"Pilot and commission were suppose to transform this clown into a man in charge, a leader, one with the strength and character to serve a noble purpose. In short, Old Chuck, as you've seen, now has the duty to do what will never come naturally to him."

"So why doesn't someone do something about him?"

"You pitifully naive Iowa farm boy. In the *real* world, where would you find that someone who is suppose to do something?"

"So what's with this real world?"

"The world of deception. In that world our hero has hypnotic beauty. Never mind that he's an empty suit, all veneer and no substance. In the world of disguise, deception, and trickery, Old Chuck is a Diva. To complete the deception, we give him a pilot rating and gold bars."

"My God, Steve! You're enough to give me a dark view of life....Seriously, back in the room you were talking like there's hope."

"There is—after we blunt his eccentric interpretation of his responsibilities and purpose. That we must do, otherwise the crazy bastard will drag us down to his level—the lowest common denominator. But I warn you: Like all of us, you were daydreaming in terms of what to expect. You are going to have to lower your expectations."

Often speaking for the both of us, Steve ultimately decided that Chuck had to be told the score tomorrow, and that Steve should tell him.

Briefing the following morning was a carbon-copy of the one before (and the ones before that, Steve assured me). I was too new to know if anyone had paid attention. I did know that we all carried a weight that bowed our shoulders. When Chuck finished, Steve rose and took over.

"Sir, speaking on behalf of all of us, I would like to remind you that we know our jobs, and that they are our jobs, not yours. Therefore, I am informing you that this is the last briefing where we arrive an hour early for the sole purpose of hearing you explain our jobs to us. We have earned our places on this crew, as we assume you have. You have, however, spent so much time looking over our shoulders that you have shown us nothing of your expertise with regard to that plane. That is what we want from you. That is what the Army wants from you. From now on, Sir, we'll do our jobs—and you do yours."

Steve sat down and waited. I had known it was coming, but the rest of the crew had been ambushed. A couple were pale, the rest anxious. Chuck was struck dumb for a moment, then he simply nodded. He looked almost relieved, as though he knew he had dug himself a hole and Steve had tossed him a line. The rest of the day went well. An approximation of quiet respect was all we got from our pilot.

That night, Steve and I went to the Officer's Club to celebrate.

"That was perfect," I said. "You had him pegged right down to his toe nails. He was a different man."

Steve nodded and looked thoughtful. "Yeah, but it won't last, unless you believe in magic. Underneath all that insecurity is a consummate jackass, although our dazzling leader can't hope to match even the charm of the rear end of a donkey." He took a long pull from his draft and slowly smiled. "But he'll be less of a pain in our asses for awhile. That's something.... When does your brother get here?"

"Tomorrow night. He should be on a crew by the day after. We talked about finding a way to be on the same crew, but there's no way. We could never get away with it and besides, I wouldn't wish Chuck on my worst enemy. I hope we got the only one like him. I'd hate to think of Rod ending up with someone like that."

"I don't want to worry you, but we don't have a corner on the crazy commander market. There are other Chuck Grands out there, and worse. There's no way of knowing what kind your brother will get.... If he *could* be on our crew, would you want that?"

"With Chuck! Are you nuts?"

"Only on weekends." He grinned. "We have an advantage. We can control Chuck and protect your brother. We can't do that if he's on another crew under somebody just as bad, or maybe worse."

My fantasies about pilots had taken a severe beating because of Chuck. The daunting truth that he might rank only a little below average on the pilot scale pummeled my fantasies into dust. "It would be good to have Rod on our crew," I said. "But Chuck will never let us. He already knows he can't intimidate me. Two of us would send him into shock. Besides, there's the Sullivan Rule." I looked into Steve's eyes for an instant solution.

"I gotta go to the john," he said, almost as if I wasn't there.

I occupied myself by staring into my Coke. There was no way we could pull this off, nothing I could do to help Rod. Steve returned within a couple of minutes. He was smiling. I returned the smile as best I could.

"Leave it to me," he said.

That I was glad to do. Maybe of all his qualities, the best thing about Steve was his two-fisted approach to making the system work for him and us.

Rod showed up on schedule. Within minutes of settling in, he had the full story of Chuck, and Steve's veiled promise. Since we already had an engineer, Rod said he wanted the tail guns. Within a day of that, he was a member of my crew. I cornered Steve about it. He had simply explained to Chuck the advantages in having a tailgunner who could double as an engineer, and the prestige and public relations value of commanding probably the only crew in the Army Air Corps that included a set of identical twins. The Sullivan Rule never came up.

"Anybody that vain can be conned," Steve said through his trademark grin. He had become a great friend. I would have hated to have him for an enemy. I believe he could have found a way to have me transferred to the Luftwaffe.

It didn't take long for Chuck to revert to his old form. Unable to attack his officers, he went after Rod. He berated him day-in and day-out about the most petty matters. Defenseless against an officer unless he was willing to take up residence in the stockade, Rod took it. But something had to be done and finally, I stepped in and cornered Chuck.

"Stop the petty crap with Rod, once and for all, or you will lose your entire crew. It's strange how everybody on this base knows how good this crew is, everybody but you. But we're a good crew in spite of you. The only reason we put up with you is that your replacement might be worse. But any more crap out of you, *any* more, and we'll take that chance."

Just as before, he said nothing. But unlike before, the relative silence that followed lasted for months. Had we been smarter, we would have been worried. As it was, we were satisfied with being left alone most of the time to become a highly-regarded crew.

At work, Rod was an equal member of the crew. Off duty, he was an enlisted man. We couldn't eat together or join each other in the Officers' or NCOs' clubs, so we found better things to do. At night, we went to the bomb trainer hanger, on weekends to the skeet range. By the time our five months of training with B-17s was up, Rod was a full-fledged bombardier, and we were the two-man team skeet champions of the base.

Just before we left Moses Lake, Steve renamed our pilot. "Hence forth, Chuck will be unaffectionately known as Le Grand Chuck," he pronounced one evening. We all laughed and asked for an explanation.

"We are his crew, but to him we are subjects to be ruled. With his regal bearing and imperious demeanor, he's a dead ringer for that pompous French general who's giving us and the British untold amounts of hell. So, what else are we gonna call our pompous ass?"

The name stuck. Rod shared my friendship for Steve. We learned he was from Fairfield, Iowa, (good quail country) and that he had a year of engineering at Iowa State. His mother instilled in him a love for reading which had built his vocabulary and insight to an often entertaining, always interesting level. He was a smart man who found much to respect in us, as well. His sense of humor made training under Chuck tolerable. He was the only member of the crew we grew close to, but even he could not work miracles.

In mid-November, we were transferred to Drew Field in Tampa, Florida, to finish our transition training. On Wednesday, December 1, 1943, I received a telegram from Mother. Ralph was dead, killed by a Japanese sniper on Tarawa on November 27. Tarawa wasn't the biggest battle of the Pacific, but it was the bloodiest in terms of the percentage of casualties. For us, it was both the bloodiest and the biggest battle ever fought. In February 1944, we went home on leave. There was to be a memorial service for Ralph.

The train crossed the frozen Mississippi and passed snow-covered farms and hamlets. We recalled our best memory of our older brother, the day he joined us in our valley. The air had been frigid and still. The snow fell in flakes the size of Mother's dollar-pancakes. They hovered, too light to fall, drifting here and there like an invasion of butterflies. Everything in the valley was covered in white, muffled into silence. Even Mike was quiet that day. The ground was trackless. We were the first and the only ones to touch it. We took refuge under the fallen cottonwood. We had our guns, but chose not to hunt. On that day it would have been a sacrilege.

Thirty miles from home, the snowscape looked nothing

like the Iowa we remembered. Our Iowa was pristine, alive even in the cold. This place was barren, a frozen wasteland where nothing could live outside except a few ragged crows. Inside, people and animals must have been huddled against the onslaught of unforgiving wind, cold, and snow.

We recognized nothing until we reached the Skunk River bridge, a mile southeast of Ames. To the north we could see the highway bridge and the lower end of our valley. As the train pulled into the station, we thought of Melvin. He had worked there as a freight handler when we were small, when he was still Dad. We had watched the people arriving and leaving and envied their status in the world. Now, we were arriving... because Ralph was dead.

We stepped down from the car. There was a bitter wind, and it was ten below. Few people were stirring. We saw no one we knew. No one came to meet us. Mother would be working. Gert and Leonard were in school. We walked home from there, in no hurry to confront the pain we knew would be there or the pain we carried with us.

We approached the house and saw the gold star in the window—the symbol of a Mother's ultimate sacrifice to the war. It was one of the first in town. Before the war was over, there would be hundreds.

Below the window was another casualty of war. Leonard had fixed up a cozy shelter on the front porch, a place for Mike to keep his daily sad and lonely watch for our return. When he realized his vigil was over, he went crazy. We hugged him, and cried for Ralph and Mother.

The house seemed empty, cold, and dark. We entered the dining room and were startled by Grandma Peterson. She was dressed in black from head to foot, seated on a straight chair in the corner. We learned later that she had come here to live from the farm where she raised our Mother and her five sisters and brothers. She was deaf and muttered only in Danish. She did not seem to know us.

There were changes in the house. Leonard lived in our old room. The Rogues Gallery on the living room wall now included newspaper clippings about us. One of them noted that we were together on a bomber crew. We couldn't help but wonder and worry: If the newspaper knew, how long would it be before the Army woke up, put its boot down and separated us? But most of the changes were about what wasn't there— no evidence of us in the form of copies of *Outdoor Life* littering the table, or the other messes and leavings after evenings of popcorn and cards. And outside, few of the young men were there, certainly no one we knew. Like a broom, the war had swept the young men of Ames to places famous, infamous, and unknown.

We tried again to talk to Grandma, but without success. Her corner was all there was in her world, it seemed. No one else would be home until late, so we went downtown looking for Mother. We never found her. She no longer worked at the Sheldon-Munn, something else we didn't know. The other employees had no idea where she could be found. But for the first time, we felt better. She must have taken a less demanding job.

We kept walking. We passed Max Duitch's car lot, empty because of the war, but his hopes remained high. The sign out front said, "Figure with Max Duitch on Your Next Automobile."

We stopped in at Paul Coe's florist shop and bought fresh flowers for Mother upon being assured that they would be wrapped to prevent them from freezing. When we got home, Gert was there waiting for us. She had changed. No longer the grouchy scullery maid, she was a tall, pretty, and confident young woman. She hugged us and cried. We cried with her. When she saw the flowers, she hugged us again. We followed her to the kitchen where she arranged the flowers and told us about Mother.

"She keeps going, which is more than I expected, but I'm worried. She stays strong during the day, the same old indestructible Louise. She reserves her crying for night. I think she cries herself to sleep every night.... You remember the Mitchells around the corner?"

"Sure," Rod said. "We used to do their lawn. The old man was sick."

Gert nodded. "He's older and much sicker now. Mother takes care of him full time."

"So what's the problem?" I asked. "It's closer to home."

"Sometimes it's non-stop for days. He's senile and

95

terminally ill and he doesn't want to die. He takes it out on her. Most of the time, he doesn't even know what he's doing." She began to sob again. She and Ralph had always been very close. "You should never have come home. You can't help Ralph and nobody can help Mother." We all cried.

Later, we learned that many people had tried to talk Mother out of caring for the old man, but she refused. She was "doing the Lord's work," she told them and no one could shake her from that devotion. Gert said she believed Mother chose to work long and hard to avoid the pain of losing Ralph and worrying about us.

"It won't be long before I know what that's like," Gert said.

"Are you joining the WACs or the WAVEs?" I asked.

"Neither. Bill and I are getting married after graduation in June. His ship leaves from San Francisco a week later. It's a small ammunition ship. Bill says it can't even outrun an enemy submarine."

We were in the kitchen when Mother came home that night. She looked smaller, and not just because we had grown taller. Her face was drawn and haggard—and bruised, we noticed to our horror. She limped. Her appearance was the explanation of what had happened that Gert could not put into words. The flowers made her smile.

The memorial service was conducted on Sunday. Melvin was there. I remember being angry that he had dared to attend. Why was he never there when Ralph was alive? I remember that neither Rod nor I talked to him. He was sad, small, old, and alone. That's all I can remember of the day of Ralph's memorial service.

We spent our last day at home, Monday, in our valley. We worried about Mother and Leonard, both devastated by the loss of Ralph. We cheered Gert's success in college and her coming marriage, although we understood more clearly than ever the fear she felt for her fiance. And we discussed the other newspaper clippings of war news on the living room wall: Harold Knight had been killed. Jim Davis was a prisoner of war in the Philippines, and his brother, our friend Gunner, was in pilot training. Our valley changed that day. We brought the war there.

We returned to Florida and awaited our flight overseas aboard our new B-17. We left February 16, but not for Europe. At the last moment, our orders were changed. We flew to Eglin Field in the Florida panhandle for specialized training.

Eglin was the center of development and testing of experimental aircraft and equipment—secret weapons. Upon arrival and settling in, we learned we were one of six crews chosen for the Azon Project. We also learned that our lives were no longer our own. We were guarded and watched day and night.

The Azon was a bomb that, once dropped, could be guided in azimuth (left and right) by the bombardier. When they worked, they were twenty times more accurate than unguided bombs. The trouble was they only worked forty percent of the time. But I was optimistic and faithful. The Air Corps must know what it was doing; the problems must be near solution or they would not be risking the lives of six crews by sending the weapon into combat.

The key human element of the Azon weapon was the bombardier. None of us knew why we were selected, but the prestige of being one of six in the entire Air Corps was impossible to ignore.

"They must think you're a world-class act," Steve joked.

Our world-class crew left for Italy in March. On the way, Chuck became dangerous.

It was hot for late March when we arrived in Marrakesh. So far our trip had gone off without a hitch. Most of the crew went swimming. That night, Rod and I went with Steve to the plane to retrieve some maps. Steve and I were in the nose of the plane, Rod in the rear. Suddenly, we heard frantic screaming. Chuck was raving at Rod, apparently trying to pick a fight. We hurried to the rear. Steve stepped between them, took a punch from our flailing pilot and was knocked down. I buried a shoulder into the back of Chuck's knees and sent him sprawling to the ground. Before he could move, I was on top of him

"Stop screaming! And if you try to get up, I'll knock your teeth out!"

Rod helped Steve. Chuck eventually stopped thrashing. He looked in shock, almost in a trance, when I let him up. Without a word or a look, he brushed himself off and wandered off into the night.

"What the hell happened?" Steve asked Rod.

Rod shook his head. "I came out the back hatch and there was Chuck, standing in the dark with his back to me. I was surprised, so I said something. He screamed like he'd seen a ghost and lunged at me. I side-stepped and he went down. I went over to help him and he got up swinging. That's when you guys showed up. I never laid a hand on him. He didn't hit me either."

We all looked at each other in disbelief. "We're four thousand miles from home and our captain needs to be committed! We're in it now, gentlemen, up to our necks!" Steve moaned.

"Us? What about Rod? If we go after Chuck, all he has to do is blame it on Rod. You know who they'll believe."

We discussed it with growing dread. Our decision was to avoid the direct chain of command and go to Colonel Paul Helmick, who was in charge of the Azon project and had come along to oversee their use in combat. The Colonel heard our story and seemed to understand. He talked to Chuck, and then called us together.

"Chuck claims he was worried about security at the plane," the Colonel said. "He said he went out to the plane to check it and wasn't aware you were there. He heard a voice in the dark and panicked. You know the rest."

"Sir, he walked off like he was in a trance, like he didn't know where he was or who we were," Steve pleaded.

"He doesn't remember that," Helmick said, clearly concerned. He frowned. "I'm glad you brought this to me and I won't forget it, but for now I think we had best drop it."

Without another choice, we did drop it. But it was now clear to us that we had at least two potentially fatal things to worry about—the Nazis and a pilot who was on the edge.

After that, for no apparent reason, we spent a week in Tunis, confined to base and a leaky tent in a North African monsoon. History had been our only good subject in high school and Rod and I longed to go and explore ancient

Carthage. No way. Azon made us special, and it also meant we couldn't leave the protection of our guards.

Our last leg to Italy, the most scenic part of the trip, went without incident. Once we got there, we soon realized we really were in it, as Steve put it, "up to our necks."

Chapter Seven

Easter, 1944 — The day to celebrate hope for eternal life in the Christian world, the day of our grand entrance, and the end of another cruel week for the 301st Bomb Group, 15th Air Force.

In the air above a square-mile field near Lucera, fifteen miles from Foggia, six new, silvery B-17 Flying Fortresses circled in tight formation. We imagined heads leaned back, eyes shaded against the sun, and broad smiles at the arrival of — not saviors exactly, but certainly celebrities. We *were* the Azons, after all.

Despite the Spartan, half-done appearance of the field, enthusiasm was high and the intercom chatter constant as we waited our turn to land. In our plane, which Chuck had dubbed FUBAR, the chatter died away as each of us spotted the blackened wreckage of a B-17.

Steve took note. "That's a hell of a fine morale booster. Why wouldn't they remove it?" Soon enough, we would know the answer: Death was a daily occurrence, and removing the physical evidence didn't purge the horror of it. As the wreck disappeared from sight, intercom traffic slowly returned.

"Anybody see a theater?"

"This goddamned place hasn't got any hangers, let alone barracks!"

"To hell with that! Anybody see any gun batteries or flak towers? What the hell do they do here during a 190 attack, throw ravioli?"

"Yeah, but it's *al dente,*" Steve quipped, "very *al dente....* Shit! We've come six thousand miles for this? It's got to be a mistake. If it were anybody but me, I'd say the navigator screwed up royally and landed us on an armpit."

"A couple feet lower, I think."

"Can it!" Le Grand Chuck commanded.

At our assigned revetment, the welcoming committee was a seedy-looking tech sergeant in greasy coveralls and his crew—a young corporal and a black private carrying an M-1. They saw us, but wasted no energy welcoming us. The Tech did survey the planes and registered approval by spewing a stream of tobacco juice with admirable velocity. Finally, he turned to us. "Them beauties sure is welcome," he drawled. "Gets a might discouragin' trying to coax another mission out these old junkers." A wide gesture of his hand took in a smattering of other planes of the 301st. It was hard to tell which *could* still fly, never mind which *should*. We soon learned that thirty flyable ones were on the day's mission.

"We've had a thirty-day slow-down on replacements," the corporal chimed in. The private said nothing and hardly moved.

Steve leaned close to me. "The colored kid must be the group gunnery expert," he whispered. "Don't worry about the Tech, though. Give these good ol' boys from the holler a monkey wrench and they can turn junk into a fine watch. Corporal's a mere kid. Nothing more than a trainee."

We saw a few people as we waited for transportation to— wherever. None of them paid much attention to us. Most seemed preoccupied, even angry. Must be because they have to work on Easter, I thought. Steve had other thoughts and took Rod and me aside.

"What the corporal said about a 'slow-down' on replacements—what would you say that means?" Steve rarely asked questions which he hadn't already answered.

"I suppose it means there's a snafu in the supply line somewhere," I said, cringing when Steve's head began to wag.

"You poor, pitiful, naive boy. You still think we're over here on a lark. As much as I *hate* to be the skunk at your picnic, I have to educate you. The corporal was talking about losses. They're losing planes faster than they can be replaced." He surveyed the junkyard around us. "Crews, too, I imagine." To judge by his tone, he might as well have been talking about a shortage of lug nuts. There was a look in his eyes I had never seen before. Rod and I glanced at each other.

Eventually, trucks rolled up and took us a half a mile on a dirt road that climbed the side of a slight rise. On top was a village of olive drab tents nestled in a grove of olive trees, a location which Steve eventually proclaimed was not an uncanny coincidence, but entirely logical to some military mind. They might actually have planted the grove, he suggested, in the interests of uniformity. It was pleasant, none the less. The calm and the greenery reminded Rod and me of City Park on a summer Sunday — minus the strolling lovers, the band shell, and playful dogs. As if in response, a pair of half-gown mongrels came wagging up, looking for hand-outs.

The area had a basketball court, volleyball net, and baseball diamond. A large tent turned out to be the mess hall, which doubled as the movie theater (when there were movies available). All in all, a good set-up for the summer, lousy for the winter. But the war would be over by then, so it didn't matter. Eventually we got our tent assignments. Rod and I, of course, would be separated. Strangely, on that first day even our uniqueness caused little more than an occasional second look. We were thankful.

As Steve and I packed our gear toward the opening of our tent, a pair of enlisted men exited carrying someone else's gear. They stopped when they saw us. Their faces were drawn, their eyes rimmed with red.

"Somebody forget to pay the rent?" Steve joked.

They stared hard at us. "You new?" one of them asked somberly.

We nodded.

"This belonged to some of Major Griffith's crew....They burned yesterday. Fourth crew this week to go down." They shifted their burdens and saluted. "Welcome to Italy," one of them said. They trudged away, leaving us in an eerie silence that not even Steve's wit could defeat.

Several hours later, Rod and I met at the mess tent for supper. We talked little, ate less. There was a wide gulf between us and the combat veterans. We were as clean, fresh, and innocent as choir boys compared to the death that exuded from them. It had a smell — sour and parasitic and unwashed. The looks on their faces came in two varieties: One was squint-eyed and tight-jawed. The other was marked by vacant eyes, slack faces, and cigarettes that dangled forgotten from thin lips.

Eventually, I told Rod about the incident outside my tent. He shook his head. I poked at my food. Several minutes passed. "Did you notice your PX card is only good for four weeks?" I asked.

"Yeah," he said. "They figure we won't be around long enough to need another one." Suddenly, the tent felt small and hot, the air inside too thick to breath. We left quickly Neither of us spoke again until we were well within the shelter of the grove of olive trees.

"Where have we been for the last year?" I asked.

"I've been thinking the same thing," he said slowly. "Guess we've been on an extended trip to the moon. It didn't take this place long to make mincemeat of that dream world."

We came across Steve, who was also out walking and thinking: "Did you notice? It was in their eyes, their dead, dead eyes. And their stunned kind of silence. Most of them weren't even there. It has stolen their souls. This place and it's daily destruction and death has stolen their souls." He looked straight at me. "It's enough to give me a dark, fatalistic view of life."

That night, Steve was sitting on the edge of his cot, brushing the dust off of his boots. I lay on my cot thinking, but unable to wander far from the events of the day.

"Lousy food," Steve said.

Grateful for the interruption, I swung my legs off the cot and sat facing him. "Yeah. I guess it could be worse, though. I hear sometimes it's K-rations."

"Great idea, canning congealed grease. Somebody somewhere is getting rich. Wish it was me."

"Yeah," I chuckled. I watched him work on his boots a few moments. "At the mess tent tonight, Rod couldn't believe what happened to us this afternoon."

"You mean them moving out the crew's effects?"

"Yeah."

Steve nodded and stared down at his cot. "Strange. Think about it: They were sleeping here last night, right here on these cots."

I looked at my thin pillow. The indentation my head had made was still there. For a moment, I felt like a burglar. "I wonder what they looked like?" I studied the pillow a moment longer and then turned to Steve who was eyeing me.

"We'll be all right," he said, smiling. "When your number's up, it's up. But I happen to know mine isn't due for..." He fished a note pad from his pocket, flipped through it, and came to a stop. "...sixty-two years. Since you're with me, your's isn't due either....Let's get some sack time." He jumped up and picked up his helmet which would serve as a wash basin. He started out the door for water, stopped, looked at his footlocker a moment, then opened it and retrieved a silver flask I had never seen before. He opened it and took a quick swig. He offered it to me and I shook my head.

"Where did you get that?"

"Outside Eglin. It just screamed class so I bought it. It adds a touch of culture to our barbaric environs, don't you think?"

"Sure," I said, shaking my head. He grinned and left. I laid back on the pillow. Out of nowhere, I realized I would have no place to sleep if the previous occupants came wandering in and the reports of their fiery deaths had all been a mistake. What would I say? They'd think I was a ghoul.

It rained cold and hard our third or fourth night there. Rod and I went to investigate a ruckus back in a remote corner of the tent area. Thirty or forty boisterous guys were lined up outside a tent. They were cracking bad jokes about sex and women. To a man, they were too drunk or too numb to notice that they were being soaked to the bone in a cold, driving rain. We stood watching for quite some time before two men came out, followed to the tent flap by two young local girls who welcomed the next pair inside. Business was brisk. We walked away.

"That scene is more depressing than our first night in the mess tent," Rod said.

"It's like Steve said, 'this place has stolen their souls.'" I said.

"Those two girls? They can't be fifteen. How can those guys do that to them? I hope I'm never that far gone."

"Me too. I don't understand why those guys are willing to risk venereal diseases."

"Whoever said 'war is hell' didn't say the half of it."

The first week passed without a mission for us Azons, and little else to break up the monotony and the apprehension. The regular crews flew. Every morning at dawn they were on the taxiway waiting. They were kids for the most part, a year or two out of high school, but at the controls and behind the guns of as many as thirty planes—a total of some nine hundred tons of steel and explosives yanked into the air by more than 200,000 horse power generated by 120 nine-cylinder, turbocharged rotary engines.

They watched the low sky for a flare—red for stand down, green for go. When it was red, they knew they would live through the day. When it was green, they couldn't be sure. Weather most often made the difference. Bad weather at home or over the target was the good news that grounded the mission. A sunny day was bad news, unless you came back, which made it another victory.

When the flare was green, they took off, one after another, climbed, circled, waited, formed up, and were gone. The Silence would follow. It lasted the longest when the targets were hell holes. The Nazis had underestimated their need for oil reserves when they plowed through Poland in 1939. They were now constantly short of fuel and lubricants. Consequently, their refineries, tanks farms, synthetic fuel facilities, and delivery systems were among the most important and best-defended targets in the Reich, along with their aircraft and tank factories. The more vital the target, the thicker was the blanket of fighters and flak protecting them by killing us. The hell holes were in places such as Ploesti, Vienna, Budapest, Blechhammer North and Blechhammer South. For Rod and me, they were just names during that first week, the names of places where Americans died.

The morning of our second Sunday at war, Rod and I set out for church. We hadn't been in one since we left Ames for training. This one was a Quonset hut that beckoned from beyond a lush pasture where sheep grazed. The day's mission had been airborne for hours and The Silence would continue until their return at about four o'clock.

The morning sun was warm, the grass green and soft beneath our boots. But there was death here, too. The burned-out hulk of a German tank squatted like a mausoleum in the heart of the pasture. Atop it was a shepherd boy, maybe ten years old, crook in hand. Black hair fell long and unruly from beneath his cap. His face was dark from long days in the sun with nothing to do but watch two dogs safeguarding the family's wooly livelihood. And thanks to our presence he could watch the trappings of a war. What he thought of war we couldn't know, but he had a grandstand seat.

"Cigarettes, Joe?" he chirped as we drew near. He stuck out his hand and smiled his most sincere appeal. We grinned and shook our heads. He tried again and again, using up most of his English vocabulary in a few words. Eventually, he was persuaded that we were just stupid or tight. Disappointed, he sulked. He perked up when Rod gave him a package of gum. He wasn't much younger than Leonard. We walked on.

"It's your turn to write Mother," I said. "For sure tell her about us going to church..."

"Better not. She'll worry about why," Rod finished, nodding. "I wonder how long it takes mail to get home."

"Or here. You heard anything about that?"

"From what I hear, we won't see any well beyond our life expectancy."

We continued in silence until the path veered west. We stopped. Off in the haze we could see the foothills of Italy's jagged spine. Just ahead was the Quonset. Nestled under a canopy of sycamores, it was painted a soft green. A plain brown cross rose from the back. We could hear an organ. Had there been snow, it was a scene that could have graced a Christmas card—a pocket of peace on Earth, good will toward men.

"Are you as embarrassed about this as I am?" I moaned.

Rod nodded, frowning. "God, we're such phonies! We haven't set foot inside a church since we left home—*two years* for me. Now, here we are. The only reason is cowardice. We're afraid we might get killed! Religion isn't something we can just turn on and off!"

Our eyes locked for a moment. His burned with anger at

our hypocrisy. I carried our shame. "Well, we're here. We might as well get on with it," I said finally.

Rod looked at the ground, then at the church. "We're gonna be late," he said.

Near the open door, over the rich chords of the organ, we heard the whistling whine of engines. We searched the sky. A single line of eight silvery P-38s slipped low across the path behind us. As we watched, they played chicken with a very low utility line. Some hopped it at the last possible minute, others ducked beneath it—a wonderful game on a Sunday morning played by young men living our dream. We watched it leave with them. Rod scooped up a rock and tossed it at them.

"That should be us!" he snarled. He stomped back up the path that had brought us here. Shocked, I didn't move for a few seconds, then I ran after him. When I caught up, I grabbed his shoulder to stop him. He spun to face me.

"We shouldn't be here!" he said in answer to my unspoken question. "We should be up there with them!"

"Yeah, but we aren't. What's that got to do with going to church? Let's go."

His face turned dark with anger and warning. "Don't tell me what to do!"

"What?"

He glared at me long enough to get to me. "You think I like this? What happened to you stinks! We should *both* be officers and we should *both* be up there right now playing chicken with those lucky guys! If I could change it I would, goddamn it, but I can't! There's not a goddamned thing either of us can do about it!" I pushed him and stormed back toward the church. I was fuming. I also wasn't done. I whirled on him. "While you're feeling sorry for yourself all scrunched up in the tail, maybe you could remember that I'm in the nose with nothing between me and a million Kraut fighters but a sheet of Plexiglass! A twelve o'clock bullseye, that's me!...At least in a fighter we'd have a chance!"

He came toward me. My hands clenched into fists. They relaxed when I saw the pain and the apology in his face. He stopped beside me and searched for words. Finally, he found some. "I'll do my best to keep 'em off you. The ones I miss you can get with the chin guns."

We stepped off again toward the church. "That's a joke. I'm worse with them than I was with a shotgun for eight years. We got almost no practice in training."

Rod slowly grinned. "We shoulda kept Big Bertha."

I laughed. "Damn right! They wouldn't have a chance!"

"Shhh! Watch your language!" We were there.

The only way in—or out—was a center aisle that separated twin rows of padded benches. Once inside, there would be no unseen escape. We moved on. Only a third of the seats were filled. None of the other Azons were there. As we sat down, the choir walked up the aisle singing *A Mighty Fortress*, one of our favorites had we been forced to admit we had favorite hymns. A sandy-haired chaplain delivered the sermon which lasted fifteen minutes. When it was over, we stood up to leave.

"What did you think of it?" I asked Rod.

"I liked it. It was short."

The only way out was the front door and it was guarded by the chaplain. He stuck out his hand. "David Anderson," he said cheerfully. "I haven't seen you around—and I'm sure I would have noticed identical twins."

You and the rest of the world, we thought, but we shook his hand anyway and introduced ourselves.

"I've been overseas two years and you're the first twins I've seen." Ordinarily, we would have been stumbling all over ourselves looking for any excuse to get away from a preacher, especially one who wanted to explain to us that we were twins. But this man, whose cultured voice had just a hint of a midwestern twang and a touch of Norway, seemed genuinely interested in us as people rather than just a sinner-be-saved doubleheader. "When did you come in?"

"Last week, Easter," I said.

"Too late for Easter service," Rod added, a little too obviously.

"One of those new Gs? Your arrival has the place buzzing about a new miracle bomb that's going to shorten the war. Would you mind staying awhile and telling me about it?"

There was nothing threatening or suspicious about his invitation, but I couldn't resist pulling his leg a little. "Do chaplains get top secret clearances?"

"Even higher....Yep, I'm cleared for hearsay and rumors, and for no good reason I can think of, I do have a top secret clearance, although mine came in a box of Cracker Jacks." He smiled broadly. So did we. Whatever this guy had, it was catching.

"Hold on while I get out of my work clothes." He disappeared for a few minutes. When he returned, he had shed his robe and was in uniform. He was a captain. We sat down at a table set up in the shade behind the chapel. There were coffee and donuts. We didn't like coffee, but Gert wasn't there to nag us about eating donuts.

David was tall. His sandy hair was as thin as he was. He appeared to be in his mid-thirties, but his demeanor was that of a younger man who had managed to be here for two years without acquiring the look of the walking wounded.

"Your chapel is nice," Rod said, "but it's kind of small."

"Not really. Weather permitting, we fly twenty-eight days out of every month. It's a rare Sunday that there are many churchgoers around."

"Do you ever get a full house?" I asked.

Sadness swept across his face like wind through a wheat field. "Last week. Easter. We were full up....It's sad in a way, but understandable in every other. My attendance goes up along with losses. Rising death toll is an awful price to pay for..."

Rod's mouth was open in surprise. I realized mine was, too. David looked first at one, then the other of us. A faint smile appeared on his lips, a look of understanding.

"You arrived here at the end of a very bad week for us. Three crews were lost in combat. That was bad enough, but Major Griffith went down here, at home. You probably saw the wreck when you came in....They hit, exploded, and burned before anybody could do anything. No one could help. So many watched it burn. It's all they could do....A lot of them showed up here. I imagine some of them felt like hypocrites. I don't think God looks at it that way." He was silent for a moment. His gazed seemed fixed on the table top. His head snapped up and his smile returned. "But enough of that. Tell me about your top-secret miracle weapon."

"For one thing, it's not very secret," I said. "Axis Sally was on the radio the morning of our second day here welcoming us and 'the Azon bomb to the three-O-first bomb group.'"

"She's a real charmer with quite a message, including a standing invitation to switch to the righteous and winning side."

"Has she had many takers?" One of us asked.

"Indirectly, yes. A few like the idea, but show a preference for Switzerland."

"Anyway, the Azon is a thousand pound bomb that we can guide in azimuth. We'll be the first to try it in combat."

"You must be proud of that — assuming it works. I hear there have been some problems with it."

I stared at him. "Does everybody know as much or more about this project as we do?"

David laughed. "I told you I was cleared for hearsay and rumors.... Does it work?"

"Well, it's not perfect by a long shot, but when it does work, it's almost twenty times more accurate than an unguided bomb."

"How accurate is that?"

"Pickle barrel! At Eglin we had an average deflection error of less than twenty feet from fifteen thousand feet. In other words, if we were bombing a road, we would come within twenty feet of the center line every time. One bomb, one target, kaput."

"I see. But there are problems with it?"

"Only about forty percent of them work and you're really limited to a single bomb drop," Rod said.

"Why just one?"

"Let's say we drop three of them. The bombardier tries to guide them with the controller. The bombs that respond at all, all move right or left, depending. Which one do you think of as *the* bomb? Whichever one it is, you correct all of them for natural dispersion, but they each are different. You could be guiding some of them *away* from the target. When all is said and done, you might as well have dropped one as three because only one is going to go where you point it and the rest may have a worse dispersion than an unguided drop."

"I see. So they don't offer much of an advantage."

"Oh yes they do," I said. "On the right kind of target—a railroad or a bridge, any long targets. They're deadly when they work."

"What about the ones that don't work?"

"Well, if we have people smart enough to invent them, they're smart enough to work out the problems. I still have faith in them. I can't wait to get going," I said.

David sipped from his mug. "It won't be long,"

"How do you know *that*?" Rod asked. "Are you telling us that if we want some answers, just come to church?"

David grinned sheepishly and glanced around him. "You got me, fellas. My roommate is in group intelligence—Jonathon White. He talked to your tech rep....I want you guys to know that I wasn't toying with you. I assumed you were proud about having been chosen for this project. You're members of a select group. When I saw you come in this morning, I could see your tails were dragging. I guess I wanted to remind you of something good."

"You knew who we were when we came in?" I asked, amazed.

"Oh, no! Not at all, which is pretty surprising when you think of it. I only knew what was obvious by sight. It wasn't until you told me when you had come in that I knew you were part of the Azon project. Jonathon never mentioned anything about brothers in the group, and certainly not identical twins on the same crew. I'm sure he would have mentioned that. I doubt that he knows—yet. That's *very* surprising."

I grinned. "Maybe not. I noticed on our way over that somebody had changed my last name on the crew list. I guess some clerk just couldn't believe anybody could squeeze past the Sullivan Rule and decided it was a mistake."

David mulled that a moment. "Probably," he said. "Or maybe he *did* know and was trying to help you out, to protect you. When you think about it, it's mighty strange that you could have gotten this far together without a little help behind the scenes."

That had never occurred to either of us. We looked at each other and at David. "Wouldn't they have told us?"

David shrugged. "Maybe it's a mystery we shouldn't try

too hard to unravel."

"Why?"

"In the real world, the squeaky wheel gets the grease. In the Army, it gets transferred."

David was right about many things. One of them was that our first mission wasn't long in coming. April 17 was our tenth day at Lucera and the most important day of our lives as far as we were concerned.

I couldn't sleep and finally gave up trying to. In the quiet hours before dawn, I walked through the windy, cold night. A light drizzle was falling. The mess tent was nearly deserted, just the cooks and me. As I ate, I prayed for the weather to clear and I focused on the successes of the Azon, not the failures. They worked fine. They would today. The rest of the group had taken to calling us the Buck Rogers Boys, which was not a compliment. Today we would make it one.

We learned at our secret briefing that only three planes would be flying the Azon mission. We were headed up the coast to the Rimini-Ancona railroad. It was supposed to be un-defended — no flak, EA (enemy aircraft) unlikely, which was best of all. Even so, we would have an escort of sixteen P-38s.

Steve snorted. "Some mission! That damned railroad must be abandoned, otherwise it would be defended. This is nothing but a goddamned joyride for the brass."

"Who cares?" I snapped, feeling the pressure. "Just give me good weather and bombs that work."

It soon became obvious that Steve was right. A brigadier general from the 15th would be flying our plane. A colonel from the Fifth Wing would be co-pilot. Other brass would be going along on Azon's debut by displacing regular members of other crews. Steve was tickled pink when he learned that Le Grand Chuck had been bumped from the mission. His mood changed when he found out the group navigator was coming along.

The inclusion of the group navigator meant that three of us would be jammed into the nose of the plane: Steve, our assigned navigator, who was very clear about not needing a babysitter on this mission; the group navigator, who didn't give a damn what Steve thought; and me, our bombardier and the lead bombardier for this mission. Being lead bombardier meant that the bombardiers in the other two planes would release their bombs when I did. The success or failure of the bomb run was riding on me. A general and a colonel would be watching me from above and behind us in the pilots' cockpit.

The general briefing ended. Pilots, navigators, radiomen, and bombardiers stayed for further briefing, the gunners left to pre-flight the planes. The detailed target briefing commenced. Our mission was to find and bomb six bridges, one after another—one bomb dropped from each plane on each target. My heart took up residence in my stomach. Finding all six targets from fifteen thousand feet was my responsibility. Our first IP (initial point) was north of Rimini. From there we would fly south along the coast, bombing one bridge after another on our way to Ancona.

The sum of my experience in finding a target from fifteen thousand feet was a fifteen foot road at Eglin, and bullseyes on bombing ranges. Today, I was lead bombardier for the first time in my life, on my first mission, on a plane piloted by a general and a colonel, and some dunce in the bureaucracy expects me to find and bomb six targets, all on the same mission. Already in a daze, I couldn't have been more devastated.

I trudged to the plane after the briefing ended. Our prestige, the project's prestige, was perched on my shoulders like an excited child, his hands clamped firmly over my eyes. Rod had installed a special trap door in the tail-gun compartment so that he could help me spot where my bombs hit. He met me at the plane and asked about target photos. I couldn't even respond. He stared at me. Steve pulled him aside and explained.

It was five-tenths (fifty percent) overcast when the green flare went up. The forecast was for solid undercast along the coast from Ancona north. We took off. I burned the target photos into my brain as we headed out over the Adriatic. Solid undercast—how would I find the bridges? With any luck, I won't even have to try.

Gunners test-fired over the water. I made my way into the bomb bay and armed the six, thousand-pound Azon bombs by pulling the cotter pins from the fuses. I went back up front where the billowing white of our cloud cover surrounded the Plexiglass nose bubble. Foreboding still hung on me like wet clothes. My head was splitting. Sucking oxygen didn't help. We leveled off at twelve thousand feet. That was one good thing. We weren't high enough to have to go on oxygen.

On the intercom, the colonel announced we were still in eight/tenths and our escort still hadn't found us. The general decided to stay at our present altitude and on our current course for ten more minutes. Steve reminded us we were thirty minutes from the IP — well inside enemy territory. The Norden bombsight was ready, but I had found no reason to believe I was or ever would be.

The ten minutes passed and the weather was worse. No fighter cover and we couldn't see. That was it. We did a one-eighty and headed for home. I'd gotten a reprieve.

"One hour and thirty-three minutes to Lucera," Steve advised.

We began descending at five hundred feet per minute and broke out of the clouds at six thousand feet. With the pressure off, I felt like we were taking a Sunday drive. Cigars and cigarettes were lit and I shut off the bombsight. I stripped off my flak helmet and vest and started back to the bomb bay to replace the pins in the fuses.

The bomb bay is the cavernous mid-section of a B-17. Six bombs dangled from racks that flanked an eight-inch-wide catwalk that ran down the center and doubled as the spine of the aircraft. Two feet below the catwalk were the bomb bay doors, which opened like a clam shell, either electrically or when something heavy enough landed on them, such as a man. Below them was thousands of feet of air. Below that was ground or water. We were over the Adriatic when I stepped onto the catwalk, holding tight to supporting struts as I inched along.

Sometimes, Rod came forward and replaced the pins. He didn't this time because of the brass aboard and our concern about advertising the two of us. That was okay. I never liked it when he put himself in danger. If someone was going to take a header through the bay doors, it should be me. Whoever was in the bay wasn't on intercom and had no way of knowing what was going on.

I had just replaced the first pin when I felt an unmistakable vibration and heard the accompanying percussion. Our guns were firing—long and continuous bursts, which was unusual enough. Our gunners were probably trigger happy, it being our first mission. I wondered with dread whether they might be shooting at our own fighters because of a bad case of nerves. But then the tail guns fired. Rod wouldn't make that mistake, no matter how scared or rattled he was.

The guns shook the plane, which made staying on the catwalk that much harder. I hugged a strut. At that instant, the pitch of the engines changed. The throttles had been shoved to full power. The plane lunged into a steep climb. The bomb bay doors snapped open and a gale filled the compartment. All six bombs dropped into oblivion. My grip on the strut became a stranglehold. Something exploded next to my head. My ears were ringing and I could smell the cordite. This was it. Our number had been called. I was terrified. The events of my life really did flash before my eyes. A dense, soaking fog swirled around me.

Suddenly, the plane leveled off and the power was throttled back. The shooting stopped. I could feel something shaking. It was me. Somebody had his hand on my shoulder and was shaking me. I opened my eyes. It was Steve and he looked puzzled.

"You sure picked one hell of a time to come back here!" he shouted over the rush of the wind. "I thought for sure you were shark food!"

I couldn't speak. I could barely move.

"We had a minor emergency. Fifteen to twenty 190s[1] paid us a visit," he yelled.

[1] German fighter planes.

Chapter Eight

21 April 1944—That morning I set out for David and his chapel, the only haven I knew. Rod was in the air—somewhere—along with the rest of my crew. Neither I, nor our plane was part of it. Rod was in danger and I was safe. Rod had some control, I had none. Rod might die and I would be forced to live without him.

The young shepherd was atop the Panzer in the pasture. I tried to talk to him—damned futile unless the conversation stuck to "cigarette," "Joe," and "gum." I'm sure he was an expert on fear, having lived all his short life under the Fascists and Nazis, but we couldn't talk about it, not that we would have anyway.

David and Captain Jonathon White were at the tables behind the chapel, indulging in the ever-present coffee and donuts. I joined them. They looked at me, then each other. They waited for me to explain the apprehension they saw.

"They left the Azon planes off the mission, but the crews'll be flying with the group, except the bombardiers. I don't understand what's going on."

David glanced at Jonathon who obviously did know what was going on. Next to nothing happened in our group that Jonathon didn't know about. Personal or official, military secret or trouble in town, he mentally catalogued it against the time just that snippet of information might become important.

Shorter than David by six inches, stockier ("Too much spaghetti.") and as unkempt as Steve, Jonathon packed tobacco into a calabash. His Zippo clinked as he flicked it open. He laid flame to the rough-cut and struck a pose like a bespectacled Sherlock Homes. Smoke swirling about his head and between us. He pulled the stem from his mouth and pointed it at me like a gun. "You're no longer expendable," he said. His eyes narrowed as if he was waiting for a reaction.

"Nice, sterile word," David said. "Men, bombs, toilet paper—all *expendable*."

"What do you mean?" I looked hard at Jonathon.

"Since you got here there's been some confusion about the status of the Azon planes and crews. The Pentagon just cleared that up. The planes and bombardiers aren't expendable, which means the group can't use your planes or you bombardiers on regular missions. Everybody else flies."

"God in heaven," David muttered.

Jonathon glanced at his roommate and then returned his attention to me. "The missions you do fly will be flak-free or at worst, only lightly defended. Part of the rationale is that guiding the Azon requires a dangerous increase in straight and level time over the target, as you are well aware."

It's hard to explain how I felt. More than anything else at that moment I was afraid for Rod, but there were added dimensions. I was afraid for me. Life without Rod was a shadow world of intolerable pain and desperate loneliness. Many times in my mind I had stepped to the edge of that bleak void and peered in. I had vowed I would never enter because I could not survive there. If one of us was to die, it had to be me, not him. Both of us would live, or he would. That was all. He felt the same way—we both would live, or I would. Aloud, we decided that the only acceptable compromise was that we both live, or we both die. That option had been taken away from us.

We had worked hard to keep from being separated by the Sullivan prohibition against brothers serving in combat, in the same unit, at the same time. We avoided being seen together because of it. Now, it was possible we would be separated by something far more permanent than a regulation, something over which I had no control. I could not be there to protect him, to back him up.

The Pentagon's ruling made Rod, an enlisted man, "expendable," but not me, a bombardier and officer. The only reason I wasn't expendable is because I had learned from Rod's single, small mistake of mentioning that he may have walked in his sleep once. Rod had made it possible for me to be an Azon bombardier, and now he might pay with his life. At that moment, I could barely speak. I was powerless, trapped in a hideous cocoon spun for me by a nameless idiot. Until that day, at least we had been equal, locked together in some awful, twisted dance of death. They had taken even that way.

"Are you all right?" David touched my arm.

I searched Jonathon's eyes. "Where are they?" My voice was barely more than a whisper. First he, then I, focused on David. No one spoke for several seconds. Jonathon's gaze was an unspoken request for advice. "Where are they?" I repeated.

David's next breath was deep enough to hear. He closed his eyes, as if he was saying a silent prayer. "Ploesti," he said finally.

I was suddenly more aware than ever before of how comfortable it was in the shade of the sycamores behind the chapel. It sickened me. I excused myself.

I wandered west through rich farm land until I came to the crest of a hill overlooking a beautiful valley. I sat down and lost myself in it. It was enough like our Valley of the Skunk to remind me of times together. I remembered the winter day when Ralph joined us. I remembered the snow and the fire we built at the windfall. I felt again how warm it was, how safe. The windfall was still there. Ralph was gone.

The valley faded. In its place was the sky over Ploesti. I had never been there, but sky was sky. This one was thick with fighters and heavy bombers. Below, concentrated in nineteen square miles of Romania, were the refineries, tank farms, and oil fields that provided nearly a fourth of the fuel and lubricants for the German war machine. Take away that fuel, and the machine soon would sputter and die.

Ploesti was the third-best defended target in Europe. Nests of German 88s and 105s dotted the ground like measles. They hurled death at the hundreds of heavy bombers that managed to survive attack by thick swarms of fire-spewing fighters. Rod was in the tail of one of those bombers. I realized I didn't even know the name of the plane he was in. Whichever one it was, he might have managed to fend off the fighters. He was helpless against the flak. It would either kill him or it wouldn't.

The Flying Fortress deserved its name when you counted

the half-inch guns it sported. The G models had two in a turret beneath the nose—the "chin" guns that were my responsibility and for which the average bombardier got training that consisted of little more than "this is the trigger." Two guns poked out from a turret on top, two in a turret hanging from the belly, one each from "waist" positions on the side, and two in the tail. The B-17 was a heavy plane empty; it couldn't carry very much. On an average mission, each gun carried only one minute's worth of ammunition. But for German fighter pilots swooping in on what they came to call a *pulk* (herd) of several hundred heavy bombers, it could be one terrifying minute.

It must have comforted them to know the B-17 wasn't particularly well armored. The most vulnerable spot was the nose. The preferred attack was straight on at the bombardier. Ironically, thirty millimeter rounds that missed everyone else as they tore through the nose bubble had more than enough velocity to make it all the way to the tail and kill the gunner.

My imagination took me to hell that afternoon. On the way, I went home where I watched Mother put a second golden star in our window while I struggled to answer questions she would never have thought to ask.

It was sunset when I returned to the compound. They were back, all of them, recalled because of bad weather. I found Rod and told him what Jonathon had told me, nothing more. I think he was relieved. Now, he had only himself to worry about.

On 24 April, the group went back to Ploesti. We Azons went back to the Rimini-Ancona Railroad, this time with the group commander and a major general on board.

Our mission was the same as before: Find and bomb six bridges. My terror was the same as before. They assured us we wouldn't have to worry about flak.

As we left the flak-free Adriatic, crossed the coast line and turned over the IP, I looked down and saw muzzle flashes. In a few seconds there it was, my first flak, in clusters of eight angry black puffs tracking us in the turn. I went rubbery in the legs. Just as we rolled out of the turn and lined up for our bomb run, the news came over the intercom that our P-38 escort had vanished. Seconds later, another bulletin: Number

Five had salvoed her bombs. I went numb. She might have been hit by flak or fighters. Whatever happened, we were sure to be next.

Nervous beyond description, I somehow found the first target through the haze — a two hundred-foot bridge spanning the Rubicon. It occurred to me that it was the same Rubicon Julius Caesar had crossed 2,000 years before. When he did, he committed to war against Rome, a decision from which he couldn't turn back.

I accomplished a near-perfect bomb run, released, and the bomb headed for earth. I made a small correction left. The bomb stuck in full left. An agonizing thirty seconds later, a huge water spout erupted in the middle of Rimini harbor — a half a mile from the bridge. Totally flustered, I searched frantically for the second bridge. I couldn't find it, but strangely, my mind wouldn't let me move on in time for bridge number three, or four, or five, or six. I never caught up. As a result, no bridge was hit that day by a total of thirty-six secret weapons. In one mission, I had made the bomb, the unit, and me a joke.

The group commander, Colonel Badjer, was in full agreement. At debriefing he said he couldn't tell which was worse, the bombs or the bombardier.

The general was more charitable: "Hap Arnold has given us a new and novel way to kill Germans. They'll laugh themselves to death."

I was devastated; we all were and it was my fault. We were the laughingstock of Lucera and it was my fault. In debriefing, a ground-pounder whose mouth was bigger than his brain tartly suggested that we ask the Partisans to paint big white Xs on the targets so the "bombardier's seeing-eye dog can spot them."

The next day, 25 April, was Rod's and my birthday. They assigned our crew, not to our gleaming new FUBAR[1], but to one of the group's relics — for bombing practice. No one could console me, not that anybody but Rod and Steve did much to try. Single-handedly I had doused the glow on our haloes. Le Grande Chuck was just itching for an excuse to pick a fight.

---

[1] Acronym, the polite meaning of which is "Fouled Up Beyond All Recognition."

I provided one by reporting a problem with the bombsight. He started in, making sure I understood just how serious had been my crime.

"Are you *sure* it's dead? Not just a fuse or a switch or something?"

My fuse smouldered. "I k*now* how to check out a bomb sight. It's my business."

He sneered.

"The horizontal gyro is out," I continued, struggling to keep control. "I know the sight. I've made a fetish out of knowing the sight....Rod knows them, too. You want him to check it out?"

"Can you bomb without it?"

I stared at him in disbelief. "I can bomb using my big toe, but somebody has decided I need practice. I imagine they intended for me to practice *with* the bomb sight."

That nasal whine shifted into low. "Damn right, you need practice! Yesterday you couldn't even *find* your big toe....How often does a crew get to lead not only its first mission, but the first Azon mission? I was honored. So was the crew. It was a great show of confidence in me—and a great opportunity for us all." He pointed his finger at my shoulder. "Me, you, Steve—we all could have gone home as captains. Now? Well, what can I say? You blew it for me. You blew it for all of us."

I was fuming, a condition aggravated by the fact that I agreed with him. "You're right! I did blow it for us all. But that was yesterday and this is today and I no longer have a goddamned thing to lose! Yesterday, I had my head up my ass, today *you* do!...The sight is dead, damn it!"

"I've had it!" Chuck said. "I insist! Stop this nonsense. What will they think of me with a pigheaded bombardier like you? I order you! Let's get out of here."

"You can insist and order until the cows come home. I refuse absolutely! Either call the tower, get someone out here to fix it, or crank up this wreck and leave without me!"

He made the call. Minutes later, a Jeep roared up. A lieutenant colonel forced his massive bulk out of the seat and stormed over to me. He knew who I was. (There were a thousand people on the base. I assumed all of them knew who I was after yesterday.) Between chomps on his thick, black cigar, he fussed, fumed, and stammered a lot. He showed total ignorance about anything technical, but great annoyance with anything Azon.

"Look, sir," I finally said. "What's the harm of getting bomb sight maintenance out here?" His face visibly inflated as he searched for the harm he knew must be there someplace. I looked over at Rod. He nodded. I saw him slip away and head for bomb sight maintenance. Meanwhile, another Jeep growled to a halt at the plane. Colonel Badjer arrived. He was certain to be in a wonderful mood.

I glanced at Steve, who was smirking. I knew exactly what he was thinking: "It's about time! Now we got the one man who knows absolutely nothing about bomb sights out here to solve the problem. Now we're cooking!" Nonetheless, he and the rest of the crew drifted away and huddled to watch the growing collection of pilots bent on skewering one poor excuse for a bombardier.

The group commander came right out and accused me — me who could never get enough practice bombing — of faking the malfunction to get out of the practice mission. I was about to tell him off, and get myself thrown in jail, when another Jeep arrived. This one carried Rod and a tech sergeant. The choir of pilots let go what may have been the second loudest huff in history as they watched them disappear into the plane. Two minutes later, they were back.

"Gyro's dead," the tech said with all the innocence of a man who really didn't know I had promoted him to saint on the spot. As he turned on his heel to get a new one, the choir turned loose the loudest huff in history. Then, they faded like smoke.

The next day, five Azon crews took off for another try at the bridges. The sixth, my crew, flew with the group to Northern Italy. They had done nothing wrong, but somebody figured we damn well had to be punished. I was protected by the Pentagon, so my punishment was to be left behind — for me, worse by far than being shot at. I skipped breakfast and tried to read. I gave up within a few minutes and went to Group Intelligence to look up Jonathon. All business during debriefing, he was relaxed and pleasant when we were alone.

He had become a confidant to me nearly the equal of David. David knew God, Jonathon knew everything else.

He put down his pipe and leaned back, hands behind his head. "Well, get a load of Mr. Sunshine this fine day! To what do I owe the honor of a visit from the 15th Air Force's most celebrated bombardier?" He was grinning.

"You mean my infamy hasn't yet spread beyond Italy? I'm disappointed. I expect to be known as World War II's poorest excuse for a bombardier." I sat down, smiling halfheartedly.

"Your mission did cause quite a stir," he said. He began fiddling with his pipe. He looked like he had slept in his clothes. Unruly, ragged brown hair framed a round, pudgy face; horn-rimmed glasses mildly distorted penetrating eyes. So much depended on this rumpled human being. Looking like a mad, but absent-minded scientist, he shifted piles of paper on his desk in search of his Zippo lighter. He saw me watching him.

"The Italians make a damn fine pipe," he said, "but no matter how well they're made, only one in twenty is worth anything." He found the lighter. "Sort of like people," he said through his teeth as he drew the flame into the bowl. "Especially those in high places."

Concerned, I shot furtive glances around me. The offices of many high ranking, certain to be humorless officers were close by. They could easily have heard him. Jonathon got up and shut the door.

"Little late, isn't it?" I asked.

He waved off my concern. "They all know I'm a heretic.... For what it's worth, I think you deserve a Silver Star for making even one good bomb run. This Azon thing more and more is resembling a Chinese fire drill. What happened to you is just the beginning."

"Why do you say that?"

"I'm referring to the most useless and destructive of all human life-forms—a committee of highly-placed bureaucrats."

"I'm lost."

"It's the high-powered group behind Azon. I call them the Azon Brain Trust. I'm their clerk/typist so I see everything they see and everything they produce. Believe me, they will only make things worse. I'm also close to Jim Miller, the Group bombardier."

"I was beginning to wonder if we had one. I don't think I've ever seen him."

"He's around and he feels for all six of you. Dropping a few practice bombs at Eglin has qualified you in the minds of the trust to be lead bombardiers. 'Insane,' according to Jim and I agree. He's searched the records of good combat bombardiers for a pattern, something they have in common. The only thing that's true of all of them is that they have at least fifteen combat missions under their belts. Jim predicted disaster before you set foot on the plane for your first mission. He was right."

I thought about that. Even though I had allowed myself to believe that I really was as good as the powers that be seemed to think I was, it was somehow vindicating to realize they were idiots and that I still had a real shot at competence.

"So you're saying that eventually I'll live down my *celebrity* status."

"Oh, hell no."

My stomach knotted. "Great."

He stared at me, puzzled for a moment. Then he understood. "You'll live down the mission, but what you did yesterday, the bomb sight spectacle, that's made you a local folk hero, a celebrity for the duration. News of it is spreading throughout the 15th."

"What'd I do?"

"Broke a cardinal rule. You, a mere bombardier, stood up to pilots. You showed them their own ignorance. You may have been the butt of a few jokes over the mission — maybe a few more than usual since everybody assumed that you must be the best of the Azons and the whole thing fell flat on its face, just like everybody expected it to and still does — but what you did yesterday was a real morale booster. It was comic relief in a place that desperately needs things to laugh at. That's what the Mr. Sunshine was about."

I didn't know whether to laugh or cry. "So I'm the W.C. Fields of the 15th, huh?"

He puffed on his pipe, frowned, and relit it. "Sort of. You

need to understand that nobody wants the Azons here, or anywhere."

"I got that hint from the first day."

"You flew in the day after a popular crew burned. Everybody's devastated and here you come, a bunch of snot-nosed first lieutenants with less time in grade than the average boot lace, in six brand new planes we desperately need, but can't use. And why? To carry out a fucking *experiment* that shifts resources and fighters away from missions where they can save lives. You get fighters just to cover your asses on milk runs — forgive me, not your asses but those of the brass who flew with you." A cloud of sweet-smelling gray smoke billowed up between us. "By the way, the brass who flew your aborted mission have been called back to the States. They've been fired, busted to their permanent rank of captain, and banished from this theater."

"You're kidding."

"Not even the Army can hide homicidal stupidity. They came out of the clouds too soon, endangered everybody — probably just so they could play tourist on the way home. What you did was stupid, but it only endangered you. What they did was beyond repair because it could have gotten you all killed. Families and their Congressmen tend to get a little peeved about that kind of thing. The only thing that saved your asses was that those 190s had Italian pilots."

I nodded, surprised I was keeping up with him. "How do you know that?"

"I don't for certain, but I'd bet dollars to donuts on it. We know there's an Italian squadron operating in that area. Their tactics were a dead giveaway, no pun intended. The gunners reported the 190s attacked only in pairs, opened fire too far away, and broke off too soon , which is why you aren't dead. Even the greenest German pilots would have attacked in waves of nine or twelve, three or four per B-17. They wouldn't have opened up until they were inside five hundred yards and would have pressed the attack to within one hundred yards. You might have survived the first wave, but not the second.

"Anyway, your first mission set the stage for disaster. If they had *wanted* to destroy Azon they couldn't have planned a better way to do it. The whole thing was so moronic in concept

126

that not even God could have made it work."

"Don't let David hear you doubting the powers of the Almighty," I chuckled.

"Good point," he said. He waited a full second to grin. "One thing you should know now so it doesn't come as a total shock when you find out on your own: There are quite a few pools going, betting on when the plug will be pulled on Azon. Prevailing wisdom gives you a maximum of fifteen missions."

At that moment, a crisp rap on the door changed Jonathon from confidant and teacher to all-business intelligence officer. "Come!"

A boy with two stripes on each starched sleeve entered, saluted, and silently handed a sheet of yellow paper to Jonathon who nodded a dismissal. The corporal shut the door as he left. Jonathon read a few seconds.

"The group is on it's way back. Your crew and one other were forced to land in Corsica. Nothing serious, mechanical trouble." He read on. Slowly, a smile spread across his face. He beamed up at me. "And we have a strike report on the Azon mission. They didn't hit a fucking thing. Nail number two in the Azon coffin." The two fingers he held up looked suspiciously like V for victory.

Rod and the crew returned from Corsica the day after my conversation with Jonathon. Later, we entered a two-on-two basketball tournament, the first thing we had done together openly since our arrival. We blew 'em off the court that day. No one could stop Rod's left-handed hook, or me from feeding him the ball.

Why we took that risk, I don't know. Most of the time we spent together we spent alone, careful not to be seen to avoid drawing attention to ourselves. We took long walks when we could, through the surrounding countryside and into Lucera, a small but picturesque town where we could buy ice cream when we wanted it. Cigarettes were among the most popular currencies. We didn't smoke, but we carried them for their purchasing power. We drew stares from the town folks — not just twins, American twins. We avoided the prostitutes and the bars. Maybe that sounds corny, but it's true. I'm not sure why we stayed away. It could have been the unavoidable power of Mother's moral compass, or the fact that we had grown up fearing and avoiding bars, or that we simply found other things more entertaining. It was probably all of those things.

Sometime in the midst of our first month in combat, we were off together with a Springfield for some target practice. The group was on a mission to which none of the Azon crews was assigned. We were on a hill overlooking the field, the only activity was a pair of B-17s shooting landings. Suddenly, Rod pointed into the distance. "There's a 109!"

I searched the sky. Rod's eyes were better than mine and it was his business to identify enemy aircraft quickly, but the sky was full of our fighters. I couldn't find an enemy fighter, nor did I notice any interest in one among ours. I shaded my eyes. "Where?"

"On the runway! Good lord!"

There he was, taxiing between the two 17s. To get there, he would have had to fly right over our fighter fields. He did have some attention by that time, but the defecting Italian pilot had flown in unscathed—and unnoticed.

Before our first month in combat had passed, four Azon missions to the same railroad and the same bridges had managed to amass a dismal record. On a Sunday after church, Jonathon, David, and I were at the tables behind the chapel.

"The whole Azon thing has been reappraised by the Brain Trust," Jonathon said. "They have made two earth-shattering observations. First, sixty percent of the bombs have malfunctioned."

"Oh, good for them." David sneered.

"And second, the bombing has been poor and the problem is the bombardiers."

"What!" David shot up out of his seat. "Sixty percent of the bombs don't work and the poor bombing is the *bombardiers'* fault?"

"I told you so," Jonathon said. "I told you they'd finally figure out the program is failing and would look for a scapegoat. Its always the same: Neurotics build these castles in the sky, dream up this shit, and then the psychos move in. Then, the inevitable: As soon as something goes wrong, its always the fault of the little guys for screwing up a theory that was just so damned elegant on paper that it had to work. It *couldn't* fail!"

Jonathon might as well have been speaking Socrates to a donkey. My head was in my hands. Whatever shard of Azon pride I had left had been pulverized into dust and was mixing into the dirt below my feet. He jumped up, his arms waving. "And that's not even the half of it. A highly placed nitwit who shall remain nameless to protect the guilty has come to the conclusion that a change in tactics is called for."

"Oh, God," I groaned.

"You better hope he's on your side, my farm-country friend. On the next mission, all the Azon bombs will be set to the same frequency. *All of them.* The lead bombardier will guide them all."

David's hands were in tight fists in front of him. "Are they crazy?"

"Certifiable!" Jonathon snarled. "And thus far they've done nothing to tarnish that image. Just think about it for a minute....Actually, its rare for anyone to get *everything* wrong at the same time, but they've done that by ignoring every plain, undeniable truth. They've actually managed to demonstrate that three heads are worse than none!"

For the first time, I truly understood and believed what Jonathon had been sure of since before the Azons arrived: The inmates had been in charge of the asylum all along. What I didn't know was that I would be the lead bombardier on the first trial of this scheme that simple physics guaranteed would be the grand-daddy of all the Azon disasters.

13 May—the premiere of the ill-conceived scheme, which had been delayed by weather, and the day I learned I would again be lead bombardier. But there was more to it than a simple Azon mission. All of the *Group's* bombs would be dropped on my release, from 23,000 feet, on a target defended by forty guns. Pattern bombing assumed that the lead plane would be flown by a battle savvy crew that included a bombardier who had proven himself to be exceptional under fire. A simultaneous release based on his sighting would decide the success or failure of the mission.

The fallacy, of course, was that on my only mission as a

lead bombardier I had done everything wrong. I had never had a successful mission. I don't think I gave those forty guns a second thought. My only thought, my constant dread, was what would happen if I made a mistake. If I did, it would be one hell of a way to blow up a pasture and a few dozen sheep.

General briefing began long before dawn. In the large hall, spirits were high. This was a milk run for the rest of the group — a few fighters maybe, only three dozen guns. Steve pointed out the consequence of that. "Since it's a milk run, notice that every seat is filled with a fanny. We'll have a lot of tourists with us on this one."

On the large map on the wall in front of us, red string marked the route to the target. It might as well have been wrapped around my neck. Now and again, I heard Azon jokes and laughter ripple through the happy crowd of young men. In my state of mind, every comment questioned my ability.

The target was huge: a great stone railroad viaduct as ornate and inspiring as a grand cathedral. The Avisio Viaduct was more than two hundred feet high and three thousand feet long. The keystone in rail traffic between Italy and Germany, it should have been a perfect Azon target. The flaw was the guns. Thought to be manned by the best gunners in Italy, the least-risk approach was from the north via the Adige Valley. From that direction, the rail line curved into the viaduct. I showed the photos to Steve and Rod.

"What's the big deal about the curve?" Steve asked.

"Cripes! You're an engineer," Rod moaned. "How is he supposed to guide the bombs around a curve?"

Steve mulled that for a moment. "Well, hell, Rolly. It's simple. Once you get 'em heading in a circle, don't try to pull them out. Just get all the bombs circling like dogs chasing their tails. We aren't going to hit anything anyway, but like the general said, 'We'll give the Krauts some entertainment.' Poor fellas have been stuck in Italy for a long time."

Rod and I burst into laughter. Whether Steve meant to raise the crew's spirits with his irreverent assaults on anything or anyone that made decisions for us, I don't know, but he had a knack for making us feel better and that made him someone to care about.

First away when the green flare went up, we climbed,

circled, and waited. By the time we were half way up the Adriatic, a thousand bombers and fighters were in the air with us. The Adriatic was like a flack-free freeway leading to targets in northern Italy and farther north to the hell holes located in the Fatherland. Bathed in the sunshine that streamed through the Plexiglass nose, I was out ahead of them all. I could see four B-17 groups to my right. The 97th was flying behind us as a combat wing. Their target was the Trento marshalling yard, just ten miles southeast of the viaduct and closer to the guns. I found myself hoping the guns would go after them and leave us alone. It's a thought John Wayne wouldn't permit, but most of us had it. Rod told me later that he counted fifteen B-24 groups from his tail gun position.

Three hundred and fifty fighters were with us. The all-black 332nd celebrated their arrival by barrel-rolling around each other. They flew the only P-47s left in the 15th—hand-me-downs from the groups now flying P-51s.

All in all, it should have been glorious—me out in front of an armada of steel, power, and determination. As it was, I spent most of the trip checking, rechecking, and checking again the bomb sight and the target photos. Above and behind me, Colonel Badjer was in the left seat, a location that downgraded Le Grand Chuck to co-pilot, meaning, according to Steve, "he's only one hundred percent above his level of competence."

I said, "Steve, why are you flattering him? He doesn't have a level of competence?"

Steve performed flawlessly that day. Nearly as inexperienced a navigator as I was a bombardier, it was up to him to get all of us there. With an undercast all the way, the pressure on him was intense, but he never showed it. His calm voice over the intercom issued position reports, and course corrections that kept us away from the flak.

As the time for the bomb run neared, my apprehension mounted: We had a fifty percent undercast, ideal conditions for me to turn this big show into a fatal flop, fatal for me at any rate. I wasn't alone. Chatter on the intercom was nearing zero, a sure sign we were getting close even if Steve had never said a word. Again I checked the sight.

Steve's voice broke the silence on the intercom: "Colonel.

You give Paulson a thirty-second window, and a bomb sight that *works*, and he'll pulverize that monster bridge for you." I cringed, wondering how good Colonel Badjer's memory was, and if he had a sense of humor. I heard laughter on the flight deck.

The colonel's laughter crackled over the intercom, but then in a calm, reassuring voice he said, "I'm *sure* we wouldn't be here if Paulson wasn't satisfied with the bomb sight. His bombing will be inspired by your vote of confidence."

"We're over the IP," Steve said, the emotion gone from his voice.

I looked off to the south toward the target. "Let's stay on this heading," I said into the intercom. "The undercast is breaking up. It's looking promising."

"I have us over the target in nine minutes," Steve said. "Six minutes to flak." Five minutes later, we saw the puffs of black smoke that followed the explosion of flak shells. The Trento guns were firing at six P-38s that had gone in ahead of us to drop chaff to confuse radar tracking. From the location of the flak, I had a good idea where the target would be.

Two minutes from where the target should be, weather conditions had improved but I still couldn't find it through the broken clouds. My heart was racing. Steve calmly leaned forward with a hand on my shoulder and helped me look. He spotted it first. There was no mistaking it. It stood out from the surrounding landmarks like the Rock of Gibraltar. Even from twenty-three thousand feet, it seemed close enough to reach out and touch.

We started the run. I didn't have time to be afraid of the outcome. It was flawless. The bombs released and I watched for the tail flares that would help me spot and guide the Azons. My hand was on the control, waiting. The flares ignited— someone had switched them. These burned red, white, and blue. Someone wanted to give the Krauts a real show. We were waving Old Glory at them.

My job was to guide those bombs around a curve, but the path of the flares was so straight and true without guidance that I took my hand away from the control. I wasn't about to screw up what I then knew was a perfect bomb run. Although certain of the outcome, the most anxious thirty-five seconds of my life passed as I watched that tight cluster of thirty-six flares. Explosions mushroomed on and around the viaduct. Finally, 186 clouds billowed up in a tight pattern. The Group's entire bomb load, including the Azons, had found the mark. Azon's only success to date had occurred because I had chosen to ignore the technology. We broke off the target.

I risked contacting Rod over the intercom. "What did you see through the trap door?"

"It was beautiful," he said.

Steve slapped me on the back; "From what I could see, it was like the work of a trained sapper; each bomb perfectly planted to do the most harm."

It never occurred to me that a perfect bomb run could get me court-martialed.

Chapter Nine

14 May 1944—The group and the "expendable" elements of the Azons, Rod included, were in the air on the way to bomb the hell out of Mantua in Northern Italy—the place to which Romeo was banished when he was declared expendable in Verona. Not expendable, but feeling pretty good nonetheless, I had just reached Jonathon's door. I was there to confess that Azon's only success thus far had ignored the technology. I had imagined him laughing about it in a low, conspiratorial voice. "I knew it," he'd say. I was partly right. He did speak in a low, conspiratorial voice.

"We have a problem." He quickly shut the door behind me. "The photo lab says none of the Azon bombs were guided yesterday."

Had I been wiser in the ways of bureaucracy, I would have understood immediately: That made me a target. As soon as word got out, they'd put up a life-sized picture of me in the shuttered offices of the Azon Brain Trust. Several hundred red mission strings would be stretched out, all of them leading directly to my butt. But I was not yet that wise. Instead, his hushed pronouncement drew a blush, no more serious a reaction than being caught kissing on the front porch.

"So? What can they do? Fire me from Azon? Big deal."

At that moment, Jonathon's pudgy face defined incredulous. "Something pretty ugly could get going here, like a court-martial and you could spend the war in the stockade!...The very best you can hope for is to never again be a lead bombardier. This is serious, my farm-country friend."

I sat down heavily, a little dizzy. "Why? There was no *need* to guide the bombs. The results prove that."

"*Need*? What's that got to do with it? You single-handedly

destroyed the Brain Trust's pet excuse for the Azon record—
it's the bombardiers' fault. Eventually, what you've done will
drop their drawers and expose their reputations."

"So? They deserve it, damn it! Besides, all I did was take
advantage of a perfect bomb run. Guiding the bombs would
have messed it up. They have to be able to see that!"

"Jesus Christ, Paulson! You seem to think the *mission* is
the important thing. It doesn't mean *shit* to anyone but us.
How can it mean anything to people willing to elevate their
pride above lives? You better get this, Rollie! When they
declared you 'not expendable,' it had nothing to do with you as
a person, or even you as a bombardier. For them, it was about
timetables and clout. They didn't want to kill *time* retraining
bombardiers. They've been able to convince somebody that it's
the project that isn't expendable. But in fact, it's their
reputations and their clout that aren't expendable. When this
gets out, both those things will be in serious jeopardy, which
will make you as expendable as a rubber and as easily
flushed. Are you getting this—*farm boy*?"

"I'm not completely stupid, so you can quit the 'farm boy'
crap. I grew up in a city."

"A *city*? Iowa doesn't have any cities. It's got silos and hog
markets that you sod busters choose to live near. The closest
you've ever come to a *real* city is flying over them. *Iowa.*
Christ almighty. Visit beautiful Iowa. Come see our toilet."

"What's the matter with you? How'd we get from Azon to
bad-mouthing Iowa?"

"Oh, well, forgive me all to hell! I didn't know you gave a
shit about the old homestead—*farm boy.*"

"Knock that shit off! Ames may not be a city by your
standards, but it's got a hell of a lot going for it that you'll
never understand."

His eyes rolled back. "Yeah, like bacon."

"It's got the best school system in the goddamned country,
for one thing! There's a college there, for God's sake! A hell of
a good one!…"

He held up his hand like a traffic cop, a thin, knowing
smile on his face. He gazed at me for several seconds. I
couldn't decide whether to hit him or hustle him to the flight
surgeon. "So," he finally said, "you do understand pride."

"What?"

"You've got pride in where you come from. It means something to you, enough to be willing to defend it…even though there's no real reason to defend it."

"Look! I'm real close to clobbering you!"

"I know." He reached for his pipe.

"You think you can go for five minutes without smoking that pipe?"

"Not a chance." He packed it. His Zippo clinked and the room was soon filling with sweet-smelling smoke. "You know what's so great about Ames? You come from there. That's it. It's yours; it's part of *you*. But lay it in front of somebody whose job it is to run the country? It's a college town in a country full of college towns. It's a small city in a state that doesn't even have a big-league team. But so what? Why should you care what anybody thinks of Ames? It is what it is. It *ought* to be self-evident to anyone, even you.

"I bitch a lot, but the few people who really run this war aren't demons—most of 'em anyway. But with the big picture to worry about, they can't get bogged down in the details of a single mission, or spend more time than they have checking into charges made by self-righteous, power-hungry, lower-level bureaucrats who think they run the war and who are pissed off because their pride has been barbecued by one little bombardier someplace in Italy. So, don't expect somebody with more clout than the Brain Trust to come to your rescue. It ain't gonna happen. All they're going to have time to know for sure is that the Azon people are pissed and the anti-Azon people are laughing their asses off and all of them want something done about it. Who knows? The battle may boil down to whether you were part of a plot to discredit Azon….Don't look so shocked. We're talking about Washington, here, not Ames. Whatever happens, one way or another, you're the goat. And there's not a goddamned thing you can do about it…unless you play by their rules."

"So, you're saying I should lie."

"In sophisticated circles, it's called CYA—Cover Your Ass. I'm saying you no longer have the luxury of sitting on that sanctimonious limb clinging to your convictions. That's the game you're in, Buster. You play by their rules, or you don't play, you pay."

"I thought we were trying to win a war here."

"We are. Fighting the good fight, freedom's defenders, the only hope for the world—we're all those things. But let's at least be honest. When we're up in those planes the number one priority is not getting our asses shot off. When this gets out, the Azon Brain Trust will be worried about the bureaucratic equivalent of getting their asses shot off. It's all about survival. We have to figure a way to keep yours from getting shot off and hanging it out the window for the world to judge isn't the way to do it."

I was getting it—finally, I was getting it. "What do we do?" I asked, a question from a student to a man who appeared to have a doctorate.

"I don't know, but this is serious. Until yesterday, all you've had from this place is bitter disappointment, in reality nothing but gentle left-hander jabs compared to this sucker punch....So, pay attention: We can't ask the photo guys to lie. Eventually, one of them would cover his ass and throw us to the wolves." He relit his pipe. His gaze was focused somewhere in the clouds of smoke he was spewing. Suddenly, his eyes sparkled. He leaned back in his chair, grinning like a witch.

"What?"

"Rollie, has an Azon transmitter ever failed?"

I hadn't quite gotten it or I would not have searched my brain and finally said, "No, not that I know of."

"Yours did."

It took a second or two to penetrate, but when it did I grinned like a witches's apprentice. "You're a genius."

"Yes I am. I'm sure your tech rep will go along. Hell, he'll love it. He's so disgusted with Azon he'll jump at the chance to nail those jerks. 'See what happens when you guide all the bombs with one transmitter? If that transmitter fails...it's just bald-faced luck that the bomb run was good enough that the target was hit anyway.' They'll *love* that."

I nodded. I still wasn't completely sure why they'd love it, but I was sure they would.

The group was back, intact, by 4:15 that afternoon. Later, I found Rod and we went off by ourselves. I explained the situation as best I could. By dark, he was getting it, too.

21 May—The group stood down. There had been no enemy-inflicted casualties in a week, but the flight surgeon still was busy every morning with doses of the clap, world-class hangovers, and other symptoms of prolonged fear. Weeks back, David urged us to find ways to distance ourselves from the war when we weren't actually fighting it—especially important for me, he said, given that I didn't often have the opportunity to get my mind off it by actually fighting it.

Among his suggestions had been one to get closer to Noah, the African-American private who guarded our plane. His isolation was near total, forced on him by bigotry. I guess David decided Rod and I weren't bigots and urged us to invite Noah to church—a neat package, when you think about it. It pulled three isolationists together and got them into church.

Noah agreed to go to church with us on Sunday, 21 May. Rod and I walked the half mile to our plane to get him. The sky was alive with 38s and 51s at play. They called it dog-fight practice. We stopped to watch.

"Cripes, that must be so much fun," I said wistfully. "They do it every day."

"I hear they're not just playing," Rod said, shading his eyes. "There's never enough ice so they take their beer up with them to cool it off. It stays good and cold long enough for the nightly parties with the WACs, nurses, and donut dollies.... You ever been?"

"Where?"

"The parties."

"No. They quit trying to get me to come. Most everybody else goes. Good old Steve wouldn't miss 'em."

How's he doing?"

I started walking again. "Not very good. He looks like death warmed over."

We found Noah at the plane. He was watching the dogfights. He noticed us and grinned warily.

"You ready?" Rod asked.

When your life depends on it, a change in the sound of an airplane engine can be as terrifying as the rattle of a diamond-back. We all heard it, but no one more keenly than Noah who spent most of his time watching the line crews coaxing and cursing a little more life out of our engines. We heard sputtering and then wind. It was as though the whine of all the other engines had been turned down so that we could zero-in on the one plane in trouble. It was the latest model 51, so new it didn't even have its unit markings. The pilot had lost his engine at low altitude and was trying to make our runway.

Awestruck, we watched the plane gliding closer. The bubble canopy should have been open all the way for landing. It was shut. The wheels were still up. The prop was dead. All were signs of disaster. Noah felt them. It took longer for Rod and me, so great was our fascination with that beautiful little plane and our envy of the pilot.

The plane cleared our boundary fence and then, like a pheasant we'd chosen for dinner in our valley, it pancaked with a blood-thinning thud. It skidded forward in a cloud of dust and a cacophony of squealing and screeching metal. It stopped and began to smoulder. We were one hundred yards away.

Fire fighters surrounded it in seconds. Noah tore off to help, but Rod reacted and tackled him before he got within what became the killing range when the plane exploded. The fire turned loose thousands of fifty caliber rounds, sending them screaming out in all directions. Including the pilot, six people died. Six were wounded. The Silence hung over the group for the rest of the day. It returned three days later.

24 May—The group was taking off on a mission. I was drowsing in bed when a shock wave rattled the tent and me. I staggered outside. My first sight was a sickening column of thick black smoke, mushrooming at the top and already the size of a thunderhead. It was Rod. I knew it. I felt it. My mind wanted to scream it but didn't dare, or it couldn't, or it didn't know how. I don't know. I suppose I ran, but I soon found myself at a better vantage point.

The smoke was billowing up from a raging fire twenty-five yards left of the closest end of the runway. Planes were still taking off. The smoke cleared intermittently and I caught sight of the tail-marking of the dying wreck. I had no idea what plane Rod had been on—that one, I was suddenly sure. I sank slowly to the ground. To call what I felt despair doesn't do it justice, not even close. Everything warm inside me—

blood, organs, thoughts, memories—all were cold as a blizzard wind. It was howling all around me, trying to freeze me to death. I was alone in it, utterly alone. Finally, it spoke in a voice both mournful and tinged with hysteria: "You don't have to tread water anymore."

The rattle of a Jeep roused me enough to notice. It hurtled down the hill. The wreck was surround by emergency crews and gear. For the first time, I realized I could feel the heat from the fire. It didn't penetrate me, I just realized it was there. I was puzzled by the efforts to put out the fire. Why bother? It was too late. Let it burn. Let *them* burn in peace. Don't intrude. That's my crew. That's my brother.

Planes kept taking off. As they neared the end of the runway, each shape became two as they rose, identical except for arbitrary markings put on them by the military—a requiem in steel and explosives. The mission doesn't just *matter* to us, Jonathon. It's *all* there is—the only sanity; the only way home, alive or dead; the only way out of here, or anywhere.

My mind watched them soar up—ten, twenty, how many? What did it matter? How did they feel at that moment, roaring away from a crematorium that could as easily have been their's, still could be in a matter of minutes or hours? Nothing. They felt nothing. At least they tried very hard to. Feeling could take you in only one direction.

The growl and clanking of another Jeep startled me. How long had I watched? What did it matter? I recognized the squadron operations officer. Did he know me? Did he want to know why I was on that road? Would I be able to speak? He stopped beside me.

"It was ol' 964. About ready for the bone yard anyway. Everybody got off before it blew. Lost a tire on take-off." He said it all in a matter-of-fact way.

I heard him. It tunneled in fast, giving me an opening to speak past my shock and relief that was so complete that I feared I would bawl. "That sure is good to know," I said, *almost* matter-of-factly. If I were only one, not part of two, maybe I too could learn to be matter-of-fact. He started to leave. "Major! Where are they going?"

"Lyon. Supposed to be a milk run." He gunned the Jeep

up the hill.

Lyon—eastern France, near Switzerland, a milk run. I looked around me. It was a beautiful day. The smoke was painting interesting patterns in the sky.

Eventually, I headed back to the tent. I found Steve there. He looked like hell lying on his cot, hands behind his head. His skin was the color of paste, his face bloated and sickly; a living groan with, from appearances, little or no pulse.

"What's the matter with you? Flak fever?" I knew the truth.

"Naw, too much Johnny Walker and cheap wine last night. Now I got a raging case of the runs. Just got back from the dispensary....I hear everybody got off all right."

I practiced being matter-of-fact. "So I heard."

"Don't give me that shit, Paulson. I know what you went through out there. You better find a way to deal with this place or it'll send you around the bend."

"You mean like getting drunk every night?" It was a rebuke. It surprised and shook me. I'd never talked to Steve that way before. He had been our rock, the one person who always knew exactly what was going on and could put it in it's appropriately absurd place.

"That's one way," he groaned. "But just now, I wouldn't recommend it."

"How about tonight?"

"Ah! That's different." He grinned, but his eyes were angry. "Let me guess. You good little boys from Ames still don't touch the stuff."

"Nope. Never wanted to. Never liked it, and don't see any reason to learn to."

"Or the people who do, huh?" He wasn't angry, more like resigned to it.

"Most of 'em. You've been an exception." I shrugged. "That's why I'm asking."

"Oh, *thank you.*" He sat up, grimacing the whole trip. "You're so pitifully naive, both of you! You think I'm unusual? Well, let me tell you: You're the ones who are. Everybody in this place drinks, most of 'em to excess, lots of 'em on missions!... That's right. I play cards with the flight surgeon, he told me. Half the pilots around here fly half-crocked!"

I stared at him, unsure of what to say, but aware of a growing anger and dread. It must have shown. He screwed up his face in a kind of apology.

"Oh, don't worry about Rod. Le Grande Chuck's blood is pure. He doesn't do *anything*...'course he doesn't know how."

I smiled at that in spite of the situation. I caught myself looking at him. I cared about this chunky comedian/philosopher, but for the first time I felt myself pulling back. It was a familiar feeling, but from long before. Decades later, I put the feeling together with a name—Melvin. But at that moment, it was just a feeling, a minor alarm in a morning too full of them already.

"Sounds like you know the flight surgeon pretty well," I said with an edge in my voice I didn't bother to hide.

"Very funny," he said wearily. "We play cards together....Damn! I gotta go again!" He half staggered, half ran to the latrine. He looked hollow and wrung out right down to the sweat stains on his flight suit. He came back in about ten minutes, mad as hell.

"I'm really fed up and damned tired of having to live up to your expectations, Paulson! I'm not your big brother and I never asked to be! So just lay off! Just lay off!"

"It's okay with me! You wanna booze yourself into the ground, go ahead, do it! I don't give a damn! I got more important things than you to worry about!...Christ, you're pathetic!" I dropped on to my cot, fuming.

He groaned. "Look, I'm sorry. I know what you went through this morning. I'm really glad...you know. Where'd they go?"

"Lyon."

He let out a long, agonizing groan.

"Now what!"

"No...no, no. It's not about Rod. It's, do you have any idea how close that is to Switzerland?"

"Yeah, so what?"

"*Switzerland*! Don't you get it? All you gotta do is head a little off course, feather an engine or two, and slam, bam, thank you, ma'am, you're out of the war; held by the Swiss in heaven. Don't tell me you don't know about the defections. We've had two this month, for Christ's sake!"

I knew, but I had refused to think about them. "You'd do that?"

"Rather than be sacrificed on the alter of stupidity? You're damn right! That's what's going to happen, you know, to you and me. If we get killed, it's statistically most likely that it'll be in the name of a ridiculous Standard Operating Procedure that puts a bombardier and navigator on every plane when only the lead needs either one! Don't tell me you haven't thought about how fucking stupid, how criminally fucking stupid that is! Don't even think about trying to tell me that!"

He was right. Anybody could drop the bombs when the lead plane let go. As far as needing a navigator on every plane — sure, planes got separated from the formation, but if getting lost was a legitimate problem, none of the fighters would ever have come back. They carried only the pilot, trained enough in navigation to get back, as were all pilots.

He was also right that I had thought about it, but I hadn't dared to allow myself to dwell on it. I looked over at this man who had come over here with me, a living reminder that I had flown far fewer missions, had gone through nothing compared to him and the rest of my crew. What would I be like in their situation? The soupy mix of guilt and fear began sloshing in my stomach. So far, this was turning out to be one hell of a day.

"You know," he said, looking far off. "I could have gone to West Point. I could have gotten in, no problem. I could have sat all this out in the world's best fur-lined foxhole."

"My God! Why didn't you?"

He chuckled bitterly. "Scruples, believe it or not. I felt like there are times you have to stand up and be counted. So I did...and here I am looking for ways to count myself out."

"You've still got scruples," I said. "Maybe...maybe you could try playing cards without drinking. Maybe that would be enough."

"Tried it. Lost big every time. On the other hand, give me a few belts and I clean clocks left and right. I'm putting together quite a college fund."

"You're going back to college when you get out?"

"Yeah, Iowa State. Back to engineering. How 'bout you?"

"I don't know. We always figured we had no hope of getting into college, let alone making it through. Now..."

"Now you got reason to believe you can. You aced military schools. You beat out guys with degrees." He looked hopeful, as though he was trying to show me my future and wasn't sure I could see it. He looked away. "I hope you do, Rollie. Both of you."

That afternoon, the group returned minus two planes. Rod wasn't on either of them. I learned later that Lyon had lived up to its billing as a milk run—no flak, no fighters. When the group dropped through low clouds fifteen miles from base, two planes collided, crashed, and burned. No one survived.

I hadn't had any nightmares until that day. From then on, I was plagued by nightmares of burning planes on the runway. I began leaving my bunk unmade in the morning. It was a popular thing among the crews to break the regulation about the condition of one's bunk, a kind of challenge to the system to do something about it. Rod never did it. He never felt the need, but understood why I did—just as I understood why he didn't, although if I tried to put it into words, I would fail.

Chapter Ten

Early June 1944—I stood at the top of the hill looking down on our planes. Some were taking off, others were waiting their turns. My attention was drawn to a far corner where an old clunker, held together with spit and bailing wire, was warming up for it's turn. Even from that distance, I could see Rod walking toward her with the crew. He turned and waved, as though he could see me. He was smiling, almost serene.

One by one, they pulled themselves into the gut of the old buzzard. As I watched, I could hear her engines turning faster, faster, faster still—then too fast! The plane began to rock and quiver. Shut it down, Chuck! Shut it down!

I ran toward her, covering the ground almost instantly. A hundred yards from her I could see Chuck's face; he was crying. Steve appeared next to him; he toasted me from his silver flask, then looked at Chuck and nodded. Chuck reached down and closed his eyes. I froze. The plane exploded with a roar and a fireball erupted into the sky. A white-hot shock wave knocked me down.

I woke up shivering and rolled over. Steve was in his bunk. That meant Rod was, too, because they always flew together. I stared into the dark. It was the fourth time I had dreamed of the explosion, and who knows what else in the dreams I did not remember, all in a matter of a couple of weeks. It was a Saturday night—or Sunday morning given that Steve was in. My most fervent hope at that moment was for daylight.

My crew flew that morning. My heart pounded as their plane lifted off. When they flew beyond my eyes' ability to guard them, I felt better, or at least normal. Normal these days on the ground was a dull feeling of dread that pumped through my body along with my blood. I went to church.

The young shepherd was in his usual place. I waved without really noticing him or caring. He had become annoying, but not because of anything he had done. He was a child, born and raised amid insanity, but still just a child. For me, he had become a harbinger, a reminder of the truth, perched atop a tank along the route to David's haven.

Even David had been unable to escape insanity. At his urging, the all-black battalion's baseball team had begun playing white teams in the 15th's league. The expectation — and I admit I shared it — was that a team with no white men would embarrass itself by being easy pickings. Instead, it proved to be a powerhouse that managed to piss-off every red neck within two hundred miles and well beyond — all the way to Congress. A powerful senator had blustered his outrage at "ehn-tah-gration bah-hind our backs" to anyone who'd listen. Given that he was a powerful senator, that meant pretty much everybody with the power to put a stop to it. Strangely, nobody did.

But David still worried that his efforts would land him before a Congressional hearing, perhaps the House Un-American Activities Committee, and a palpable undercurrent of polarization continued, sometimes flashing like lightening. Rod never told me about it, but I learned from Steve, who learned it from the flight surgeon, that Rod decked Big Red. He was one of our gunners, his nickname a perfect description of his neck. Noah had come to church with Rod and me several times and Red didn't like it. He called us "coon lovers," or words to that effect and Rod leveled him with a left hook. Red apparently complained to the flight surgeon, who politely told him to pound grits up his ass, or the clinical equivalent.

After church that day, I joined David and Jonathon at the picnic table behind the chapel. The conversation eventually turned to the baseball debacle, via David's simple question about Rod's welfare.

"I've lost him to baseball," I said. "If he's not flying, he's playing."

"That's good for *him*," David said, concerned.

"Yeah. Why aren't you playing?" Jonathon asked.

"Not good enough. Ever since we were kids, he's been the

athlete. In Junior Legion, coach Rit put Rod in center field, and me and another weak sister in left and right. Rod ended up covering all three. We were small, but what an arm he had. All I managed to do was get us kicked off the team."

"How'd you do that?" Jonathon asked.

"I didn't think the coach knew sickum about baseball and I told him so. He kicked me off the team. Rod wouldn't stay without me."

"So, Rod wasn't kicked off, you were," Jonathon said in his most analytic tone.

David cringed. "Someday you're going to get it — for them, one or the other is the same thing as both. There's no difference."

"Not when they have a choice," Jonathon countered with the calm of a lawyer who already knew the answers to his questions.

I sometimes felt as though I was a project rather than a person for these two. Not me so much as "twin-ness" or "oneness," a subject they both found fascinating, but one I couldn't help them with much because for me, it just *was* — as natural as breathing.

"And they don't have a choice now," David said, nodding.

"Rolly doesn't. He's not good enough to make the team. But Rod does. He could choose not to play, but he's chosen to play."

"Would you want him to quit?" David asked me.

"No! Not at all. I'm proud of him."

"And he know's that, right?"

"Sure."

"So, if he did quit, you'd figure he did it out of sympathy for you?"

"Probably."

"And what would you do then?"

"Kick his butt — I mean, I'd tell him to get back out there. It's good for him. It gives him that distance from the war and our situation you said was so important."

David nodded. "And it gives you some distance, too, right? At least you can watch him and root for him?"

"Yeah, absolutely."

"Are you getting this, Jonathon?" David asked, just a hint

of anger in his voice.

Jonathon sighed. "Yes. Forgive me, Rolly. One of the reasons I keep my pipe in my mouth is that it leaves less room for my foot."

I wasn't sure why, but I felt vindicated—for about thirty seconds.

"I've watched Rod play," Jonathon said. He's damned good. He might have a shot at the majors."

"He hasn't had enough experience," I said, a recently-born guilt growing in my belly. "If I hadn't shot off my big mouth and gotten us kicked out of Junior Legion, he might have made it."

"You don't know that," David corrected.

"Yes I do. Those three or four years would have made all the difference. Now, it's too late."

"Bull shit," Jonathon growled.

"It's not bull shit. You know a lot about a lot of things, but you don'tknow shit about me or us." It was the first time I'd gotten angry at either of them. Jonathon was fuming.

"Listen, I'm trying to help you."

"Knock it off," David snapped. "Jonathon, it's a *fact* that we can't really know what being a twin is all about, especially here where it's darn near impossible to know what *anything* is all about. But Rolly, you might give us a little more credit for being able to see things you can't see *because* you're a twin. We've been talking here about neither of you having any choices, that your connection dictates what you *must* do. From what I can see, that's not completely true. The fact is that Rod quit Legion baseball because there was no place he'd rather be than with you and you couldn't be there. You're both here because there's no place you'd rather be than with Rod, even in hell, and him with you. And someone—a clerk, a commander, God—someone made that possible. Since then, you two have turned yourselves inside out, in effect choosing to separate to prevent someone from taking that choice away from you. That's love. It's love so deep that few people have ever experienced it. It's love so deep that it can seem like something else I like completion, as though you aren't a complete human being without Rod.

"You say Rod feels the same way and I'm sure he does. But

the fact that he *is* playing baseball, that he *is* finding ways to survive without you, means that the separation you two have chosen to create has allowed him to learn something about himself. He may not be aware of it, I don't know."

My head was spinning. I was angry. He didn't get it at all, and yet something he was saying seemed right. Jonathon lit that damned pipe.

"What do you do that's just for you?" Jonathon pressed.

"What do you mean?"

"Rod plays baseball. What do *you* do?... I'll tell you what you do, you wait for him. When you're not together, you wait for him. You fill in by reading my copies of the daily war diaries and learning all you can about just how dangerous this place is — for him, mostly. It's damned clear that you'd far rather it was you up there every day and him on the ground worrying and waiting. I think you need to ask yourself two questions. The first is, if your situations were reversed, would he go ahead and play baseball? If your answer is yes, than he's learned something you need to learn. If it's no, then we really *don't* know what the hell we're talking about.

"The second one is, given the way each of you feels, who has the tougher assignment, you or him? You've never mentioned it, but he'll have his missions in long before you do. One way or another, he'll go home before you and you *will* be separated."

It would be weeks later that I fully understood, in words I could have expressed, exactly what they were missing. At that moment, I could only brood.

"I think we've taken this farther than we should," David said, an apology in his tone. "Let's just be glad Rod has baseball — and that there's still a league for him to play in."

I took a deep breath, thankful for the change of subject. "Cripes, that still going on?"

"Oh, yes," David moaned. "They still want my hide. All I can figure is that they can't decide how to take it without causing an uproar in more liberal circles."

Jonathon laughed. "Did you hear Axis Sally? She agrees with our esteemed senator. What you did has played criminal havoc with the natural order of things."

David shook his head in disgust. "They keep telling me I

have to find a way to fix 'the damage you've done.' How was I to know their team would kick butts and take names?"

"You did a good thing and you know it," I said. Both of them looked at me in surprise. "Don't look so shocked. I've been known to think!"

We all laughed hard for the first time since we had come together for our social circles. When the laughter ebbed, David picked up on his favorite subject.

"So, how are you doing these days?"

"Okay, I guess. I've been having nightmares since the plane blew."

"Bad ones?"

"Bad enough. I don't wake up screaming or anything, but it's getting to the point I'm afraid to go to bed."

"Have you seen the flight surgeon?" Jonathon asked.

"What for? What's he going to do? Besides, he's got more than enough people going there with real reasons without whiners like me."

"I'm not sure trying to do something about nightmares qualifies you as a whiner. He might be able to give you something to help you sleep, right David?"

"Some kind of sedative, usually."

"Usually?"

David smiled wearily at me. "The ones who *don't* have nightmares are either brand new or in deep trouble."

David and I went to lunch in Lucera that day. Jonathon was the primary topic of conversation and it was David's contention that I might know too much about our little corner of the war, that as good a man as Jonathon was, his attitude rarely allowed for hope or a respite.

I understood him, but he was wrong. There could be no respite for me, not as long as I was stuck on the ground while Rod faced danger. My only defense was to know as much as I could, to be involved in every way I could.

On a stand-down day, Rod, some of the other Azons, and I went to Foggia. We were with Sammy Gambino and George Yarbrough in a bar. While Rod and I drank lousy lime soda, Sammy and George drank wine and practiced their Italian, with unusual intensity, on a young girl. Somehow, Rod and I came to understand that they were trying to find out why she was a prostitute. We joined in, adding our vast experience with the evils of prostitution, which was exactly nothing at all. For her part, the girl hadn't been one long enough to dump us and move on to a paying customer. Instead, she vigorously defended her choices.

The air was getting pretty thick when George finally brought a halt to it. He had a Master's degree in psychology, but I doubt that had much to do with his sudden realization. "Wait a minute," he said. "We're sitting here passing judgement on her and we don't know the first thing about what she's faced. We've been here what, three months? She's spent her whole life under the thumb of Hitler and Mussolini. Her country's been destroyed by war, her family ripped apart, and we have the nerve to tell her what she's doing is wrong! When we leave, she'll still be here and nothing will have changed. Hell, it'll be worse because we'll take our money with us. All she's doing is surviving the only way she can." A look of shame and regret swept over his face. "She's just doing what we hope to do—just survive."

The conversation stopped and we could barely look at her. Confused by what must have appeared to her to be total rejection, she left angrily. We didn't see her again.

Whether being fellow warriors was the equalizer or we simply looked easy to talk to, I can't say, but later we were joined by a lieutenant colonel in full-dress uniform. Among his ribbons was the Silver Star with cluster. He introduced himself as Sonny—a youthful, all-American-handsome P-38 pilot. We three first lieutenants and Rod soon learned that he carried his rank and prestige on his uniform, not in his demeanor. He may have been the most unaffected man ever to admit to being a command officer and fighter pilot, but he *could* tell a story.

He kept us spellbound for hours with stories of the P-38 and the Desert War, Cairo and the Holy Land, the Palm Sunday Massacre, Rome and Capri, and dogfights at thirty thousand feet. He *knew* Richard Ira Bong. He didn't tell us how he earned his first Silver Star, or his second, and it didn't seem right to ask. He might have earned one of them leading one of three P-38 groups in the daring surprise attack that was instrumental in evicting the Luftwaffe from the airfields around Foggia, which made it possible for us to be sitting where we were.

That happened in September 1943. They flew most of the way on the deck and caught the Germans by surprise. When it was over, they had destroyed more than two hundred enemy aircraft on the ground at ten airfields. He moved on in time and experience to something closer to us—the execution of the 483rd.

"If there had been even one fighter group with the 483rd," he lamented, "we could have cut their losses in half."

We knew about the 483rd. Every bomber crew in the theater knew about them. Like bubonic plague, news of their decimation over Memmingen in southern Germany had swept through the theater. Heavy weather had separated the B-17 group from the massive force in the sky that day. Without fighter escort, the 483rd was easy prey for German fighters. An estimated two hundred of them shot down fourteen of the 483rd's twenty-nine planes in less than ten minutes.

"The Krauts aren't strong enough to take us on everywhere," Sonny said. "They've changed tactics to selective defense. They mass everything they have to defend selected targets, and we never know which targets they've selected.... But we're getting better and they're getting worse. Their losses are now clearly unsustainable."

Slim comfort, but there was hope in it.

My crew and the group closed out June with a mission to Bleckhammer. In terms of numbers of guns, Bleckhammer wasn't the most hellish of the hell holes my crew faced without me. Two hundred guns defended it, compared to Ploesti's 250 and Vienna's 340. What gave it special significance was that it was a smaller area, with the guns packed closer together and their fire more concentrated. The result, Bleckhammer was the Fifteenth's deadliest target.

Seeing the red target string stretched from our field to Bleckhammer was more than enough to draw angry shouts from the crews gathered for briefing, more than enough to send some men stomping or trudging out of the hall before they were dismissed. Nothing was done to them, no disciplinary actions lodged against them. The commanders allowed nearly anything a man found necessary to do to prepare himself for another round of Russian roulette.

I spent some of that day with Jonathon, learning more about Bleckhammer, complaining about the Azon project, and preaching to the choir about the lethal stupidity of tactics that did not use fighters to attack gun batteries. Every day, our forces were reducing the strength of the Luftwaffe and taking back real estate from the German army and armored units. But as anti-aircraft units pulled back, they took their heavy guns with them. Less ground to defend meant more guns per square mile and more shrapnel in the air trying to kill us — and succeeding.

In the midst of it, someone delivered a message to Jonathon. He read it and frowned. "We lost one — not your crew."

An all-too-familiar ache fanned out from its home in my gut. "What's the total?"

"Another lousy month," he said. "In the nine missions since the fourteenth, we've lost twelve planes and eleven crews."

2 July 1944 — A beautiful Sunday. All six Azons were in the air to bomb a railroad bridge in Hungary. We had an escort of eighteen P-38s. Flying at eighteen thousand feet, twenty miles from the target, we flew over a German fighter base. Our fighters were itching to take them on, but not one came up to greet us. Over the intercom we agreed that they must have felt it was just too nice a day to die for the Third Reich. To my lasting regret, many innocent residents of a Hungarian village were about to die for the Azon project.

The attack plan for the bridge was for the six of us to form-up in trail and fly around and around the target, each plane dropping one bomb at a time. My first run was perfect, but the bomb hung-up and went out late. I had no idea where it would land so I did what I could to guide it along the rail line. It guided to perfection, following the tracks straight and true right into the very heart of a tiny village. A thousand pounds of RDX lit up that entire hamlet. How many people died, I don't know. Nor do I know the name of the place, or the

155

names of any of the people who died. I do know they lived miles from our target, miles from any target.

The plane was silent. Nobody blamed me then, or later. It was a mechanical foul-up in a project pock-marked by mental and mechanical foul-ups. The irony was that the Azon technology had worked just enough to kill innocent people. It wasn't my fault. I knew it then and I know it now. But the survivors in that village didn't know it. All they knew was death. Many times since I've wanted to find out the name of the hamlet and send them an explanation so they would know that the destruction of their homes wasn't the act of a barbarian. On that day, I did what I could to put it out of my mind. Our route back took us near Sarajevo, a city of red roofs in a beautiful valley. I explained the significance of that city over the intercom. I don't know how many people on the plane cared that Arch Duke Ferdinand had been assassinated there thirty years before, and that his death had been the spark that ignited World War I, but I told them anyway. Suddenly, flak guns that weren't supposed to be there opened up and crippled Phil Oliverie's plane. Two engines belched smoke and fire erupted all along the trailing edge of the right wing. George Yarbrough was Phil's bombardier. The tail gunner was one of Rod's buddies, little Billy Floyd from Kentucky. They barely made it to the Adriatic and ditched dangerously close to the Yugoslavian coast.

We circled and watched life rafts opening in the water near the plane. Some of the crew members gave us reassuring waves. If you had to ditch, the B-17's huge, low wings made it the best in the world in which to do it. Suddenly, we saw three enemy patrol boats heading out from shore. A half dozen P-38s dove down and sank them in one pass. The fighters maintained cover until an Air-Sea Rescue PBY[1] plucked the crew from the water.

15 July 1944 — We got our first mail from home. Mail call was right after evening chow. Rod and I took our half-dozen letters to our favorite spot, alone beneath a sycamore tree. Five letters were from Mother and one thick one from Gert. All of

[1] A twin-engine navy amphib, nicknamed the "Catalina."

Mother's letters had been written on Sundays, the latest one May 21.

"Why does the mail take so damn long? Rod complained. "A slow boat would be faster."

I shrugged. "She still only writes on Sunday. You suppose that means she's still putting in twelve hours a day the rest of the week?"

"I hope not. She shouldn't have to with only three mouths to feed."

Her letters caught us up on those Ames residents who had died in the war, and those who had survived and where they were. Our brother Leonard was thirteen and working hard at the odd jobs we used to do. Unlike us, Mother pointed out, he was making good grades in school.

"You suppose she wrote that just to needle us about our grades, or because she thought we'd want to know?" Rod asked bitterly.

His tone puzzled me. I was the angry, sarcastic one, if either of us had reason to be. "I think the latter," I said, studying him. "I'm sure there were times she wanted to kill us over our grades, but not now....She says Gert will graduate from college and be married. Cripes, that means she already is and we didn't send her a thing."

"Yeah, we got off scotfree on that one....I still can't believe it."

"What?"

"Any of it, but especially that Gert graduated from college. That must have been hard, what with having to work all the time."

"At least she got room and board living at home," I said. "What I don't understand is how she got into a sorority. You have to be somebody and have money, don't you?"

"I'll bet you anything Gert got into some dump of a sorority that they set up at Iowa State just for the nobodies."

"That's ridiculous."

"Okay. You tell me how she did it, smart ass."

I glared at him, but decided not to push. "Forget it, Rod. I'm not even going to try to figure that one out....What I want to know is how she graduated. She's smart, but I didn't think she was that smart."

157

"Yeah. I thought it took straight As just to get into college. She had a few Bs."

"Maybe it's because she majored in home ec," I ventured.

"That's got to be it. If boy's home ec in high school is any indication, there's no way home ec in college could be as hard as some of the men's courses like engineering, vet medicine, even forestry.... What do you think we should do if we get out of this alive? The war isn't going to last forever. I'll bet we have a year at most to decide."

"Right. We probably don't even have that much time. I think we should get serious about Alaska. I think we missed the boat on that one."

Rod shook his head. "Alaska's not in the cards. There's an awful lot going on up there because of the war. By now it's been ruined; all the timber cut and the game killed off. If we were pilots, maybe we could have made a living as bush pilots. So, where does that leave us? Maybe getting a job with Herb?"

That thought made me cringe. "That would be like admitting we're not good enough to get jobs on our own. Besides, who says he'll be able to hire us? Everybody says there's going to be another depression after the war. Maybe we could hide out in the service."

"Oh, there's a hell of a good idea!" Rod roared. "Do you actually think I'm going to spend the rest of my life taking shit from people like Le Grande Chuck—that's what you call him. I call him Shit for Brains, which flatters him!"

I had never seen him so furious. It took several seconds for him to calm down enough to continue. "I not only wouldn't stay in the service, I don't think we'll have the opportunity. The Air Corps will never be hard-up enough to keep us!"

"What's so bad about us, all of a sudden." "There's nothing sudden about it. We're losers with no place to go and only ourselves to blame. You remember when you sent me my high school transcripts while I was in training? I never could understand why you did that, but I figured my average. You know what it was? A good, old fashioned, all-American D-plus! If it hadn't been for the plus, I would have been really depressed. Did you ever figure yours?"

I nodded. "C-minus." He was staring at me, waiting. "It sounds better than a D-plus, don't you think?" We broke out laughing. We laughed until our sides hurt. Worn out, Rod laid back in the grass. It was too dark to read Gert's letter. Rod's mood soon darkened, too.

"I don't know what's so damned funny. What are we going to do?"

"Jonathon thinks the government will help veterans go to college."

"So? No amount of money is going to get the D-pluses and C-minuses in the door."

"He thinks there'll be some kind of probation program."

"Great. I've got a fat picture of how that will work. Let's say there are ten openings and twenty vets apply, ten officers and ten enlisted. Guess who they'll pick?"

I was worried about him. I'd never seen him so down. "I suppose that could happen. But I can't believe that you getting shafted once is going to ruin your life forever."

He sat up, furious again. "No? Well it's damn easy for you to be blasé about it! You weren't the one shafted!"

"Wait just a damned minute! Okay, you were shit on. There's no doubt of that. But look what's happened because of it. You're a mechanic. You've got skills they'll pay for in the real world. I'm a goddamned bombardier! There'll be one hell of a lot of demand for that outside!... Damn it, you're the one who's impressed everybody here with how well you play baseball. With your arm, you could become another Bob Feller, even better since you're left-handed. The Cardinals won't give a damn about your grades. Hell, I couldn't even get a job as a bat boy! While you're feeling sorry for yourself, maybe you could remember that.... You *know* I'd trade places with you in a second if I could!"

Rod hung his head and struggled for a reply. "And you know I wouldn't let you. I know it's not your fault. I don't even know why I said that."

"None of this is like you. Has something happened?"

He looked at me with the look everyone had too often. "Two of my baseball buddies were on the one that went down over Ploesti yesterday. We'd talked about maybe sticking together after the war and trying some semi-pro or minor league ball."

"Were there any parachutes?"

"Only three." He got up and walked away.

20 July 1944 — Five Azons went to the French Riviera. Our target was a 1,200-foot viaduct just northeast of Toulon. The mission was tricky. Our bomb run axis was from the northeast at about two hundred degrees, directly toward the sprawling city. At bomb impact, flirting with the hundred Toulon guns, we were supposed to break hard left, back out over the Mediterranean. Our crew was leading the mission with Le Grande Chuck in the left seat.

The bomb run was routine. On bomb impact, everybody broke left except us. Chuck broke right. Instead of being safe over the Mediterranean, we were headed for a mid-air collision with our wing man. Fortunately, the wing man was slightly out of position and a little late. Otherwise, all twenty of us on both planes would have been history. Our troubles were only beginning.

Our course took us right into the heart of the Toulon flak field and we were the only target. It was like flying through a bed of red hot coals. Shells bursts rocked FUBAR constantly. At only 15,000′ and not on oxygen, we choked on the foul-smelling cordite. Steve calmly offered Chuck a course to safety. It was as though Chuck didn't hear him, didn't hear any of us. Ray Dominy, our co-pilot, also an Iowa boy, tried to take control, but Chuck fought him, as if battling an invisible demon.

The plane was severely shot up, but still in one piece. Somehow, eventually, we staggered out over the water. Steve tried to give Chuck a new heading. Again he refused it. We got as far south as Corsica, headed toward Sardinia and Africa. Steve tried again. At the sight of Corsica, Chuck seemed to snap out of it. He accepted the course change.

That night in our tent, Steve summed up how the entire crew felt: "He'll get us long before the Krauts do."

3 to 21 July 1944 — The group flew sixteen missions, every one to a hell hole. Miraculously, we lost only three planes. Two of those were last seen under control and headed toward paradise (Switzerland).

22 July 1944—Rod and our crew failed to return from a mission. I was too numb to function, yet I somehow did what I had to do the next day. I wrote to Mother.

Sunday, July 23

Dear Mother;

I'm writing this from Rod's tent. Both tents are empty, mine and his. Mother, Rod and our crew didn't come back from yesterday's mission. It was Rod's thirty-fourth. I just know they are okay. They didn't make an emergency landing at one of our other bases, or we would have known about it by now.

Their plane lost an engine, fell out of formation, and was being chased by 109s. It was last seen entering a layer of clouds. Once in the clouds, they were safe from the fighters. Their plane was under control, there was no fire, no one saw any signs of an explosion. One chute was seen just as they entered the clouds.

Since the plane was under control, I believe they were all able to bail out. They were over enemy territory, but the area is controlled by Partisans. It's wild and rugged, but that's good. It's harder for the Krauts to round them up. I can't let myself think of Rod being locked up like a caged animal in some POW camp.

Rod has a better chance of surviving in the wilderness, even behind enemy lines, than anybody I know. We've been learning how to survive in the wilderness our whole lives. It's like an adventure that he's been trained and prepared for. He'll do just fine and'll be home in time for squirrel season. We have people showing up all time who have been shot down and rescued by the Partisans.

Rod has a regular emergency kit—rations, maps, and money—and he made his own survival kit. It has special maps that he gets from Steve, extra food, matches, a good hunting knife, first aid kit, extra socks, toothbrush, and a good little compass. Don't worry, Mother. He'll be good at evasion and living off the land. The rest of the crew is lucky to have him. They'll all be back here in a week or two, and then they can come home.

Over here, if you are picked up by the Partisans, its an automatic ticket home. Otherwise, if they rescue you twice they think you are a spy. I'm probably not even supposed to mention Partisans. Oh, well, nothing ventured...Sometimes we get word right away if they rescue someone.

Here in Rod's tent it's quiet and cool. It's not even seven yet. The group has already left on today's mission. Our six gunners all live together in this tent. The place is not very neat, no way up to your standards, except Rod's area. All his things are neatly arranged. Even the baseball bat he brought over is clean. It's a thirty-six-inch Stan Musial.

His only picture is one of you and us when we were about three. It's our favorite for several reasons: You were smiling in spite of all the trouble we were. We were in overalls and cute little caps. I can't even tell which of us is which. We both have mischievous smiles. No doubt we already had our next misadventure planned. I know you remember that at that age our favorite daredevil thing to do was a trip all the way up the alley, one whole block, to Yikky Way. With all that traffic, it was an exciting and scary place to be. If we survived that, don't you worry, Mother, we can survive whatever they throw at us over here.

Rod made his bed yesterday before they left. He always does. Nobody else over here ever does that, makes his bed before a mission. They all figure if they don't come back at least they have finally beat the system once. Rod's not trying to beat the system. All he wants to do is beat the odds. He knows more about that than all the rest of us put together. He has learned how to welcome each new day as though it was the rest of his life.

When he's not flying, baseball is his first choice. We've been to the beach. I guess I'm not even supposed to tell you which one. I'll give you a hint:

There aren't any palm trees. Once in a while we go to the big town. The main attraction is the Red Cross ice cream.

Mother, you would be so proud of Rod. Even though only the tail gunner, he's the leader of the enlisted men on our crew. He leads them by example. Nobody takes any better care of himself or his guns, but it's more than that. He is always neat and clean.

He's ready to listen if they need somebody, and we all do sooner or later. He's patient and has a positive, up-beat attitude. He's a good mechanic and likes to help out at the plane. Rod is really grown up.

He's outgoing, makes friends, and enjoys his friends. He seems to have total confidence in himself. Maybe its because he's a great baseball player, easily one of the best over here.

Our chaplain, David, says he has never seen anyone in this situation handle it any better than Rod. He handles it a lot better than I do, and he's the one who's at risk, not me. David says Rod is the best thing that has ever happened, or is ever likely to happen, to Noah. He has become a big-brother figure to Noah.

Another thing. Since we've been in the service, I've had every break, Rod none. Yet, it hasn't made him bitter. In spite of his bad breaks, he has pride and confidence in himself. It must come from you.

I think you would like David. He has helped both of us a lot. He says he can tell by us what kind of a person you are.

I put the pen down. I had thought of so many things, and there was so much I more I wanted to say, but I couldn't bring myself to write any more. If I could have, I think I would have written something like this:

I can't figure out how you do it. You've had three of us to worry about. How can you even keep going? I just have Rod to worry about (I don't even have to worry about me!) and in only four months I already have nightmares about things that have happened or may happen.

Since yesterday, I've already had feelings of relief; no longer every day the worry and dread about what might happen. Is that a terrible thing? Have you ever felt that way? Am I relieved because if he's gone, I no longer have to worry, or is it because I really believe that he's okay, which also means I no longer have to worry?

We knew the day we got here that we weren't likely to live through this. That's when we realized how lucky we were to be together. Flying together, on the same plane, we would have about the same chance, either way. Then, for reasons I'm not allowed to write about, we haven't even been able to do that. Instead of flying together, Rod's in danger and I'm not. I'm the one that's getting the free ride.

Now, it no longer matters. If Rod's okay, he gets to go home. If not, I can't even feel or imagine what it will be like. Which will be worse, having him to worry about, or not having him? I may not be able to go on. I may not want to go on.

Why were we together in the first place? We didn't plan it that way. The whole thing is crazy. There's a law against it and everybody knows about us. It's even in the press clipping you sent us. They had to have been written right here. There is stuff in those press clippings we can't put into letters. It's all so crazy. All along we've had to worry about how long we'll be together. Sooner or later, they will separate us. Will it be another bad deal for Rod?

I felt a little better. In a very real way, I needed to write that letter, even though I couldn't finish it. I re-read it and suddenly realized I had described for Mother a Rod I had completely taken for granted. I stuck the letter in my shirt pocket. I had to finish and mail it that day. I took another look at Rod's picture of us and picked up his glove. It was so clean and soft. He must saddle-soap it every day.

Out on my perch above the field I tried to think of Rod and couldn't. Steve came into my mind. We'll miss him. He was our leader and big brother. From the beginning he was our eyes, ears, and voice. Even if we knew what we wanted to say, he could say it so much better. Losing Steve will be like losing Ralph all over again. We have to write Steve's folks.

I was worried about Mother. If only I could get home before the telegram. It was mid-morning on a blue-bird day, but the sky was deserted. The only thing moving was a harmless old Goonie Bird[2] approaching from the east. Poking along at low altitude it was like something going nowhere and in no hurry to get there. Otherwise the whole world was at a standstill. Quietly and probably unnoticed, the Goonie came in and landed without even bothering to circle.

What am I going to tell Noah?

The Goonie parked. Nine new guys loaded their stuff into a covered truck.... Silver was the wrong color for the Goonie. It should have been black, except it brought them in alive. Nobody had to come and take them out—a very efficient system we have worked out with the Germans. It's amazing. We lose a crew one day and a new one shows up the next. Why can't we be as good at saving lives as we are at replacing them?

Oh, oh—they didn't get the numbers exactly right. Nine for ten is a ten percent shortage. At that rate, in a few months we'll be down to nobody...and our losses will be down to zero. How clever of someone. As Jonathon would say, "Never underestimate the bureaucratic mind's capacity for absurdities."

In the back of my mind I was aware of a truck grinding up the hill. It stopped beside me. I looked up. I was stunned. There was Le Grande Chuck in the right seat. Something in my mind said, "That figures. Even in my nightmares he grabs the front seat, everybody else rides in back."

A B-3 bag came out of the back end, followed by Rod. He looked as clean and fresh as he did every morning. More or less the same old nightmare, said the voice in my mind, but it wasn't. He was safe. As it turned out, it took hours for me to

[2]C-47, twin-engine transport. The military version of the famous Douglas DC-3.

165

fully comprehend that. But at that moment, his flying suit looked as if he had put it on fresh and clean that morning. The truck moved on.

Rod looked at me. "You look awful. When did you sleep last? And shower, and change clothes?" He saw the envelope in my shirt pocket. "Mail from home?"

I handed it to him. "Not exactly."

He sat down on his bag and took his time reading it.

The Goonie Bird came lumbering down the runway toward us. Once in the air its wheels slowly disappeared. It came by, almost level with us. I waved. It dipped its wings, gracefully turned, and headed back east. Silver was just the right color for that Goonie.

Rod finished the letter, looked at me, and tore it up. "You won't be needing this or any others like it. After yesterday, we know for sure, the crew I mean. We were meant to see this thing through to the end....Let's take the rest of the day off. You get cleaned up, we'll hike into Lucera for some ice cream."

"Jonathon said one parachute was seen. Who bailed out?"

Rod grinned. "Big Red. He panicked just before we made it into the clouds. I waved to him as he floated away."

26 July 1944 — Back from a good day of skeet (ninety-nine out of one hundred), I was alone in the tent. Gibbon's *Rise and Fall of the Roman Empire* had again put me to sleep. I was awakened by the sound of engines. Outside in the late afternoon sunlight I had to shade my eyes to look up. All I could see circling overhead was a flight of seven in an unusually tight formation, like they were passing in review. From the ground I could tell by the tail markings that they were not all from the same squadron. Peculiar. I wondered how they managed to get all mixed up. Three of the seven each had a feathered engine. What was going on? Usually the cripples land first. This is highly unusual. I assumed the rest of the group had already landed.

I went to Rod's tent and waited for him to get back from de-briefing. I recognized him as he came into the dappled sunlight under the olive trees. I have no idea how, but the minute I saw him, even from thirty yards away, I knew something was terribly wrong. He came slowly along the shady path between the tents. He was alone.

Where was the rest of the crew? I still had no idea what had happened on the mission. When he was close enough so that I could clearly see his face, I didn't even have to ask.

That is all I remember about Rod on that day. I don't remember what he said. Maybe he was in a daze, or in a state of shock. Maybe he walked right by me without saying anything. I don't remember what we did later, or what we talked about.

I don't even remember when or how I found out that Steve was gone. For some reason, Steve flew with a different crew that day. I don't remember when or from whom I found out about the mission:

The whole Air Force was assigned to targets in a thirty-mile area near Vienna. Before the group got to the IP, there wasn't much going on, except for small groups of enemy fighters all over the place engaging our escort fighters. A reported 160 fighters, mostly 109s and 190s, hit our group at the start of the bomb run. In five minutes, we had lost eleven shot down and two more to a mid-air collision during the attack.

Our squadron lost three planes. Steve was on one of them. That's all I remember about Wednesday, 26 July 1944 — the day we lost half of the group in five minutes. I did learn what that seven-ship formation was all about. Of the fourteen that came back, the seven that were in the worst shape or that had wounded on board landed first. The formation of the remaining seven was Colonel Badjer's idea. It was his message to the survivors up there with him, and to all of us down below: The Three-O-First may be battered and bloody, but it sure is not broken! That was his way of beginning to pick up the pieces. Tomorrow would be just another day.

That night my nightmare returned. There was a burning plane and I couldn't find Rod. I woke up at five. Ray was in rest camp, and Chuck was up and gone. Rod's tent was empty. They were on the mission. By six-thirty the group was gone. By eight they had several teams packing-up and taking the personal effects of thirty people out of the tents. When they came to get Steve's things, I left for the chapel.

A B-25 was circling. Even then I would have known it

anywhere by the distinctive throaty rattle of its engines. It was the first one I'd seen close-up since we had been there. David wasn't at the chapel. Hardly surprising. He had to help write letters to the next of kin of 130 people.

Back at our tent a note was on my cot. I was to report immediately to the orderly room. I knew why. The ax had fallen. They'd blown the whistle on Rod and me.

The other five Azons bombardiers were already there, with their bags, waiting on me. I had fifteen minutes to pack. All any of us knew was that we had been exiled to Corsica. When I got back, packed and ready, a member of the Azon Brain Trust and Colonel Badjer were there to see us off. All sweetness and forgiveness, as a farewell gift, they sent with us that damned monstrous albatross of an unguidable bomb project.

Chapter Eleven

27 July 1944—We six Azon bombardiers arrived in Corsica, assigned to the 446th squadron of the 321st bomb group, 12th Air Force. My new nightmares began about two weeks later. They were always the same. I would look long and hard for Rod, but never find him. Sometimes, I would be searching in our valley, other times on a military base. Many times, I visited a nightmare-post office in the hope of finding a letter from him and would wake up terrified that none was there. The latter wasn't far from reality.

Every day I waited among the throng at mail call as the clerk called name after unfamiliar name. Every day, there was nothing from Rod—no letter, no postcard to tell me he was still alive. Nothing to tell me he was dead.

Two weeks after our arrival, I wrote to David. Surely, he would know something. I got no answer. The fourth week passed and I was desperate to know, one way or the other, alive or dead. I had never before taken a personal problem to a commanding officer. Under normal circumstances, I never would have considered it. My problems were not things to be shared. Life wasn't fair to anybody in the middle of a war, and I certainly didn't expect anyone to understand what it meant to be a twin. But this was different—worse, harder, consuming. Finally I went to our squadron commander, Major Paul Cooper, who may not have understood, but was understanding. The next day, the end of my fifth week on Corsica, I was in a B-25 headed for Lucera.

The shaded path was cold and forbidding as I approached Rod's tent. Memories and emotions from the first time I had faced the possibility of losing him came howling back like a hurricane that had changed it's mind about moving on. Most of my will and energy drained out of me into the Italian dirt beneath my feet. It took all I had left to get close enough to the tent to look inside. When I did, the effect was like a thunderclap. My energy returned with a bonus measure: His cot was made up.

His glove and bat were in place, the photograph of us was still displayed. He was alive—or at least he had been when he'd left that morning. I sat on his cot and let the evidence of him surround me for a few moments. Still, none of that could begin to eliminate the mystery of why I hadn't heard from him. Two questions remained: Where the hell was he, and why the hell hadn't he written. I vowed at that moment to kill him if he wasn't dead by the time I found him.

No one in the Orderly Room knew anything about him, which was as surprising as dawn. I went to the chapel. The shepherd boy and his flock were where they should be. Unfortunately for me, David also was where he should be—home in the United States. I headed for the flight line. Noah was there and so pleased to see me that I felt important, and then scared when I saw he wasn't guarding our plane.

"FUBAR, she's gone," he said sadly. "But Rod, he wasn't in it. He's in the hospital."

Relieved and petrified at the same time I said, "What hospital?"

"Over to Foggia."

"What's wrong? What happened?"

Noah didn't know.

I wanted to stay and talk with this young man who, without meaning to, had expanded our world, but I had to get to Rod. I broke for the road at a run. Once there, I hitched a ride with a captain from maintenance.

The fifteen miles from Lucera to Foggia crosses lush green fields. Streams hurry around them, ponds shine among them. Orchards and vineyards held tight to the bordering slopes. As usual, 51s and 38s played above us that day, their contrails a crazy-quilt fluffy white against the blue sky. I had forgotten how beautiful it all was.

"How's it going?" I asked the captain, a question rooted both in nerves and in my obsession with keeping track.

He grunted. "August's been even worse than July."

"Are you still getting fighters?"

"Naw. This was a clean war when it was fighters. Most of the damage was to the planes that didn't come back. Now, its all flak." His voice sounded like the gravel under the tires. "The ones that get back are flying coffins—riddled by shrapnel and full of wounded and dead."

I promised myself then and there to quit keeping track of the war.

"You going anywhere special in Foggia?"

"Yeah. Do you know where the hospital is?"

"You don't look sick, Lieutenant. You got something going with a nurse?"

"Uh uh. I should be so lucky. My brother's in there."

"I'm sorry. I'll take you right to the front door. Was it flak?"

"I don't know, nor does anybody else, including the Orderly Room."

"So, what else is new? Whose crew's he on?"

"Chuck Grand. Do you know him?"

"Then it has to be flak....Do I know him? Grand he isn't. Flak magnet, he damn sure is. That's what he's known as in the Group, Chuck The Grand Flak Magnet. Every time the Group gets flak, Grand seems to be the one the Krauts are after, like he was their special project. It's eerie. Any combat guy who is slightly superstitious, and they all are, would gladly go to Ploesti rather than be on the same mission with Grand."

We'd been together less than fifteen minutes, but this guy had managed to whip me back and forth between hoping for the best and expecting the worst. If Rod was still alive he's shot up, crippled for life, and barely hanging on.

"Far as we're concerned, Grand is a disaster certain to happen. Crew chiefs sweat blood every mission day in fear of him. Finally we found the answer."

His inference frighteningly clear to me, I mumbled, "I know I'm going to love this."

"When Grand flies, he's assigned a relic long overdue for the boneyard. That way we in maintenance are guaranteed winners. If he brings it back shot full of holes, we don't even have to fix it. If he doesn't bring it back, our worst nightmare is behind us."

"Are you crazy? Are you telling me it's okay for my brother to get shot up just so you jackasses don't have to do your goddamned job! With you bastards for friends, who needs the Krauts for enemies!"

He blinked and slowly his eyes narrowed into a glare, but he didn't say a word.

At the front door of the hospital I said, "I'm really sorry. I'm not myself. For over a month I've had no way of knowing if he was dead or alive."

He shrugged.

I found Rod quickly. The jerk was sitting up in bed reading — tanned, relaxed, and smiling from head to toe. No wonder. A tray of snacks was nearby. At least the 'bottomless pit' was probably getting enough to eat. Both arms and hands were present, attached, functioning, and not in casts, so why in hell didn't he write?

"So," he said, " you got my letter."

He was a dead man. "Did I get your letter? You think that's funny? You know damned good and well you haven't bothered to write! I'll give you a chance to explain that before I break your damned arms!"

He kept smiling, as if how I felt didn't matter. I considered knocking his teeth out.

"I'm through," he said. "I finished up on the twenty-seventh. I sent you a letter that day — exactly a month after you left. Didn't get it, huh?"

"You're through?" Never had I dared to speculate on that possibility. I'd been grimly plodding ahead, somehow carrying on in the hope that he was alive, but far from being out of danger. Until that moment, *milk run* had been the finest, most lyrical words in the language. Suddenly, they were second on the list. *I'm through* was by far the best phrase ever uttered. Rod was going home! But the math was wrong. It would have been impossible to fly that many missions in a month.

"What do you mean? Were you injured? Are you getting a medical discharge?...God, Rod! Can you walk?"

"Hell yes! I had some boils on my neck and they lanced

172

them. That's why I'm here...and in no particular hurry to leave!" He was giddy, almost hysterical. "What a luxury! I'm off death row. I have my life back. I've won. I *beat* this godforsaken place!"

"Then I don't understand. There's no way you could have flown that many missions."

He looked at me thoughtfully. "After you left, I tried to fly every mission. It so happened that the mix was heavy in doubles." His smile faded. "Most of us who came back on the twenty-sixth (of July, following the catastrophic mission to Vienna) felt we'd been handed a death sentence. For the first time, I gave up. I was going to die—maybe sooner, maybe later, but it was *going* to happen. Once I figured that out, I decided not to prolong the wait. Just do it and get it over with. It seemed so right at the time, so natural.

(Years later, I discussed a short story by Sartre in a great books seminar. The essence of the story was exactly the decision and understanding Rod had come to: Death is natural and inevitable. It shouldn't be all that troublesome, even if it comes early, at age twenty. Like Sartre's character Emil, Rod had figured that out.)

"Did you talk to David about it?"

"Of course. He helped, but after that mission he really had his hands full. According to him, life without hope was a nearly unanimous condition throughout the group....I was numb, in a state of shock. David called it 'extreme trauma.' And then you left. We didn't even get to say goodbye. One trauma piled on top of another and somehow I got to the place where both traumas were connected. I was going to die, but at least you were going to be safe. I even know why I thought that: *Anywhere* was safe compared to this place.

"Then it hit me that it was all we ever expected anyway. It was the hand we were dealt not long after we got here. I was expendable and you weren't. It was being played out just the way it was supposed to be. It all seemed so logical and orderly."

I nodded. I understood, but not as clearly as he did. "What made you decide just to get it over with?"

"I started having good dreams, dreams about us and Mike, mostly out in our valley. Sometimes I dreamed about

Ralph being with us. David said I was in a state of grace. He said he'd seen it many times with people who were very old or terminally ill. My dreams were about the hereafter. They weren't threatening, they were pleasant expectations. Why wouldn't I want to get on with it?"

I sat down on a chair near his bed. What he was saying made sense, but it was painful to hear. He had gone through an experience so profound that it was nearly beyond description. He had talked to David...but not to me.

"Does this square somehow with no letters? I've felt like I was being punished for something I didn't do. Or maybe you couldn't write. Maybe you were dead. How was I to know?... Why didn't you tell me about all this?"

As he studied me, regret and tears began to fill his eyes. "I'm sorry. I thought...I thought you knew. It was so clear and obvious to me that I thought you'd be tuned in too....I'm really sorry."

I understood, and while we talked about other things, I occasionally wondered why I hadn't been tuned in.

Later that day, he was discharged from the hospital. Before we left, I met his cute nurse—no doubt another reason why he had been in no hurry to leave. We spent the following day together. We had a fine meal at our favorite restaurant in Lucera, a place where the tables were on the roof and the view was fabulous. It was just the place to dare to start living again, to relax with a glass of fine wine. We had our usual lime soda. As tranquil and fairy tale-like as the whole thing was, our conversation came back to the war.

"Have you heard anything about Steve?" I asked.

Rod looked sad and nodded. "We heard from the International Red Cross. He was killed. There was a direct hit in the nose on the bomb run. Steve and the bombardier were killed. Some of the crew bailed out and survived....I wrote a letter to his folks. That was the hardest thing I've ever done." He stared down into his empty glass.

"With you and Steve gone, I was afraid Chuck would start giving the rest of us all kinds of hell, but he didn't. I don't know what happened, but he's been okay. Even better than okay. What drives a jerk into becoming a good guy? I guess a few bad experiences are enough to change anyone for the better.

Actually, Chuck's transformation has been remarkable. On the twenty-sixth, we were flying squadron lead. Our squadron was in the slot. I don't know how he did it with everything that was going on—planes dropping like flies, parachutes, the flak, and all—but he kept us right where we were supposed to be. I think he saved our lives. Our squadron only lost three, the whole second element. The high squadron lost five out of seven. I think Chuck saved our necks. What counts is that Colonel Badjer also thought so."

"How so? I must say, all of this is a bit hard to swallow."

Rod grinned. "Since then, we've flown lead every time except once. On that one, Chuck had the humbling experience of flying with Colonel Badjer—as his tail gunner."

"Steve would have busted a gut!" I laughed. "Chuck's falling-out with the Colonel?"

"No way. The Colonel was fed up with the sloppy formations and he had Chuck back there as his spy."

"At least he was a natural for that role. Enough of this fairy tale, Rod. What's this I hear about Grand the Flak Magnet?"

"It's been like a nightmare in hell," Rod groaned. "Every time the Group got flak, we came back looking like a sieve. But he *always* brought us back. He has two reputations: Fly with Grand and you'll get the hell shot out of you, but he'll bring you back—dead or alive. "

"You guys are flak happy. This can't be the Le Grand Chuck we knew and loathed."

"Rolly, I swear every word's true. He has several Purple Hearts and a Silver Star. Any lesser man would have found a way to get himself grounded. I think he'll make captain before it's over....So, what's happening with Azon? What's the B-25 like?"

Azon. Actually, I had arrived at Corsica with renewed hope—lower altitude, maybe different attitudes without the Brain Trust hovering over us. All of that had turned out to be true, but the damned bombs still don't work. I was sick of it. Why didn't they just go ahead and kill it?

"The 12th (Air Force) is mostly B-25s and 26s and P-47s. I've only flown five B-25 missions so far. It's a good plane, fast and the engines are loud and mean. Our missions average about three hours and we never fly high enough for oxygen or frostbite. Often the 47s escort us in. With no Kraut fighters in the air, they go after the guns. I haven't even seen an enemy plane since I've been there—except on D-day (the invasion of southern France, 15 August 1944). An ME-210 flew right under us on the bomb run, from back to front. I saw the damn thing through the bomb sight. I almost fainted. All he had to do was raise his nose and blast us out of the sky. That was a thrill I can do without."

Rod brightened. "You were in the air that day, too? Wasn't that something? At Frejus we saturated the beaches with hundred-pounders just before the landing craft came in. Man, that was something! A twenty-mile string of Goonie Birds bringing in gliders and paratroops; all those battleships, cruisers, and destroyers. Did you see the aircraft carriers? First I'd ever seen."

I agreed and mentioned that we'd flown right between Arle and Nime. Each of them has a two-thousand-year-old Roman coliseum. (Thirty-five years later, I went to southern France and to Arle. An international gymnastics tournament was being held in the coliseum.)

Rod stared out into space. The smile I'd seen the day before returned for a moment, then faded into concern. "What about losses with the B-25?"

"No Bleckhammers or Ploestis. In fact, B-25 loses are only one-fourth of 15th losses." I was lying. The fact was that B-25 losses were about half those of the 15th, but I didn't want him to spend months worrying about me. "Our standard tour is fifty sorties, no doubles. With my fifteen missions here, and five so far over there, I'm nearly halfway. I could be done by December, if the war lasts that long. As far as Azon goes, one of the guys said it pretty well: 'We brought the same old whore wearing the same old dress to this party.' Has Jonathon heard anything new from the Azon Brain Trust?"

"He went home, too. He told me to make sure you were making friends with somebody in the photo lab." We laughed at our private joke.

"I already have, but I don't know if it's going to make any difference for me. They've stuck all six of us Azons in the same tent like we're lepers. The chances of any of us flying lead are slim to none, not with our reputations as foul-ups. My group claims to be the best there is in bombing accuracy. Hell, they may be. The bird in charge is an obnoxious bastard. All he cares about is bombing accuracy. He's darn sure getting it, but the pilots get all the credit, never the bombardiers."

"That doesn't make any sense. What do you mean?"

"Ol' Snuffy—that's what we call him because he's short and sloppy—ol' Snuffy believes in keeping people motivated. So, every month they write up what they call the 'Raid of the Month,' which obviously means the best bombing of the month. The pilot flight leaders get the credit, the lead bombardiers aren't mentioned. Same with the daily war diaries. Rarely is a bombardier even named in the write-ups."

"That's absurd! That's like...if the *Tribune* back home wrote up the Iowa State football team for a win on the road and gave all the credit to the bus drivers! It's nuts!"

"I'll have to remember that one," I laughed. "But it gets worse. Three days after the invasion, there was an urgent mission to bomb a destroyer, heavy cruiser, battleship, and submarine in Toulon harbor. They sent all three B-25 groups, but our group was the only one that completed the mission. The other two chickened out. Weather was their excuse.

"Anyway, the flak was far worse than I'd ever experienced, even worse than that day old Chuck blundered right into it. You remember that. But we sunk all four boats without losing a plane. Every damn one of us—all forty-eight planes—was shot up, and seven people were killed, but every plane got home. It was the most successful medium bomber attack on war ships since the beginning of the war. So, naturally it was written up as Raid of the Month. It also was submitted for a Presidential Unit Citation. All four lead pilots were named in the citation, and get this: All four of them got Silver Stars. Not one of the four lead bombardiers was even mentioned by name, except the one that was killed."

"God all mighty."

"Lieutenant Kukowski. Ski had to get killed on the bomb run to get his name in the paper. I'm telling you Rod, a psycho runs the place." I shrugged. "My pal Andrew—by the way he's in charge of the photo interpreters—said Ol' Snuffy is like a cemetery: 'You have to be dead before he'll even give you the time of day.'"

Rod nodded, clearly concerned for me.

"Hey, it's not all bad," I said. "Corsica is beautiful. Of course, our little part of it is next to a swamp thick with mosquitoes that carry malaria. Taking atabrine every day is mandatory. I was taking mine until I found out it doesn't do a damn thing to prevent malaria. It only suppresses the effects so you can still fly—the fly now, die later plan. When I found that out, I quit taking it on the spot. I'd have to be pretty stupid to knowingly suppress something that could kill me. All the natives in the area look sickly, but they have better sense than to live right next to the swamp. We were out looking around one day and some old guy stopped us and shook his finger at us. 'Mosquit no good,' he said." Rod chuckled at my attempt at an accent.

"To the west of us is a thick jungle called the *maquis*. I'd like to do some exploring, but I don't know about fighting my way through all that stuff. About a mile from us, there's enough of a dam left to form a deep, clear swimming hole. There's a nice beach a half-mile down stream. A blown-up ammo carrier in the middle of it reminds us to watch out for leftover mines and booby traps....Oh, you'll like this. On Sundays the families come out of their stone shacks to go to church. They look just like we used to marching down the road in single file. Papa's at the head of the line with a shotgun slung from his shoulder. Mama's next, followed by a string of kids and maybe a mongrel or two."

"Wait a minute. The men carry shotguns?"

"Yeah, a lot of them do. And a pistol stuck in their belt. They all seem like they're spoiling for a fight. We hear stories about vendettas and murders. It seems their favorite pastime is killing each other. Sometimes, the way they look at and treat us, we get the feeling they'd shoot us if it would get us out of there faster....But the men live like medieval European nobility. They hunt boar, deer, rabbits, partridges, and ducks, and they fish. Maybe we should move there after the war."

"Heck, why wait? I'll sign up for another half-tour and we'll get us a couple of boar," he kidded. "We'll drop a couple of Azons on 'em. Might as well put them to some use."

"Bull shit! You're going home. Tell you what, I'll mail you

a couple and you hire on with some farmers. I can just see the advertisement in the paper: 'Instant field plowing—not necessarily *your* field.'"

We broke up. Our laughter turned heads in the restaurant. Some people smiled and others shot us looks whose implied messages had something to do with deportation. We calmed down eventually.

"Now that you've come back from the dead, what are you going to do?"

"What are you getting at?"

"I'm not sure. After a miraculous, spiritual experience like yours, some people...you know what I mean. They become ministers, priests, missionaries, whatever."

"I haven't had that kind of conversion, not yet anyway. Meanwhile, I plan to live every day to the fullest, hope that I'll always be thankful for what I have, and pray that you will be as lucky as I've been."

"I will be! Meanwhile, what *are* you going to do when you get home? I've heard that some guys are being recycled to the Pacific when they finish up here."

"Not me. I'm going into B-29 flight engineer school. It takes about a year and there's a commission at the end of it. I hear it's quite an airplane."

"That sounds pretty good, but why not try for pilot training? As fouled up as the system is, they may never figure out they've already had a whack at you. They may even have figured out that sleep walking as a kid doesn't make you a walking time bomb."

"Maybe. Like Steve used to say, 'If you don't like today's rules, just wait a month for a new set of them.'...I'm going to miss him."

"Yeah. He was a great guy."

Several moments passed in silence. Each of us knew the thoughts of the other. We were going to miss each other, but it didn't need to be said. And we also knew that our roles had been reversed. Rod would go home and spend the next few months looking for ways to take his mind off the fear he felt for me. He would have the added responsibility of reassuring Mother and Leonard. It would be a staggering burden.

But my burden was gone. I returned to Corsica that day,

flying higher and freer than my plane. *Rod was safe.* My cares were gone, vanished. Thirty more missions and I was through. And they would be a snap, I was sure. Just ride along as a togglier and let somebody else take all the responsibility for when to hit the switch. My war was over. The only thing left was everybody's war, by comparison, no worse than a little one-on-one.

During the course of the months that followed—many more months than I expected as it turned out—I got many letters from Rod.

Mother was doing well. She had just one job, in the Iowa State cafeteria, and that for only eight hours a day. Thirteen-year-old Leonard was busy with odd jobs that mirrored what we had done. Both of them still mourned Ralph. Leonard had a tough time adjusting to his loss, but his grades were good and his family life far less chaotic.

Gert, now Gertrude Armstrong and a college graduate, was working in San Francisco, waiting and worrying for her Bill, who was a sitting duck on a slow ammunition ship in the Pacific. We hurt for her.

And Mike, who Mother said nearly died of loneliness when we left, rediscovered his will to live when he saw Rod walking up the street.

Rod's letters talked about hunting with Mike in our valley, and his first quail hunt, which turned out to be a humbling experience for him. The hunt was arranged by Uncle Herb. When the first covey broke cover, their numbers surprised him and he missed them all. Herb taught him to concentrate on just one bird—a lesson German flak gunners were teaching us in spades at the time—and he soon bagged his limit.

He was accepted into flight engineer school and I was happy for him. But I could also read his worry for me in what he wasn't saying. And there was something more in the letters. His definition of *home* had changed. Before the war, home had been many things, but it had never been a haven, never a place to be safe.

It was now. Safe from madness, carnage, unimaginable violence; safe from the terror of the real danger of the moment and the unknown danger of tomorrow; safe from dreading missions to hell holes and the shock of red lines leading straight to them; safe from laughing with a friend one day and staring at his empty bunk the next; safe from the ever-present spectre of sudden death. He was home, a place where there is a tomorrow.

But no one comes home from war unscathed. Rod's time in hell was during the worst six months in the history of the 15th. Nightmares about past missions and about the next one plagued him. Beyond that admission, he never said anything to me about the horrors he had witnessed.

Chapter Twelve

1 November 1944

Dear Rod,

It's been two months now and things continue very slow. Not only does this hot outfit look down their noses at us because of the Azon mess, our squadron really didn't need six more bombardiers. We fly an Azon mission once in awhile, otherwise we just try to find something to do. I'm finally in the second volume of Gibbon — and there's Andrew Jenks. I got to know him on one of my junkets.

Andrew's in charge of the photo interpreters and he lines up rest camps. He's twenty-four, a college graduate, history major, with an OCS commission. Thick-lensed glasses prevented him from even thinking about flying. He's been overseas with the 32lst nearly two years, still only a first lieutenant, and doesn't seem to care that he's not likely to get any farther. About his job, he says, "I pretend to work and they pretend to pay me. Along with my negligible assigned chores, I'm the group's Egg Head at Large, a carry-over from BS — Before Snuffy."

He's become our Corsican tour guide. He has the time, knows where to go and what to see, and he can handle the blend of Italian and French like he was born here. He's become a source of great Corsican food.

You were right. Six of us in a tent is too many — by one. Two in one tent would be fifty percent too many, if one of them was Joe. Thank God, for his sake and ours, most of the time the little bastard is off pestering others. Otherwise we'd have no choice but to find some Corsican who makes a living causing people to disappear. We understand there are a few of those around. The tangled mat of brush and vines known as the maquis, which covers most of the lower slopes of the island, has a reputation as the ideal place for mysterious disappearances.

I've finally found the perfect solution to Little Joe and boredom. The group has non-combat B-25s that are always going somewhere. Between Azon missions, I make sure I'm on one of them. I'm gone so much they think I'm a coward, deliberately trying to avoid missions. So far, I've been to half a dozen places, including Rome and Naples, even Tunis. By the way, I heard a good story there.

We spent a whole day touring ancient Carthage. Our guide claimed that during the Tunisian campaign, General Patton paid a visit to the Carthage amphitheater, older than the Roman coliseum. It seems that George modestly professes to having been a Carthaginian in a past life. I assumed he came to compare his battlefield experience with such past heroic warriors as Hamilcar and son Hannibal. Not so according to our guide. Patton was there for counsel and inspiration from his former self—Hannibal, naturally. Why would he settle for anything less.

In other words, in two thousand years as a warrior, George has gone from plodding over the Alps on six-ton elephants to racing across Europe in forty-ton tanks. That doesn't strike me as meaningful progress.

We leave early, spend the day, sometimes two. But that's not the best news. I've gotten to know quite a few pilots. Arnold Kimble and Carl Fisher are two of my favorites. Every time we take a trip, as soon as the flaps and wheels are up, they let me take over in the right seat. So far, I've logged over twenty hours, most of it over water, right on the deck. My most recent trip was to Naples. Just off the Anzio beach was a single-masted, commercial fishing boat. We see them often.

I lined up on this one and made like I was coming in on a skip-bombing and strafing run. As I relentlessly bore down on that imaginary enemy, our big props were so close to the water they stirred up their own spray. At the very last second I pulled up. Our prop wash flipped that sail boat like it had been struck by an Oklahoma twister.

Arnold said, "We could have used you when we were knocking Rag Heads off their camels."

After that trip, Dan, the crew chief who goes everywhere his plane goes announced, "I had the best gol-darn gravy-train ever invented until that Kamikaze bombardier started trying to kill us all. To hell with it. I'm going back to crewing combat airplanes."

Rod, I hate to tell you how much fun I'm having in the right seat of a 25, so much fun it must be sinful. Arnold says I've missed my calling.

On a recent Rome trip—you aren't going to believe this—I ran into three from Ames: Bill Giese, Bob Phillips, and Cramer. (Do you remember his first name? I was too embarrassed to ask.). Cramer acted like he didn't know me, which was fine. I don't blame him for his negative attitude toward a D student and ex-janitor who now out-ranks him. As a social science teacher, he should know better than anyone: "Where is it written that life is supposed to be fair?"

I ran into Giese on my way to the Red Cross Club for ice cream. He complained it was too far to walk and flagged a cab. What he said to the cabbie sunded to me like fluent Italian. I was impressed and I told him so. For some reason, I was in no way prepared for his explanation.

"No big deal. I'm sleeping with an Italian dictionary."

We met Bob Phillips in the club. He was flying P-38s and hated it! How could you get any weirder than that?

The show at the airport was the ultimate weirdness. We were outside operations getting ready to go back to Corsica. I noticed a plain-Jane, olive-drab Goonie Bird land and park well away from everything else. The props were still turning when a small figure in dress uniform hopped out of the back and hustled off in our direction shouting, "Attention! Attention!"

We assumed it was a USO[1] troop announcing their arrival by putting on a little skit. Too bad we were leaving. When the shouting, strutting little figure got closer we could see a star on each shoulder—for sure USO. No real BG would be running around acting the fool.

Well, behind the BG came a much larger figure, ramrod erect, swaggering along at a fast clip. His costume included a shiny steel helmet, waist-length jacket decorated like a Christmas tree, cavalry breeches and boots, and ivory-handled revolvers. Pretty standard stuff for a USO skit.

When we saw the three stars on the helmet and recognized the face of chiseled granite beneath it, we knew what was up. Georgie (General George S. Patton, Jr.) was making one of his routinely grand appearances. He wasn't about to be upstaged by the historic grandeur of Rome.

About that little show, Andrew said, "But for the grace of God, there goes God." That was a good one. I hoped he would never run out of them. He didn't. After that exhibition, why should any of us take this war seriously?

Rod, wish you could have seen all those places with me. After the war we'll redo them.

—Rolly

In October, somebody finally pulled the plug on Azon and I descended to the brain-dead role of togglier—released my bombs when the lead plane dropped his. That was it. Go in straight and level, big gap between flights, praying you make it to bomb release so you can drop the load and get the hell out.

[1]United Service Organizations

186

We got shot at the whole way. Big gaps and flying straight and level gave the Germans plenty of time to site in on following flights and shoot them down. Someone must have thought it was the sporting thing to do. George Yarbrough put it better than anyone: "Dying the Snuffy way is one hell of a poor way to make a living."

Meanwhile, winter was coming and we were told to winterize our tents, which amounted to putting in a wood floor, and maybe some wood walls to raise the four-foot height of the canvas ones. But when the word came down, four of the six of us were on a two-day excursion. No matter. I was naive enough to believe the powers-that-be would do the logical thing and shorten our missions by moving us back to Italy. Heck, we might be able to fly two missions a day and get home that much sooner. By the end of October it was wet and cold and clear that I was wrong. And the lumber was gone.

All that cement experience Rod and I had finally paid off. I found some and laid a concrete floor. While we were at it, I decided we might as well have a fireplace. The one I built worked so well I was talked into building one at the officer's club. I had two warm places to kick back, read, sip lime sodas, and flick my cigar ashes.

If it sounds like I was having fun it's only because I was. Without Rod to worry about, I could truly enjoy the rich scenery, history, and culture around me. Missions were another thing, but up until then, I hadn't gone on very many. That would soon change, however, and I was going to be in the middle of it.

As Jonathon had predicted, flak had become the number one killer of men and planes. German gunners were among the best, and their '88 was the finest anti-aircraft gun in the world. They also had developed a multiple-radar fire control system. Not only was it more accurate and harder to jam, it could track several formations simultaneously. As the lead formation reached bomb release, it took only a throw of a switch on the ground and with instant and deadly accuracy, they were pumping rounds into the following formations. They also could track us in a turn. The best guns, packed into smaller and smaller areas to defend, aimed with high-tech radar systems — that's what we faced on every mission. They were slicing us up.

In response, and with few German fighters still in the air, our fighters were shifted to "anti-flak." They flew in ahead of us to knock out the guns. It seemed like a great idea, but most of the fighters were assigned to ground support and the push to Berlin. There were never enough to do the job for us. Our losses in October and November were bloody proof of it.

I had been writing Rod once a week since he'd left. I never told him how high the losses really were, but I did tell him about the utter stupidity and boneheadedness that led to some of them. Our bombing accuracy was second to none. Under Snuffy, accuracy increased from just over forty percent to ninety. He did that by demanding tighter formations, which naturally resulted in tighter bomb patterns. And with the manner and mouth of a barnyard dog, he flipped aside at will any lead pilot or bombardier who did not perform up to snuff.

From my perspective, Snuffy's only challenges were supplying warm bodies on cold mornings, and honing bombing accuracy. What else could explain the deadly gap between the flights he tolerated — "Snuffy's gap," I had begun calling it. In defending a target, the flak guns could take on each flight as it came in. A gap of only thirty seconds between succeeding flights was enough to give the Germans time to pump hundreds of additional rounds at each lead plane as it came in. Lead planes were three times more likely to go down than any other position in the formation.

Andrew mentioned a partial solution he had proposed. We were having lunch near Frejus. In one direction, our view was a sparkling white beach littered with junk left from the August invasion of southern France. In the other direction we could see segments of an aqueduct built by Roman ingenuity some two thousand years before.

We made the stop during a Jeep trip from Nice to San Tropez. We were going there to check out rest camp possibilities on the French Riviera. Rest camp was the World War II equivalent of R and R. One of Andrew's jobs was to set up places for us to go during our week off. It was tough work, ferrying him from resort to resort, but we hung in there.

On 1 November, the 170-mile Brenner Route became the

9 B-25's of the 321st Bomb Group hit the Ponte Di Piave Rail Diversion Bridge in Northern Italy on February 4, 1945, knocking out the northernmost span and badly cratering the north approach.

nearly full-time occupation of our 150 B-25s and varying number of P-47s. Andrew filled me in on its importance: "It's their most vital connection with the Fatherland — for bringing in supplies, and exiting troops and loot from Italy."

"Exiting loot?"

"Spoils have always been a big part of war. Right now, there are more trainloads of loot going out than supplies coming in. The Nazis have turned on their former ally and partner in crime with a vengeance. As they retreat northward, they're frantically stealing Italy's treasure of art and antiquities. Anyway, compared to the Po Valley, the Brenner will be one hell of a battle."

"I've been to Verona and Bulogna. I didn't think the Valley was any picnic. How can the Brenner be worse?"

"The terrain may be the world's worst. The high and steep mountains and deep valleys limit line of sight to little or no bomb run — plus clouds, haze, shadows, turbulence, and smoke pots.

"Smoke pots! Shades of Ploesti."

"Oh, hell yes. Especially in the lower Adige where the valley widens out a bit. In the whole 170 miles, there are only about a dozen key targets that we can really get at. They'll set them up as killing fields."

"Killing fields?" I knew what he meant, but it was the first time I'd heard the term relative to airplanes.

"First of all, the Krauts have already deduced the obvious: With us switched to the Brenner all those Po targets are no longer targets. By the hundreds, those guns will end-up in the Brenner defending only a few targets. On most of them, we have only one workable axis of attack. Those are the makings of a killing field, with some special twists, like placing guns thousands of feet above the valley floor."

"Damn! How much difference will something like that make?"

"Guns at five thousand feet will be three times more effective than those on the valley floor. Four guns become the equivalent of twelve. Worse yet, they'll have an enormous line-of-sight advantage. Guns at five thousand feet or higher will be shooting at you long before you can even pick up the target. It all adds up to a classic killing field."

"Great. I can't tell you how happy I am that we're having this conversation."

"I know. You don't want to hear about it. Exactly the reaction I got from our reptilian knot head."

"Who?"

"Snuffy.... Like most of the main characters in this war, he's a recycled warrior from The Great War."

"So what's so bad about having leaders with plenty of training and experience?"

"Experience? Ha! With the post-World War I military in a perpetual moribund state, the officers on active duty existed at the level of knock-about sharecroppers, and there was no money for equipment or training. The result is exactly what you'd expect—officers who are stone-age, brain-dead has-beens with one year's experience twenty times. So, what would you suppose happened when the parabolic rises in rank were handed out after Pearl Harbor?"

"I give, Andrew. You tell me."

"A mess! Those who didn't make general suffered severe cases of humiliation and suffering from what I call Thwarted High Ambitions. When in his cups, I've often heard Snuffy lament, 'I could still be a general. I paid my dues, put in my time, but I get no respect. Even my old buddies treat me like Texas roadkill.' Some of the bitter ones, like Snuffy, are bound to compensate with erratic behavior."

"You mean Snuffy unloads all that stuff on you? How chummy."

"My friend, you'd be surprised what one can learn late at night, sipping vintage scotch. You should try it sometime. Deep thinker that he is, Snuffy has even figured out that wars are useful. I'm embellishing the way he explained it, but he actually believes wars provide a necessary outlet for young men—for their aggression, their yearning for adventure, their weariness with prosaic routine. Why not let them die for their country in the anesthesia of battle amid an aura of glory?"

"My, God, Andrew. So Snuffy believes he's doing us all a great favor by tolerating the Gap. In his grand scheme of things, the sooner we're dead, the better off we are."

Andrew's cultured voice rose a decibel or two with disgust. "When the Wing was committed to the Brenner, I fired off a memo simply pointing out the obvious: Losses may become unsustainable and here's what we can do about it. All that did was make Old Blood and Guts mad. He went into a tirade, declared me 'a gutless ninety-day wonder, meddler,' and 'the war's greatest source of useless information.'"

"What did you expect, Andrew? You probably needled him with something obscenely cowardly, like let's declare victory and go home?"

"If I only had. He'd have hemorrhaged over that one and we'd be rid of our 'Beloved Mediocrity.' Our choices are limited. We could try evasive action on the bomb run, which would reduce losses, but also drag down bombing accuracy."

"That went over like a lead balloon," I said. "Nothing is more sacred to Snuffy."

"The only other real choice is to overwhelm the guns."

"How many P-47s would that take?"

"Three, maybe four times as many as we have."

"That's crazy! With no German fighters around, taking out the guns should be a snap."

"Says you! You think anti-flak will be a picnic for the 47s? Forget it. The killing fields set up for them are quad 20s. On each mission, just to suppress them, will require at least half the fighter-bombers we send in."

"Now that you mention it, I do know about them. Quad 20s: twelve hundred rounds a minute, deadly up to a thousand yards. But what about our five-inch HVAR's?"[2]

"Thank God for them. At least they make it a more-or-less fair fight. But hey, all this is irrelevant and won't happen. Ever since Normandy we've been loosing P-47s to Ike—one of the costs of being a sideshow. Besides, the 5th and 8th, our two great, 'Going Nowhere at a Glacial Rate' armies, have first call on the few that remain. In the numbers we need, even with the HVARs, our fighter losses might be unsustainable. The Krauts can build and deploy quad 20s five times faster than the 88s."

"Damn, Andrew, there has to be a way....Like, why not ask the British to drop a few twenty thousand-pound dam busters—plug the Brenner with well placed landslides. Then

[2]High Velocity Aircraft Rockets, accurate up to 1,000 yards.

we could sit out the war on the Riviera. My choice will be to stay right here."

"Wait till you see San Tropez. There's the exotic place for holding a victory shindig. Actually, there are landslide possibilities. Meanwhile, don't hold your breath waiting for that herd of independent minds that lead us to endorse it. Another possibility I like—supply our own anti-flak. Send 25s in ahead of the formation and take out the guns with massive doses of phosphorous or incendiaries."

"You're out of your mind! We'd have to recruit the Nips as volunteer Kamikazes. Have them crash-dive the guns for us!"

"Exactly what Snuffy said. You are both dead wrong, pun intended. With proper evasive action I'd a hell of a lot rather be anti-flak than leading a flight, especially the first. Leading the first flight, there's your suicide spot."

"So you've sold yourself on a crazy idea. How many anti-flaks would it take?"

"Just to make sure, two per battery. At Rovereto that would mean six anti-flaks. Let's say we send in three flights of nine. Anti-flak would be about twenty percent of the total."

"I can imagine Snuffy's enthusiasm for that one."

"Oh, Christ." He hitched-up his drawers and bellowed, 'You gutless wonder! We're here to kill Krauts, not mollycoddle our crews! You'd of had us chicken-out at Toulon like everybody else and I wouldn't have gotten us our second Presidential Citation.' At which point I said to myself, And you, you bloody bastard, wouldn't have your second Silver Star for gallantry—make that butchery!"

Andrew was fun to have around. He had a rare combination of amiability, intelligence, and wit, but those were mere details. The important thing about him was his trappings—he didn't have any. He was a well-bred Ivy-Leaguer with contempt for all affectations.

We set a record in August for the highest number of sorties flown. We lost only four planes. November weather reduced our sorties to a record few, but our losses climbed to twelve planes and crews. Andrew told me the rest of the wing didn't fare any better.

"It must have taken a couple of lobotomies, but finally

someone at 12th Air Force did get it," he said. "Death and a higher authority have overruled Snuffy's objections to anti-flak. Word came down that our group will put together and implement an anti-flak plan."

I don't know whether Andrew had anything to do with it, but our squadron was chosen to pioneer the effort for the wing.

Lieutenant Colonel Cooper (promoted while we were there) asked me to volunteer. I don't know why. I hadn't done much since I'd been there. No doubt he was impressed with my fireplaces. In any case, I jumped at the opportunity to do something useful — anything but be a togglier, and anything that would take it to the Krauts for a change.

We decided to simultaneously develop three bombardier/pilot anti-flak teams. I had to find two more volunteers and I uncovered a couple of aces: Fred MacCollough was a confident old guy of twenty-five from Chicago. Bill Cimino was a refreshing, exuberant lad of nineteen from Brooklyn. Both had about fifteen missions. Neither had ever flown lead. They were rare: cool, enthusiastic, and terrific with a bomb sight. I thought I was good. These guys were better.

My pilot was Arnold Kimble, who brought with him the relaxed, sophisticated attitude of his hometown of Santa Monica, California. Our three anti-flak teams would go in together, ahead of the formation. Still out of range of the guns, we would separate and attack from different headings and altitudes. The trick as we went in was our evasive action — to randomly change altitude, heading, and air speed, and find the guns. Then we would fly a straight and level bomb run of no more than thirty seconds on an assigned flak battery. Take longer than thirty seconds and the risk increased ten-fold.

We coordinated with the P-47s. From our altitude they would roll over, dive, and go in on the deck. We would follow staying above ten thousand feet. Some of the 47s would carry HVARs, five under each wing, fired in pairs. The others, a napalm tank under each wing, each capable of scorching a football field. With a bomb-bay load of phosphorous fused for ground burst, one B-25 could saturate an area larger than a football field. Later, with busters and air bursts, we could cover four football fields. Phosphorous burned and smothered the bastards. The napalm incinerated them.

We worked on our technique for two weeks. On 13 December, ready or not, we were scheduled for our first anti-flak mission. Our target was the Avisio Viaduct, the place of my one and only personal Azon success. Sixteen P-47s and three B-25s would be going after forty guns dispersed in seven batteries. Bad weather forced us to sweat that mission for ten days. We were briefed five times. The longer the wait, the more nervous and unsure we became.

We approached the target from the east, skimming the deep and wild Brenta Gorge, on Christmas Eve morning. The main body was four flights of nine. We anti-flaks and the P-47s were ahead and out on the flank. For the first time in my combat life, I was part of the fighter pilots' world. I could look across at our old world. The formation was all too familiar. Each flight was tight, but the second, third, and fourth flights were lagging, creating the usual deadly gap.

We anti-flaks were detached physically, but not emotionally. For the first time, I was responsible for the lives of others. That day, there were 216 people depending on us, on me. Could we take out those guns?

Finally, it was time. There was nothing left to do but go and do it. The P-47s went first. Their leader was so close we could see his wide smile. He stuck his thumb in the air, rolled over, and was gone. The rest rolled after him. The first eight carried rockets, the second eight, napalms. What an awesome sight. I envied them, but also felt for them. There were fifteen sets of quad-20s lurking down there.

Arnold called after them, "Good hunting guys! Be sure and leave some for us!"

They seemed invincible, maybe even overkill—sixty-four .50 calibers and eighty rockets going after the quad-20s, and sixty-four .50 calibers and sixteen napalms for their assigned batteries. What an act to follow. When the last one started his dive, I called Arnold on the intercom. "Instead of screwing around up here, let's follow them down—make sure we get it done right."

Arnold laughed. "If it was left up to you, I think you'd be just crazy enough to try it." (As it turned out, that crazy idea was tried at least once. Benny Gale, one of the Azons, was the bombardier). Our joking fooled no one. We both had been on the edge for weeks.

Insignificant compared to the show we had just witnessed, we anti-flaks nonetheless spread out and began evasive action. My worry was finding my eight-gun battery. The amount of flak changed my worries instantly. The clear, faded-blue sky above the Adige was suddenly alive with ugly orange and black bursts, as though all forty guns had singled me out. The air was saturated with slashing bits of metal. I was sure we'd be torn to shreds; we wouldn't last long enough to drop our bombs.

It clearly was time to panic, but somehow I managed to block out everything else and search for the guns. The fiery wreck of a P-47, at least one of those guys died trying to help us, and the napalm fires lit by them helped me pinpoint my target. We released and got out. One engine was hit, but we made it home.

The official report of the mission listed our results: "Flak light and inaccurate. No losses." In the anti-flak business, that's the highest praise we could get. We had done it.

Not all our missions were as successful as the first. Even so, news of what we had done spread and we were celebrities overnight. Even Snuffy applauded us. Within a month, we often sent out two anti-flaks for each gun battery. Group losses dropped by two-thirds. Zero losses seemed possible. That became our goal. Maybe even Snuffy's gap would no longer matter. But the Germans had other ideas.

Europe suffered under one of the worst winters in history in 1944-45. Bad weather kept us on the ground, but more important to us, it made it impossible for reconnaissance to pinpoint flak batteries. As aware of that as we, and with predictable zeal, the Germans began shuttling hundreds of guns from place to place. Overnight we went from a flak location system that was ninety-percent accurate, to having no idea where the guns were. We called them "loose cannons." One of them was responsible for the first Azon casualty.

Before 1944 ended, Charley Kaenzig—a happy, joking, Kentucky-bred version of Huck Finn—was shot down. We waited for word from the Red Cross, but none ever came. For us, no news was good news. We held out hope he was hiding and running, trying to get back, but only four parachutes had been seen leaving his burning plane.

12 January 1945 — Rod was in B-29 flight engineer school. I was studying target photos at fifteen thousand feet above the Po Valley. I glanced over at the three-quarter-inch aluminum plate our crew chief, Sam, had installed on my left. The fixed, twin fifties on my right were unusable as guns precisely because they were fixed, but they could stop a chunk of flak. The floor in the nose was three-quarter-inch case-hardened steel. The effect was like being in a metal foxhole. It was my first mission since Sam had volunteered to give me that extra protection.

Our mission was to incinerate three flak batteries at Rovereto. Navigator Dick O'Conner — every bit as talented as Steve — announced we had cleared the Apennines and were in the Po. An explosion as loud as a lightning-strike rocked the plane.

Stunned by the concussion and gagging on foul cordite smoke, neither of us moved for several seconds — not until we realized the smoke had suddenly disappeared and we were freezing to death. Icy air was shrieking in through a gaping hole in front of the bomb sight where there had once been an inch-thick glass panel. We couldn't hear the engines, there was nothing on the intercom. We were suspended in empty sky with only the frigid air for company. Dick and I stared at each other. How bad was it? As if in answer, a bloody face appeared in the crawl way. It was Pete, our top-turret gunner. We couldn't hear him, but he seemed to be there to check on our welfare.

"Christ, Pete! You're the one who needs help!" I yelled in vain. None of us could hear a damn thing over that howl. I looked more closely at his oozing face and discovered that the cuts were mostly superficial. Pieces of Plexiglass had raked him when his turret dome was shattered. It took some doing, but he was able to convey a message from the pilot: The intercom was out and Arnold needed a heading to get us the hell out of there. Happy to oblige, Dick gathered up his maps and gear and scooted out of the nose.

The higher you go, the colder the air. At fifteen thousand feet in January it's at least twenty below. Throughout the war, frostbite probably maimed more of us than the enemy. Hands, fingers, feet, and toes could be frozen in minutes. Electrically heated flight suits were available, but they failed as often as not. All of this is by way of introducing the fact that I hadn't done anything about plugging up the hole and I was in real danger of freezing to death. I headed that off by stacking our heavy flack vests against that gaping square-foot hole.

We were headed for home. As I settled back, my left thigh began to burn. It might have been the cold that kept me from noticing before, or adrenaline, or both, but a chunk of shrapnel the size of my little finger from tip to knuckle had tunneled into my leg about a half inch. I yanked it out and clamped my hand over the wound. I looked around. There were three, jagged, two-inch holes in the aluminum plate. I found another piece of shrapnel in the heel of my left boot, the broken-in pair Rod had sent me so many months before from Santa Ana. A total of three chunks of flak had barged into my foxhole. The three pieces of aluminum they tore out of the plate made a total of six jagged projectiles trying to kill Dick and me. Only two hit me. The thought of what would have happened without the makeshift armor made me shudder more than once. Later, I was very pleased to be alive to see my first Purple Heart.

I flew my tenth anti-flak mission in late January. It was textbook all the way — our textbook, but perfect nonetheless. I had doused six guns with a full load of phosphorous. On that day, all twelve of the Rovereto guns were burned into silence. I was on top of the world at debriefing and I wasn't alone. The other crews were overjoyed that the perilous run past the Rovereto guns was finally flak-free. Even Snuffy was all smiles.

Colonel Cooper approached me. "How'd you do today?"

It was a strange question, one he had never asked before, but I choked down the donut I was chewing and tried to appear cool. "Colonel, after what we did to those guns, they couldn't possibly have gotten off another round. Our results prove it. Practically no flak and no losses." He smiled and walked away, leaving me wondering.

As was my routine, I walked down to Operations to check the posted "official" results of the mission. What we saw and reported counted for nothing. The official results depended entirely on what photo interpreters decreed. It often took until 10:00 P.M. for them to finish examining the hundreds of photos taken of missions. I scanned the posted results. They said I missed the guns.

Angry, embarrassed, and sure they were wrong, I hunted down and cornered a tech sergeant whose dearest wish at that moment was to go to bed.

"Sorry, sir. All we can do is call 'em as we see 'em." He was giving me his ass-kissing, servile act, but his tone and manner came damned close to insolence. "And besides, *sir*, I'm sorry but you have no right to even question our findings. You know the regs! Our independence and objectivity are at risk if you even question our work. Sir, according to the photos, you should have stayed in the sack."

I came perilously close to losing it. I wondered if this self-anointed piss-ant was beyond reasoning with.

"Did you make a determination of the amount of flak encountered on the bomb run?"

"There was none, *sir*." The sergeant made it plain he was being assaulted by a nobody.

"How many flak batteries at Rovereto today, and how many anti-flaks?"

"Three of each. *Sir*, its really getting awfully late—and there are regs about this."

I pointed my finger between his eyes. "That better be the *last* time you try to hide your incompetence behind the regs! I'm not just another stupid bombardier born yesterday. If I missed the six-gun battery, why no flak on the bomb run? Did the Krauts run and hide? Or maybe the tooth fairy intervened!"

"I'm sorry, *sir*. In our work we're not allowed to indulge in subjective speculation."

I almost smacked the little twerp, but I walked away fuming and did what I should have done in the first place: I got Andrew out of bed. He was annoyed, but he understood my anger. While we were going through hundreds of photos I asked him why he put up with the smart-aleck sergeant.

"Have you ever tried to fire the general's nephew?" Several hours and hundreds of photos later we found the

BEFORE

DURING

AFTER

DESTROYED

24 B-25's of the 321st Bomb Group successfully attacked the Brexlegg rail bridge in Southern Austria on 22 March 1945. All bombs dropped fell in target area. Four Bridge spans completely destroyed, at least two piers damaged, and the west approach cut.

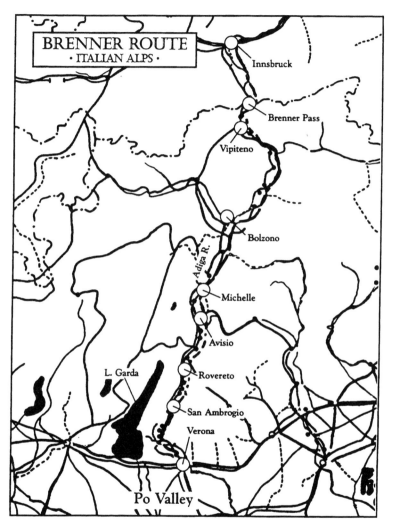

150 B-25s pounded the Brenner route for six months, playing havoc with German's most important rail supply and escape route out of northern Italy. The area became one of Germany's heaviest concentration of anti-aircraft defenses. Flak became the prominent killer along the Brenner route.

proof I needed.

A few days later I found out what Colonel Cooper was up to. Jack Mayo, our squadron bombardier, would soon finish his missions and go home. My squadron, the 446th, had the best bombing record in the group. Jack would be a tough act to follow. Based on my anti-flak work, I had been asked to be his replacement.

I couldn't believe what I heard. Colonel Cooper wanted *me* for squadron bombardier. I was thrilled, flattered—and I wasn't sure. It would be my only chance of making captain. Promotion to first lieutenant was automatic and the end of the line for all bombardiers and navigators—except for the squadron job. Less than one in thirty got the opportunity. In our highly imperfect and phony world, my promotion to captain would be real. I had earned the opportunity. Not once had I resorted to the tried and true method of gaining recognition and promotion—nightly drinking with, and sucking-up to, the brass.

And there were the bragging rights. It was something to be a squadron bombardier. It was something special in the record-setting 321st. And I would be one of the dozen who had a place at the head table in the officer's mess.

On the other hand, I would have to give up anti-flak. I had helped to create something that worked, something of value. Accepting the job would mean going back to the stupid and incredibly dangerous world of flying straight and level and praying for the best. Even worse, I had to commit to flying thirty more missions. I had forty, that would mean seventy missions if the war lasted enough. I could fly ten more anti-flak missions and go home. *I'd be through.* What kind of idiot would choose to plant his butt back in danger—in the lead plane, no less—and stay there three times longer than he had to? Not me. Mother didn't raise a fool.

I signed on.

Other than flying lead missions, my biggest responsibility was maintaining an adequate supply of anti-flak and lead bombardiers. Before the war ended, I developed a total of ten. In my system, the progression was from anti-flak to leading a flight. If they could find and hit the guns, they could find and hit anything. The ten I found were world-class. For the rest of the war, my squadron led the group in bombing accuracy and number of bridges destroyed. So petty had score-keeping become, however, that the record for number of bridges destroyed didn't come without a fight—on the ground, with our own people.

It was a cold day in late January. My target was a fifty-foot stone bridge near the Austrian border, an area where the Brenner rail line snaked it's way south through deep, narrow canyons. I was leading a formation of nine planes, each carrying four, thousand-pound general-purpose bombs. The target wasn't defended, so after bombs-away, I had plenty of time to look for results. My first bomb detonated in the middle of the bridge. The remaining three from my plane, and all thirty-two from the other planes in the formation, pummeled a sheer cliff beyond the target. The resulting landslide buried the bridge beneath thousands of tons of rock.

That night, my favorite tech sergeant posted results claiming I had *missed* the bridge. This time it really hurt because I was nearing a milestone—most bridges destroyed in a month. I stormed to the photo lab and searched through several hundred photos before I found the one that showed my bomb exploding in the middle of the bridge. Controlling my temper, I presented it to the tech sergeant.

"So what?" he said. "The landslide buried the damn bridge. How could we verify your bomb *destroyed* the bridge?"

"A thousand-pound bomb goes off in the middle of a fifty-foot bridge and you can't *verify* the bridge was destroyed? You pitiful jerk....Well hell, let's just call up the Partisans and have them run over and check it for you. I'm sure they'd be glad to risk their lives to keep your record clean."

February was a month of change, strange happenings, and extremes—good and bad. The weather was typical of the previous three months. We were briefed twenty-five times, took off twenty times, completed only fifteen missions. Two were violent and bloody.

On the second, we lost three at Avisio. On the fourth, we went to Rovereto. Unknown to us, the Krauts had put a four-gun battery on a 4,500-foot-high ridge we had to cross early in the bomb run. Going in, all four flights would be less than

9,000 feet above those four guns. In the first flight, the guns killed the lead bombardier. Captain Jack Remmel led the second flight, his sixty-ninth mission. He and his two wing men were shot down. The leader of the third flight was shot down. Arnold and I were leading the fourth. On the bomb run, we were right where we belonged — tucked in tight just below and behind the last element of the third flight. In other words, there was no gap between the third and the fourth flight. We were in and out before the Krauts could target us.

In February, the group lost twelve planes and eleven crews, six of them lead crews, all in Flak Alley — forty miles of the lovely lower Adige River valley from Avisio south to Verona. Flak there had thickened to a world-record seven guns per mile. For six months, it was our special hell hole, particularly Rovereto and Avisio.

Enroute, we flew the full length of deep blue Lake Garda, thirty miles of spectacular flak-free beauty, then crossed a high ridge over into the Adige to confront the guns of Rovereto. A Michelin three-star resort, and Italy's largest and most beautiful lake, fjord-like Garda was separated from our five-star hell hole by five minutes of flying time.

In the six-month Brenner campaign, our 150 B-25s never ran out of targets. The ever resourceful and energetic Germans saw to that. Just in the forty miles of the lower Adige, ten thousand conscripts and massive amounts of heavy equipment worked night and day to replace bridges nearly as fast as we could knock them down.

For us, the Big Show — the Battle of the Brenner — became a fatal contest of wills, ours and the Germans. A place of great natural beauty, the Brenner would swallow up at least one hundred B-25's, half that many P-47s, and serve as a burial ground for nearly a thousand American boys. It became a place of terrible memories. Every day, every mission, became agony — a nightmare with no morning to come.

Worry began to dominate my life, day after day, night after night. I slept badly or not at all. I tried to control it, but I couldn't. It grew like a tumor and invaded my dreams. Fear of dying — never underestimate it. Once unleashed, it spreads like a living thing; a merciless monster that feeds on itself. My fear spread like a killer virus feeding on my insides.

Very few of us professed to being frightened, but the tell-tale signs were there in faces, voices, actions. Mealtime was marked by the quiet and calm of exhaustion and of death. There was nothing I or any of us could do to relieve the growing, paralyzing fear.

Over and over my mind was telling me: I should have gotten out. I had done the unthinkable—agreed to seventy missions when I could have gotten out with fifty. I was crazy to do that. Certifiable.

We all knew we were facing an enraged beast. Sometimes it spoke German and shot at us, sometimes it spoke English and gave us nightmares. Long before the end of February, group morale dropped into the gutter. We were exhausted and out of touch with things unrelated to the war, hanging on as best we could. I was sure we were running out of time. Every day our fear of flying grew, yet every day we went back out. Fear and despair were total, yet there were very few turncoats. Why?

"It has to be the group thing," Andrew said. "It can be a powerful force. Loyalty to the group, to each other, controls you. Not fear, or obedience to the system."

One morning about five, I was alone in the secret briefing room. Suddenly, I realized I had company. Looking on was a tall, attractive blonde of about thirty. She was wearing a leather flying jacket, complete with a star on each shoulder. In the military and in Corsica in particular, blondes and stars were rare and highly unlikely to come as a package. I thought she might be a nurse, which answered every question but how she got in to what was supposed to be the most secure room on the field.

She was charming, cheerful, polite, and very curious about our affairs. How did I like Corsica? How long had I been there? What was my name, my job, my age, how many missions, where was I from, where were we going today? For all I knew, she was Axis Sally's girl in Corsica. Then, General Knapp came in. Commander of our bomb wing, we all knew the old boy was a BTO (Big Time Operator). He lived in grand style in Bastia, toured the island in a Lincoln. In England, Ike had to settle for a Ford and his driver wasn't a sexy blonde. Later, I found out this blonde was Doris Duke, richest girl in the world, according to the publicity. She was a "war correspondent." General's stars must have made her job much easier.

13 February 1945 — We were dangerously late getting back as our flight of nine approached the Corsican coast. Nerves were frayed, tempers short, and senses dulled after five hours of fighting weather and dodging loose cannons. Down to fifteen hundred feet, we were still being batted around by scattered storm clouds.

At last we crossed the coast, only ten miles out. The sky around us lit up like the Fourth of July. The gathering dusk was ablaze with vicious orange streaks lashing at the formation, accompanied by long, roman candle-like strings of brilliant lights. Tennis ball-sized burning globs drifted up toward us. The fireworks clearly illuminated their source: an American PT boat.

For an eerie eternity our formation seemed paralyzed, frozen in space. Then we exploded like a covey of Bob White. It was a miracle there were no mid-air collisions as B-25s scattered all over the southeast coast in the dark. Everybody was low on fuel, there were no alternate fields, and no runway lights. Truck lights, and each plane's landing lights guided us in. It was a hairy business. Resorting to short, fighter-like landing patterns, all nine planes got safely down in record time.

That night, Arnold and I talked about our latest joust with loose cannons.

"What all were they throwing at us?" I asked.

"Those blobs of fire were two sizes. I think forty and twenty millimeter. The tracers were fifty caliber."

I still couldn't believe what had happened. "How do you account for it? They've been here at least as long as we have."

He shook his head. "I hear those PT guys are natural-born hell-raisers — worse than we were as anti-flaks. After the scrapes they get into night after night, they're bound to be trigger happy."

"Bull shit. That's no excuse. We have to do something about it."

"What do you mean, 'we?' Have you lost your mind?"

He looked seriously shocked, so I changed the subject. "We're getting stale after all of these dry runs. In the morning, we're going up and get in some practice bombing."

Loaded up with Blue Whistlers (hundred-pound practice bombs), we did just that.

That afternoon, Arnold and I were playing one-on-one when a battleship-grey Jeep carrying a pair of determined-looking sailors cruised through the gate and came right at us.

"Oh God! They're SPs. We're going to the Brig. How could they possibly have figured it was us?" I gasped.

Arnold groaned. "You idiot! I told you not to hit them. Just get close enough so they got the message."

"That's what I did? Cripes! That string of ten didn't get any closer than fifty yards off their left beam. They may be mad as hell, but no one got hurt."

The Jeep came within ten yards of us. It was flying a white flag. Painted on it in red letters was one word: TRUCE. The Jeep stopped at the officer's club. The sailors carried some packages inside and left.

Greatly relieved but still anxious, Arnold started for the club. "We better get over there. Maybe they've delivered a time bomb!"

Major Smedley, operations officer, was inside studying a note. He acknowledged us with a nod and pointed at a case of scotch and twenty gallons of ice cream, the only ice cream we'd seen on Corsica.

"I assume that's their response to Snuffy's message," he said

"What did he say," I asked.

"Vintage Snuffy—short and sweet. 'How long does it take you numskulls to figure out who the enemy is? Now we damned well know: The Krauts are our adversary. You bastards are the enemy! Scotch and ice cream will go a long way toward healing the 446th's wounds. Strong letter and bill for triple damages to follow.'"

He read the note from the Navy: "'Your messages received loud and clear. Enough already. Let's declare a truce.'... Messages? I only know about one." He peered at us.

"How'd your practice mission go?"

"Great. All ten were exactly the right message."

"Message to whom, Paulson?"

I turned to leave. "To loose cannons wherever we find them."

25 February 1945—I flew my fifty-seventh mission. I remember because at dinner that night Colonel Cooper presented me with an old set of his captain's bars. What a surprise. I'd been on the job less than a month. He made a big deal of it in front of everybody. I, who never drank, had to buy everybody else one—an added embarrassment. It seemed to me getting promoted was a costly proposition.

March 1945—An all-around good month and a long time coming. The group set a monthly record of sixteen bridges destroyed. As usual, we led the Wing in bombing accuracy. Losses were only two planes and one crew. The morale-boosting drop was mostly due to fewer encounters with loose cannons. As the weather improved, so did photo recon and our data on gun locations.

Colonel Cooper invented the Milk Run Club. To the extent possible, any crew member with five or fewer remaining missions finished his tour on undefended targets. We had a few of those, even with the five hundred heavy guns now guarding the Brenner. In early April, my first mission as member of the club was a long one—north of the Italian border, nearly to Innsbruck, in the heart of the Tyrolean region of the rugged Austrian Alps.

Between Bolzano and our target, the landscape grew increasingly wild and remote. Up there, the worst of our difficulties would be finding IPs and targets. That day we had six-tenths cloud cover in the mountains. Only rarely could we see the occasional tiny village or road in the deep valleys. At best, navigation was limited to brief glimpses of steep, rugged hills. Dick O'Conner demonstrated that he could find his way around up there better than most of us could on a clear day over the Po Valley.

He got us to the IP. We turned, leveled out, and started the bomb run. Almost instantly four guns opened up on us. So confident were we that this one would be a milk run as promised, neither Dick nor I had on flak vests and helmets.

Normally, my bomb-run time was consumed in finding the target and making a good run. In that sense, lead bombardiers were lucky. The required concentration blanked out everything else. But this one was too easy. Long before bomb release, with literally minutes to spare, I was synchronized. The cross-hairs stayed locked on my aiming point. All I could do was wait and listen to the hammering of those guns — and that crazy guy on the intercom.

Use of the intercom was strictly forbidden on the bomb run except in emergencies, such as the approach of enemy fighters. The tail gunner was jabbering away and nobody could shut him up. He gave us every gory detail of what was going on with the six planes just slightly behind and below us in our nine-ship formation:

"Number three in the third element is on fire, out of control. So far no chutes. The element lead feathered number two, number one is smoking. They are bailing out."

I screamed at Arnold, "Will somebody go back and shut him up? We still have two minutes to go!"

In a shaky voice Arnold replied, "I can't send anybody back there now. What if we go down in the meantime? How would he get out?"

Like punctuation for the gunner's frantic sermon, every three seconds we were hammered by four more rounds of flak.

"Third element is gone. Number two in second element hit in tail. Going down."

Dick cut in. "Can't somebody drown him out with the national anthem. Even if you can't sing, anything would be better..."

"Old Dad just bailed out," the radio operator interrupted. Old Dad, a thirty-year old waist gunner, finished one tour and volunteered for another without even going on leave.

I finally snapped. I was convinced we could not make it to bomb release and certain I had already waited too long. I turned, intending to find my chute, go down the crawlway, and bail out. Dick would be long-gone. To my utter shock, there he sat, blocking my access to the crawlway. Seeing him sitting there, seemingly unconcerned by our situation, daring me to try to get past him, jolted me out of my panic attack or whatever it was.

Somehow calmed and under control, I finished the bomb run. As we broke out of that nightmare, I looked down and saw only three strings of bombs. We had started the bomb run with a formation of nine. I was surprised our lead element had survived.

We lost an engine thirty minutes from home. Jim Ratliff, one of our wing men, crash-landed six miles north of our base. He and his crew survived a wheels-up landing that came to a violent end in a drainage ditch.

After debriefing, such as it was with only two crews there to debrief, O'Conner confronted Arnold and me. "To hell with the Milk Run Club! It should be called, the Panic Club. If the slightest thing goes wrong, you flak-happy old guys come unglued!" He glowered at me. "I'd a hell of a lot rather take my chances flying regular missions with the beginners!"

21 April 1945 — My seventieth mission. Rumors about the war's end had been flying for weeks. Our target was San Ambrogio. Again leading the Milk Run Club, we were to try and block the lower Brenner by starting a landslide from a three hundred-foot high limestone cliff. It was our eighth attempt. Where was Joshua when we needed him?

About half way through the bomb run, one gun started to pop away at us, but the bursts never came close. It was like somebody down there believed the rumors and no longer wanted to hurt anybody.

Like most of the others who had tried to start that landslide, I couldn't find the exact aiming point. I aborted the bomb run and announced to Arnold that we would go around and try again. What happened next, according to our own propaganda, never happened in all of World War II. As we came around for our second bomb run, the tail gunner said our second and third elements — six planes — weren't with us.

"What's going on? Has the war ended? Was there a recall we missed?" I shouted.

"No recall," Arnold insisted. He started to laugh. "One gun chased them off the target. They're high-tailing it for home. As Dick said, we Milk Run Clubbers are all flak-happy."

The three of us completed the second bomb run. For the eighth time, no landslide. On the way back to base, I thought about what had happened. How dare those cowards turn tail and run when confronted by one measly gun! Then the light dawned: Some of us know when enough is enough, and some of us don't. Even the German with the flak gun had it figured out.

Four days later, on my twenty-first birthday, B-25s bombed in the Brenner for the last time. After two false alarms, the Germans officially gave up on 2 May 1945. Every one of our planes had a flare gun and red, green, and white flares. That night the hundreds of flares we fired off left a thick, pungent layer of smoke hanging over the base. That's all I remember about what we did when our war ended.

Most of the flying personnel went home in B-25s. I would have if I hadn't been grounded by Major Smedley for flying violations. I had become overly exuberant in celebrating the end of my year-long ordeal of having to go out and get shot at. My last experience piloting a B-25 included three low-level, high speed passes over historic Florence. I might have been forgiven had I actually been a pilot, but a bombardier could not intrude on that sacrosanct province without severe retribution.

As a result, I waited three weeks for a slow boat from Naples. But I was through and on my way home. Rod and I had survived, even prospered in some ways. Nothing could separate us now unless we wanted it to.

I passed the time by rummaging through intelligence reports. One of them stunned me. It concerned the use of Azon in Burma.

In seven missions, 127 Azon bombs were dropped. Fourteen bridges were confirmed destroyed, one probable, two possible, all in fifteen days. The bombing was done from below ten thousand feet. There were no multiple drops. Mechanical bomb failures were under two percent.

Fourteen bridges destroyed with 127 bombs. That's an average of nine bombs per bridge. How good is that? Our bomb wing, the Fifty-Seventh, so far as we know, was the hottest bombing outfit in World War II. In the last eight months of the war, on average, we used 280 bombs per bridge destroyed. According to that data, Azon in Burma was a mere thirty-one times more effective.

Based on Burma results, five Azon equipped B-25s could have replaced our 150 B-25s. Even more interesting and novel: In the Brenner, and other routes, wherever there was a half mile of undefended track or road, we could have cratered it with an Azon bomb as often as it took to keep the route blocked.

What went wrong with Azon while we had it, before it went to Burma? All of Azon's strengths and weaknesses were clearly evident before we left Eglin. What to do and what not to do should have been obvious. In the absence of a clear and devoted adherence to those realities, the project became hopelessly bogged down in increasingly absurd exercises in futility. The ultimate absurdity, thought to be a success, was the Avisio Viaduct "Flock Shooting Scheme."

Chapter Thirteen

Autumn 1953 — Rod and I were in the vicinity of where we wanted to be.

I had first seen this area a decade before from a B-25 and many times after that from a B-36: the Salmon River, Clear Water Range, Selway Wilderness Area, Bitterroot Wilderness Area — a northern Idaho treasure trove of thousands of square miles of rugged mountains, virgin forests, and pure water.

Our plan was to nibble away at its edges and do some elk hunting, a significant step up from deer hunting. We could do that by taking back roads from Spokane to the small Idaho towns of Headquarters and Pierce. Both of us were stationed at Fairchild Air Force Base, Spokane, and assigned to different B-36 crews. We had taken a week of leave. It was the week of the 1953 World Series, but neither of us cared about the Series because the Cardinals weren't in it and we hated the teams that were. The Dodgers seemed to specialize in keeping the Cardinals out of the big show, reason enough to hate them. And the Yankees? We hated them on general principles.

The back-way southeast from Couer d' Alene Lake comprised narrow, gravel, logging roads that followed crystal streams through valleys vibrating with fall color and skirted lakes that glistened like tears on the cheek of Nature. Virgin timber mixed with various ages of second growth and recent clear-cuts told the story of over fifty years of logging.

Along the streams, willow, maple, and species of brush unknown to us were aflame with cool fall fire. Higher up, the larch was golden brown, softening the scars left by single-minded mining. With almost no traffic to worry about and so much to see that you really didn't have to look to see it, we settled in for several hours of conversation about what had become our favorite subject: Why the hell were we still in the service? Not that it had been an uninterrupted hitch. It had been broken up by disgust and enough years at Iowa State for both of us to get degrees in forestry, neither of which we found to be of great value.

I started pilot training in the fall of 1945. Rod was nearly finished with flight engineer school. From San Angelo, Texas, where I was in primary training, I took a bus to San Antonio to visit him. He was still a staff sergeant at the time. As I approached his barracks, a young sergeant came running up.

"Rod? Have you lost your mind? You can't run around impersonating a captain!"

No amount of explanation would persuade him of who I was. Rod was up and gone, working out with the baseball team. I found the field and watched. He was the starting center-fielder and batting clean-up. Later, we said our hellos.

I imagine it might have surprised those who saw us together at that moment to learn we hadn't seen each other for a year, so low-key was our reunion. We were glad to see each other, of course. We had much to catch up on, but at the core of whatever it is that makes each of us living beings, in that place where I suppose the soul must live, we hadn't been apart for a year, not even for a second.

People have asked me if we had some sort of ESP link. It wasn't like that. Had I known what he was thinking, what was happening to him, I would have known he was in the top ten of his class and about to quit the Air Force.

"What do you think the odds are of my having another Le Grande Chuck in my life?" he asked finally. His wry smile told me that he already knew the answer.

"Oh, God. You have your pilot already?"

"Yeah." He shook his head. "You're gonna *love* this!"

"What? Tell me, damn it!"

"Don't rush me! I want you to savor this moment. We've been doing a lot of on-the-job training the last few months — post and pre-flight, and trouble-shooting on B-29s. They show up regularly. Last week, I headed out to get to work on one that had just come in. By the time I got there, the crew was already in formation outside being lectured by this tall, gangly character who was droning on about something. Just like that," Rod said, snapping his fingers, "something told me to get out of there."

"*No.*"

"Oh, yes. Le Grande Chuck in the flesh. But it was too late, he'd spotted me. I knew at that instant it was time to get out."

"Wait a minute. I thought you told me he'd changed for the better."

"He did, but apparently it was flak-induced. He was back in old form. He greeted me like a long-lost valet and announced, as if it was an imperial boon, that he would request me as flight engineer for *his* crew."

"God."

"It get's better. I told him that was fine, but as before, I'd only come as a package — the both of us."

"I'll bet he *loved* that."

Rod grinned. "He *did*. He kept smiling even after I told him how glad I was that he wasn't going to have a problem with a bombardier that out-ranked him!"

I groaned.

"Don't worry. It's not going to happen. Seeing him woke me up. It's been like that year before we actually landed in Foggia — asleep, in a dream world. Seeing him was enough to make me take a hard look at what the Air Corps is really all about. Flight engineer school was fine while the war was on. It gave me something to do. But the war is over and the fact is that the Le Grande Chucks of the world are everywhere. In the real world, you've got a choice. You can quit and move on. In the military, you don't have a choice. Right now, I've got a choice."

"Isn't this a little drastic? Are you sure the cure won't be worse than the disease?"

"I still have time to get into Iowa State this fall."

I thought for a moment and nodded. "You'll do great at Iowa State. Just like before, you'll be the guinea pig. If anything goes wrong in pilot training, I'll join you there."

I was court-martialed out of pilot training. A few months before that happened, in the spring of 1946, I was home on leave and went to visit Rod on campus. He had a flare for chemistry, math, physics, and as always, sports. He had a B average and was a comer on the baseball team. The coach, "Screwball Charley," was obsessed with turning him into a left-handed Bob Feller. I had asked George Hartman if they called him Screwball because it was his best pitch.

"Hardly. He's been diagnosed as having been beaned too many times by wild pitches."

As I approached the practice field, Charley saw me and came over, sending a signal that he was out of sorts about something. I assumed he knew about Rod and me, and he knew I wasn't Rod.

"Why aren't you suited up?" He sounded somber, more like he was going to funeral than coaching baseball.

I thought it an act of some sort, or that he was thinking that I was as good as Rod, so I played along.

"I just couldn't get into the spirit of it. Too nice a day," I said with a grin.

Screwball lived up to his name. He exploded into a rage in front of the entire squad and then kicked me off the team. It was the second time I'd gotten Rod thrown off a baseball team. Stunned and ashamed, I went looking for Rod and told him the story.

"I'm not surprised," he said. "He's done that to everybody this spring. Then he takes them back."

"Well, maybe we should go and see him to make sure," I said.

"Forget it. I'm through with that dimwit and his crackpot staff. They say it's still too soon after the war. The demand for coaches exceeds the supply, so this is what they get."

At the end of his freshman year, Rod hitchhiked to Oregon and went to work at a Weyerhauser logging camp near Beatty, in beautiful south-central Oregon ponderosa pine country. In less than a month, he was head scaler, the best-paying hourly job in the camp. In the fall, he tried to enter Oregon State, but even his three-point Iowa State average didn't make the high cut forced by the influx of GI Bill students. He stayed on with Weyerhauser until the following fall.

That same summer, we student fighter pilots got caught

doing what student fighter pilots did — dogfighting. It was a violation of the regulations. I was number one in the class, Mike Hill was number two. Because of our standing, and I suppose because two seemed like a nice, easy number to handle, we were the only ones court-martialed.

At the trial, our commanding officer, Colonel Howard Craig, had the courage to take on the system on our behalf. "What purpose is served punishing the best in the class for the conduct of the entire class?"

"We're setting an example," one of the Fat Five (full colonels) on the board sneered.

"Couldn't such a lofty purpose be served just as well by drawing straws?" Colonel Craig challenged.

Apparently not. With three weeks to go, I was kicked out of pilot training. At least I had proven to *myself* I could fly with the best of them. Rod's words about the reality of the Air Corps had been haunting me since I heard them. I quit and signed up at Iowa State where he had done so very well.

In the fall of 1947, Rod returned to Iowa State and we received our degrees in foresty in June of 1950, an accomplishment made possible in part because he took a final exam in chemistry for me.

For reasons I don't remember, Rod took an ROTC commission and went back into the Air Force and pilot training. Rod was among the seventy percent of the class washed out in primary. Among them were two dozen West Point and Annapolis graduates. He was assigned to navigation school at Ellington Field, midway between Houston and Galveston

The week the Korean War started, I headed to western Oregon as a trainee in the lumber business. My training began in a saw mill with the absolute worst job in the place. After four months of that, I decided there had to be more to life than a job no one else was willing to do. I volunteered to go back into the service. I didn't ask for it, but I landed in navigation school at Ellington. By accident we were together again.

After completing the school, Rod went to a B-36 recon wing. When I graduated six months later, I went to a B-36 bomb wing in Spokane. A year after that, Rod came to Fairchild. We were together again. I had been promoted to major. Rod was a first lieutenant. He was assigned to a newly-formed B-36 crew and one of our old, nagging worries returned: Right from the start, I regarded Rod's aircraft commander as weak a hanger-on who had no business being an aircraft commander.

Rod frowned out the window at a stand of virgin white pine towering seventy feet to the first limb, each trunk at least four feet in diameter.

"So, what's wrong with being the youngest lieutenant colonel on the base?" I growled.

"We've had this conversation. There's nothing wrong with it as long as the service needs you. I'm just saying that the Pentagon doesn't know from day to day who they need or can afford. You'll always be at risk. Unless you apply for a regular commission, you'll never know if the next RIF[1] will get you thrown out or set you back to your permanent rank of first lieutenant. Imagine supporting a wife and brood on my pay."

"We're twenty-nine and still haven't got a clue as to what we want to do," I said angrily. "Hardly the time to think about a family."

He shook his head. "Don't change the subject. Why haven't you applied for a regular commission? Whether you stay in or not, what do you have to lose?"

"Whether *I* stay in? Sounds like you've made up your mind about you."

"I guess not.... Here's what I see: We grew up second-class citizens. In the military all that seemed to change, at least for awhile. The uniform was the great equalizer, right?"

"Right."

"Wrong! War was the great equalizer. Now that it's gone, we're back to being second-class citizens of the service because neither of us has the right credentials. We're not pilots and we're not West Pointers. We're on the outside, Rolly. We're not first-class citizens of the military and we're not first-class citizens of the country because we're in the military." He

---

[1] Reduction In Force.

watched the scenery a moment. "Never mind all that. At least you have a shot with all your time in grade as a major, so I'll ask you again: Why haven't you applied for a regular commission?" He looked at me hard. He wouldn't buy an excuse.

"I'm afraid I won't make it."

"That's stupid."

He was right. I was better qualified than most. I had a good combat record. I made captain at twenty, major at twenty-seven. Unlike the majority of reserve officers who had made regular, I had a college degree. And I was the only major on a crew that was up for Select status on our next Strategic Air Command evaluation. If we made it, I would be eligible for spot promotion to lieutenant colonel. I would be the first senior observer of that rank in the squadron and the youngest light colonel on the base. At that moment, there was only one answer for my reluctance.

"I guess I'm gutless."

"Baloney.... The hell with it. Let's drop it."

We did, leaving unbroken our two-year record of being unable to resolve this dilemma. Hours later, about two in the afternoon, we got to where we wanted to be. We could see the magnificent Bitterroots in the distance, monarchs of this mostly unspoiled kingdom of big game and giant trees. Hoping to get more information on the area from a local, we turned onto a grassy lane that should lead to somebody's home. It did after a mile of meandering and gradual climbing.

He was the image of Gabby Hayes—Levis, full white beard, battered cowboy hat. His neat log cabin was tucked into a grove of virgin white pine. A window planter vibrated with color. A group of apple trees were in the midst of losing their color out on the well-kept front lawn. A brook gurgled below, framing it all.

When we stepped onto his property, he opened the door of the screened porch and began bellowing so loudly we couldn't tell what he was saying, but we were pretty sure it wasn't complimentary. We turned to leave.

"Don't run off!" he yelled. "My bark is worse than my bite! Come have a cold drink!"

As we approached again, a black and white Springer

spaniel lying among the yellow leaves of the apple trees raised it's head. It was curious, but not enough to get up.

"I'm Nels," the old man said at a normal volume. "Sorry 'bout the yellin'. Spent a lot a time on a ship where ya gotta yell to be heard." He offered his hand as he flip-flopped down the stairs in a pair of slippers. "I must be goin' loco. I'm seein' double!"

With anyone else, that would have drawn a polite, but forced chuckle from us. But he meant it and so did we when we smiled warmly in response and introduced ourselves. He sat us down in comfortable arm chairs on the porch. He darted into the cabin to get refreshments and we surveyed the surroundings. Although a hundred miles from civilization, he had modern plumbing and electricity. On a small table beside a brown recliner was a copy of Peter Drucker's *The Practice of Management*. Classical music wafted out from the interior of the cabin. He appeared from inside with iced tea and cookies.

We told him about ourselves and how and why we had shown up at his doorstep.

"I see them B-36s flyin' over and makin' vapor trails almost every day," he said. "How high are they? How come they sound so funny."

"Probably forty thousand feet or more," I said. "The strange noise comes from the six props behind the wing that push rather than pull."

Rod got down to business. "How's the elk population?"

"Down, but I know where some bulls hang out nearby. How much time you got?"

"Five days — six counting a day to get back."

"I'll make it as easy for ya as shootin' fish in a barrel — assuming you can hit a barn from fifty yards. You'll have just enough time."

"I thought you said they were nearby," I said.

"They are. Round here, nearby means anything within a day's walk. It'll take a full day to get there. How much time it takes after that depends on how many and what size. Regardless, you'll spend several long, hard days skinnin', quarterin', and packin' 'em out. You're first-timers, don't forget."

A little miffed, Rod said, "It must be pretty obvious — that we're first-timers,"

"Sure, but I didn't mean it as a put-down. There always has to be a first time, right?"

Still uncomfortable with our role as tenderfoots, we changed the subject.

"We thought all the Swedes out here were seven-foot, three hundred-pound loggers."

"Logger I'm not," Nels said, apparently pleased by the fact. "Grew up down in Lewiston where my dad worked in the big pine mill. He started at fourteen and worked his way up from the bottom. At thirty-two, he was the head sawyer, youngest around for that big a job. I worked in the mill summers from age twelve, the year my mom died.

"Came up here in '15, after my junior and last year in high school. Dad thought we was sure to get into the war. He was always tighter 'en a tick — an Old World habit — and had saved up enough to build his own saw mill on an old mining claim. He thought the war would be a long one and figured the price of everything would inflate, including high-grade lumber. We made good money during the war, sailed through the roaring twenties, and right on through the crash of '29."

"The Depression put you out of business?" Rod asked. We knew from school that most mills hadn't survived.

"Naw, Dad's business was damn near Depression proof. We made it through '30 and '31 without much trouble, then we sold out. Dad was fifty-four and worn out. Sixteen years of working long days and weeks had taken their toll. We sold the mill and leased the land with the stipulation that none of the trees be cut. And they ain't been," he said with a sweep of his hand.

We weren't sure we completely bought the story. Anything that made it through the Depression and was strong enough to be sold at a solid profit was either a fairy tale or something special. Fascinated, we questioned him further and the hours drifted past. When the conversation wound down, what we had learned boiled down to three things:

• Nels' father had kept his business small enough to allow him to control every aspect. He knew his market and his product, and he worked harder and was smarter than other mill owners. His success proved it.

- Nels was no backwoods Rube.
- It was too late to set out hunting and we had no place to sleep.

"Bunk here," Nels insisted. "Tomorrow, I'll fix you up with pack mules."

Pack mules? Rod and I looked at each other and grinned. "That'll be a first."

Nels was up before dawn making a breakfast of pancakes, juice, and coffee. While we ate, he drew a map of our route to the bull elk sanctuary. Later, as we got acquainted with the mules who seemed annoyed at being stuck with us, he gave one last bit of advice.

"You've never taken an elk. This one time do it my way. Shoot only one—not one each, just one. Pick the smallest thing you can find with horns, in other words, a spike. It will be the least work and the best meat."

By seven o'clock we were on our way into the deep woods, headed toward the Bitterroots, leading mules that knew more about us than we did about them. The trail was easy and stayed that way for the first hour, but the mules became skittish and contrary. We stopped, savvy enough to know that they might sense something ahead.

"Could be a mountain lion or bear," Rod said. "I'll take the mules off the trail and hobble them. You go up ahead and see what you can find."

A hundred yards farther on the woods opened into a five acre meadow—a feeding ground from the look of it. A young bull moose was the only diner at that moment. He was on guard at my end of the meadow and gave every sign of being particular about who he'd let by. He glared and snorted and pawed the ground, his breath steaming in the early cold. He charged and stopped, and charged and stopped. His warnings were clear. I fingered my .270, hoping I wouldn't have to kill him. There was no season on moose, but I couldn't allow him to stampede the mules.

He tried again, but I stood my ground and he gave up with a parting snort and shake of his ample antlers. Frustration, I could understand that. He headed for a patch of skunk cabbage and began to browse. I returned to Rod and the mules and we kept going. The mules stayed calm, even though the moose was in sight. Apparently, they understood, too.

We figured we were about an hour from the camp site marked on the map when the trail dropped into a deep gully and headed up the equally steep other side. The trees were high and thick and kept the gully dark, moist, and smelling of pine and mold. In the lead, I reached the bottom and carefully and slowly started up the other side. I could feel something beneath my feet, a vibration that was growing stronger by the second. I began hearing a sound like thunder, rolling closer, coming from up the trail above me. Suddenly, a huge beast broke through the trees at the top and hurtled down the slope at full speed. The moose's fantastic head and antlers were down low, like a great cowcatcher. That crazed bull had no hope of stopping, even if he wanted to.

"Look out!" I yelled, diving behind a tree and trying to drag a hysterical mule along. It brayed in terror and bolted in the other direction. Rod's mule did the same. From my cover, I watched the moose lose control at the bottom of the gully and crash in a great heap of antlers and legs. We watched for a few seconds, wondering if we might have to put the great beast out of its misery. It struggled to its feet, shook a couple of times, then glowered and snorted at us. He had no fight left in him, however. He limped back up the trail in the direction we had come.

A couple of hours of frantic searching and we found the mules peacefully grazing in a meadow, proving once and for all that they knew more about these woods than we did. It was too late to do anything but set up camp.

After a meal, we sat by the fire, smoking stogies to ward off swarms of mosquitoes.

"So, is today what's known as having a hell of a good time?" Rod asked wearily.

"Yeah, right," I said. "Why are we doing this? If we get lucky and don't get run down by a pissed-off moose, we'll get an elk. Then we'll work our butts off butchering it. Then we'll pack the meat back to the cabin where maybe we'll eat some of it. And we'll do all that for what? The privilege of shooting a majestic animal.... Do you realize we've spent the past twenty years looking for something to kill—including cats, for God's

223

sake? Maybe in the beginning killing for food made sense, but now? Maybe we're finally at a place in our lives where enough is enough."

"Maybe. I know for sure I'd rather be talking to Nels. He's a once-in-a-lifetime fountain of wisdom, don't you think?"

The elk and the moose were safe. We spent the night and at daylight headed back.

"There's hope for you two yet," Nels said when he saw us approaching. "What's so damn great about killing an elk or anything else?...You can stay as long as you like. Tour the country. There's a lot to see. Most of it's been finding a way to stay alive for a lot longer than the human race."

That afternoon, we drove to the top of a 5,500-foot round-top mountain that offered a view beyond spectacular. We stayed for hours, looking, relaxing, and having the same arguments about the service. A pickup with Montana plates drove up. Out of it stepped tall, blond Carl Hackinson, a forestry classmate from Iowa State. The odds against it were staggering, but it happened.

"What are you doing up here?" Rod asked.

"I work for Diamond Match and you two troublemakers are on our property."

"You came up here to arrest us?" I laughed.

"Only if you're still killing cats. Seriously, the company owns about one hundred thousand acres up here. My boss and I manage all of it—harvesting, reforestation, rehab, protection and recreation."

"Sounds like the perfect job," Rod said. "You're actually practicing forestry. Where do you live?"

"In Superior with my wife and my daughter, Julie, she's two. It is great. We really enjoy the small-town life. Hell, I'm on the school board. It's still unspoiled and we have great camping, fishing, and hunting—even skiing on Lookout Pass. That's about forty miles from here."

"What can we say?" Rod said. "You've died and gone to heaven."

"Almost—but heaven doesn't pay all that well. If it wasn't for the non-monetary benefits I'd have to get out. Actually, the pay is pretty sick. My God, half the mill workers make more than I do. Foresters have a lot in common with school teachers. They earn a college degree for the privileges of low pay and being an underclass."

"That's funny," I said. "We were just talking about something like that."

"Yeah? What did you decide?"

"Nothing yet."

"Let me know if you figure it out, will ya?"

"Have you figured it out?" I asked Rod on the drive back to Nels' cabin.

"I don't know. Half the foresters we know hate what they do, and none of them make much money. Carl is making less than I do and about half what you do. No wonder we can't make a decision. We're damned if we do and damned if we don't."

"Yeah, but Bud Schlick and R.T. seem to feel pretty good about the Indian Service. How long will that last? Do we know anyone working for the Forest Service?"

We couldn't think of anyone, but we realized that a lot of foresters we did know were going back to school to change careers.

We talked it all over with Nels that night over a gourmet meal of green salad, elk steak (although we suspected it was moose), cherry pie, a French gamay, espresso, and Havanas. We sat listening to him amid a cabin full of classic birds-eye white pine furniture and cabinets hand-crafted by his father. He was proud of his father and had every right to be. We had no similar feelings to offer, but we had never wanted to share that with anyone and we didn't with Nels.

"Boys, going back to school at thirty and starting over would be a long, hard row to hoe, but it's been done. As I see it, you're really worried about your credentials in the service. Service or corporate world, credentials are just as important. So is monkey see, monkey do. It's no accident that most big corporations look the same. What's hot, the latest management fashion and fads, are a damn serious matter to them, not the least of which is the *right* credentials.

"What it boils down to I think is where you can do the

225

most about establishing credentials. You've already said there's nothing you can do about them in the military."

"Which leaves the corporate world," I said. "What we need is the corporate equivalent of West Pointer and pilot, and we shouldn't make a move until we're darned sure we know what that is."

Less than a year later, I decided that meant Harvard Business School. Rod never got the chance.

29 March 1954 — Six months after we left Nels, my crew and I were in Fort Worth, Texas. Rod was back in Spokane. It had been a good day, the third day of a two-week SAC[2] evaluation. It was a long time in coming and the last hurdle before being accorded the status of a Select Crew, which brought prestige and eligibility for spot promotions.

Dave Caudle and I were having dinner at the Carswell Air Force Base Club. Dave was the flight engineer on our crew, and a great friend; actually the only member of the fifteen-man crew that I was close to. We were joined at 7:00 P.M. by Carl Townsend, one of our pilots. Carl told us there had been an accident that afternoon at Fairchild, but he had no more information. I shuddered at the word "accident." Perhaps it was because of the look on my face that they both studied me

"Rod's okay or we would have heard about it by now," I said, reassuring myself.

They both agreed, but dinner was noticeably strained. We left for quarters a little early. Dave and I were sharing a room at the transit Bachelor Officers Quarters. I went to bed at ten. The following day promised to be a long and tough one. Dave stayed up to write a letter to June and Dixie, his wife and their three-year-old daughter.

Dave shook me awake at midnight. "You're wanted on the phone," he said, obviously irritated at having been awakened at that ungodly hour. "It's at the far end of the hall."

Barely awake, I staggered from wall to wall down the hundred-foot hall, picked up the phone and mumbled a hello.

"This is David Wade," a voice said.

The name cut the fog in my brain. The only David Wade I

[2]Strategic Air Command

knew of was a general.

"Yes, sir?"

There was a long pause, and then the last words I remember clearly: "Your brother has been killed."

The next thing I knew, Dave was shaking me. I was sitting on the floor, the phone receiver dangling over my head.

Dave took care of getting me from Fort Worth to Des Moines. I don't know how I got from there to Ames. At six the next morning, Mother met me at the front door. She hadn't heard about the accident yet, but she knew immediately why I was there. The week before she had told Aunt Dorothy of her bad feeling concerning us. We both broke down and cried. I'm sure the house was as dark and empty as when Ralph was killed, but I don't remember.

Rod's body came home by train, escorted by Dan Youngblade, Rod's roommate at Fairchild. Earl, George, and I met him at the depot. The casket remained closed. I never knew if there was enough left of Rod inside to bury. Nobody said anything. I didn't ask.

The funeral is a blur. I remember the oaks, then a beautiful grove of fifty-year-olds. There must have been bird song and insect chatter, but I don't remember. I do remember looking across the valley to where Mike was buried, and I remember feeling badly that George had to come all the way from Burn, Oregon. He was missing work and had spent all that money to get there.

Carl Townsend and other friends of ours came from Spokane on a B-25. Rod's aircraft commander wasn't among them. They wore their uniforms. I didn't. My uniform stood for the system that had killed Rod.

A reserve or ROTC honor guard was there. I wondered whose idea that was. I resented them and their uniforms, and that they were complete strangers. Who invited them and their stupid little .30-caliber carbines? Was it Melvin or the American Legion? Rod wasn't just anybody. How dare they show up and perform one of their Memorial Day rituals! This day was only about us, Rod and me. They played *Taps*, normally a beautiful tune to hear at the end of the day. Not then and never since.

After the funeral, I desperately wanted everyone to go away. I had a terrible, aching longing to be alone with him — just Rod and me. But I couldn't. I was cheated out of it because they didn't understand. They couldn't understand. No one ever could.

They didn't let me say goodbye. I think it would have made a difference. Maybe the awful, painful longing would have gone away by now. Maybe the nightmares that began then wouldn't have continued for fifteen years. They were always the same: I couldn't find Rod and there were no letters from him. Maybe I could have found peace with his memory instead of being cut down by it. For forty years I've had to force myself to go to the cemetery. There have been visits to Ames when I haven't gone to the cemetery. I feel guilty about that. Maybe the guilt I still feel about his death wouldn't be as hard.

Where was I when Rod decided to go back into the service? Why wasn't I more positive and assertive about his natural talents — the success he had at Weyerhauser, the ease with which he could achieve, make friends, take over? He was a natural leader. Why didn't I tell him about all those things, remind him that they were his real future?

Why hadn't I acted on my first impression when Rod was assigned to that crew and been more forceful in getting him off of it? There had to have been a way. We often talked about why we were still in the service. All along, the great urgency was why he was still on that crew. I certainly should have known.

I learned later that Rod wasn't even supposed to be on the plane when it crashed and burned.

Every SAC unit had a monthly quota of flying hours. At the end of every month, any remaining hours were burned up just for the sake of the quota. I heard it cost taxpayers $30,000 per hour, per plane. Rod's crew was burning up some of those hours by doing touch and go landings. That didn't require a full crew. Rod was supposed to have the day off, but a crewman who was supposed to be there begged-off. An always generous Rod volunteered to fill in.

Trying to go around after a landing, the plane went out of control, crashed, and burned. Half the crew was killed.

Everybody on the flight deck survived. The Accident Review Board cleared the commander and gave him a new crew. I couldn't clear him. I thought then the crash was one hundred percent pilot error. I still do.

I stayed with my crew through the SAC evaluation, although what good I did them I can't imagine. I had a hard time doing the simplest things. My crew made Select anyway. Somehow, I must have come through for them.

After evaluation, I had to do something about Rod's things. I remember his three guns and his Pontiac. I couldn't part with the guns. Dan sold the car and dealt with Rod's bank account for me.

Six months later, I was still in the service. I had been unable to decide even simple things, let alone my future. Dan and Dave helped me decide. When I did, I was out in a week. They had to help me through the separation process.

During seperation, I remember someone commenting, "With your rank and years of service you should definitely sign up for the Reserves."

And I remember saying, "My God! Why would I want to do that?"

Finally, Dan and Dave helped me pack my car. The nightmares had come every night since Rod's death: I couldn't find him and he hadn't written.

An MP saluted as I drove slowly out the gate for the last time. I headed for Spokane. I don't remember feeling anything. Ahead in the pre-dawn gloom I could see the lights of a plane on final. I pulled over and watched. It was my crew delivering Fairchild's first B-52. It's eight jet engines flamed as it screamed past. The B-36 and I were relics of the past.

I drove on. Just after the exit to Indian Canyon Golf Course, an exit we used often, I dropped into the canyon and onto 195 headed south. The highway was dark and empty. Above me, brilliant sunlight was slowly spreading down from the top of a five hundred-foot, sheer rock wall. It reminded me of my final mission in Italy—the rock wall we bombed eight times but never brought down.

Just south of the city limits, a large, healthy coyote emerged from the rocks and trotted across the highway. Our guns were in the trunk. I pulled over and pondered which gun to use. Rod's super accurate 22-250 was on top—custom barrel, burled walnut stock he had selected and finished himself. By the time I got it out of its sheepskin case and the scope caps off, the coyote was three hundred yards away, sitting on its haunches in an alfalfa field. I looked at him and searched for the ammunition, but I couldn't find it. And suddenly, I couldn't find a reason to keep looking. I remember wondering, "Why am I doing this?"

I put the weapon away, took a minute to admire the beautiful animal, then drove on.

The sunlight had reached the highway.

Epilogue

It was chilly and quiet, not a breeze under the 90-year-old oaks. I found a dry spot at the base of one and sat down.

Fluffy clouds and a dozen crows shared the late afternoon sky. North across the road and up the hill, the site of our first squirrel hunt was now covered with streets, houses, and lawns nearly all the way to Camp Canweta. The cabin was still there, still in use and surrounded by woods. It was perfectly preserved with, I suppose, at least twenty coats of forest-green paint. Maybe it would remain a permanent symbol of the way things were for two eleven-year-olds that fine fall of 1935.

East Thirteenth, now asphalt, traveled down the hill and split the still-rich, coal-black bottom land. I watched a John Deere putting back and forth, planting corn. The same steel bridge spanned the Skunk. North of the bridge, the hillside where I buried Mike was still protected by a fine stand of mixed hardwoods.

Cardinals and finches sang in the branches above me. Bees were busy in the flowers. In front of me, a vase of freshly-cut tulips had been placed lovingly on Rod's grave. Earl had been there. He'd come on this date — the anniversary of Rod's death in 1954 — every year for forty years .

Aunt Dorothy had been there the week before. Eighty-four and the only survivor of the six in Mother's family, she drove up from Des Moines every year to attend to the perennials she had planted at the head of Mother's grave.

I looked out over the Valley of the Skunk, all aglow from the setting sun, and I felt alone. I looked down at Rod's grave. I couldn't say goodbye, not to him. Maybe I didn't have to.